Union with Christ

COLUMBIA SERIES IN REFORMED THEOLOGY

The Columbia Series in Reformed Theology represents a joint commitment of Columbia Theological Seminary and Westminster John Knox Press to provide theological resources for the church today.

The Reformed tradition has always sought to discern what the living God revealed in scripture is saying and doing in every new time and situation. Volumes in this series examine significant individuals, events, and issues in the development of this tradition and explore their implications for contemporary Christian faith and life.

This series is addressed to scholars, pastors, and laypersons. The Editorial Board hopes that these volumes will contribute to the continuing reformation of the church.

EDITORIAL BOARD

Shirley Guthrie, Columbia Theological Seminary

George Stroup, Columbia Theological Seminary

Donald K. McKim, Memphis Theological Seminary

B. A. Gerrish, University of Chicago

Amy Plantinga Pauw,
Louisville Presbyterian Theological Seminary

Columbia Theological Seminary wishes to express its appreciation to the following churches for supporting this joint publishing venture:

First Presbyterian Church, Tupelo, Mississippi

First Presbyterian Church, Nashville, Tennessee

Trinity Presbyterian Church, Atlanta, Georgia

Spring Hill Presbyterian Church, Mobile, Alabama

St. Stephen Presbyterian Church, Fort Worth, Texas

COLUMBIA SERIES IN REFORMED THEOLOGY

Union with Christ

John Calvin and the Mysticism of St. Bernard

DENNIS E. TAMBURELLO

Westminster John Knox Press
Louisville, Kentucky

Book and cover design by Drew Stevens
First edition

Published by Westminster John Knox Press
Louisville, Kentucky

This book is printed on acid-free paper that meets the American National Standards Institute Z39.48 standard. ∞

PRINTED IN THE UNITED STATES OF AMERICA
94 95 96 97 98 99 00 01 02 03 — 10 9 8 7 6 5 4 3 2 1

Library of Congress Cataloging-in-Publication Data

Tamburello, Dennis E., date.
 Union with Christ : John Calvin and the mysticism of St. Bernard / Dennis E. Tamburello. — 1st ed.
  p.   cm.
 Includes bibliographical references and index.
 ISBN 0-664-22054-1 (alk. paper)
 1. Calvin, Jean, 1509–1564—Contributions in doctrine of mystical union. 2. Bernard, of Clairvaux, Saint, 1090 or 91–1153—Contributions in doctrine of mystical union. 3. Mystical union—History of doctrines—16th century. 4. Mystical union—History of doctrines—Middle Ages, 600–1500. 5. Bernard, of Clairvaux, Saint, 1090 or 91–1153—Influence. I. Title.
BT767.7.T36   1994
248.2′2′0922—dc20   94-9324

CONTENTS

ACKNOWLEDGMENTS

This book began as a doctoral dissertation that I wrote at the Divinity School of the University of Chicago. Its appearance now as the first title in the Columbia Series in Reformed Theology is something I never would have imagined when I wrote it. Many fine people are responsible for bringing me to this point, where I have the opportunity to share my work with a wider audience. I would like to acknowledge some of them here.

First and foremost, I thank my adviser, Brian A. Gerrish, who introduced me to the excitement of Calvin studies and was of enormous help in forging a viable dissertation proposal. I also thank my dissertation readers, Bernard McGinn and Jerald C. Brauer. Bernard McGinn guided me through the complex history and theology of Christian mysticism, and Jerald Brauer offered me a model by sharing with me his own dissertation research on a Puritan mystic. I thank these men for their teaching, for their scholarly expertise, and for their friendship, and I dedicate this book to them.

I am also grateful to my religious community, the Franciscan friars of Holy Name Province, who offered both financial and personal support throughout my doctoral studies, and continue to sustain me in my life and work as a friar. In particular, I thank my friar classmates, many of whom have also pursued doctorates and have firsthand knowledge of the joy and the pain of giving birth to a Ph.D.

A special word of thanks is due to my friends, colleagues, and students at Siena College, where I am now privileged to teach as an Associate Professor of Religious Studies. They have been unflagging in their support of my scholarship, urging me to keep it as a top priority as they saw me being pulled in all directions by the many demands associated with teaching and pastoral ministry. The Department of Religious Studies has been especially patient and supportive. I am also deeply grateful to my students, whose enthusiasm and support mean more to me than they probably realize.

The H. H. Meeter Center for Calvin Studies at Calvin College, Grand Rapids, Michigan, and the staff of the Siena College Library in Loudonville, New York, provided invaluable research assistance for this study. The staff at Siena was particularly helpful in locating rare and valuable information on very short notice.

For the appearance of this study as a book in the Columbia Series in Reformed Theology, I owe a special debt of gratitude to William E. McConville, O.F.M., president of Siena College, for encouraging me to send the manuscript to Westminster John Knox Press. Davis Perkins was kind enough to send the manuscript out for review, despite his justifiable reservations about publishing a doctoral dissertation. Cynthia Thompson has been extraordinarily helpful as a liaison with the series board and editorial staff at Westminster John Knox.

Finally, I thank my parents, my brother, and my sisters, whose affection and support have sustained me through this and so many other important events in my life. They have always helped me to realize that there is more to life than books and academic degrees.

A NOTE ON THE LANGUAGE OF THE TEXT

For most citations from the primary sources, I have used the best available published translations. All translations were, however, meticulously compared with the original-language texts, and I occasionally suggest better renderings of certain phrases in the notes for each chapter.

Since these translations are copyrighted, I have not taken the liberty of amending quotations to eliminate sexist or archaic language, but in my own translations and in the body of the text I have attempted to be as inclusive as possible, though I have generally used the male pronoun for God, following the custom of Bernard and Calvin themselves.

Scripture quotations are cited as they appear in the translated works of Bernard and Calvin, rather than in a modern translation like the New Revised Standard Version, in order to reflect as closely as possible the texts as Bernard and Calvin understood them.

1
CALVIN AND MYSTICISM:
THE STATE OF THE QUESTION

INTRODUCTION

In recent years, Reformation scholars have devoted a great deal of attention to the question of relationships between the major Reformers and the many late medieval movements to which they were exposed, for example, nominalism, humanism, and mysticism. With regard to mysticism, much of the discussion has focused on the presence of mystical themes, and sometimes on the direct use of medieval mystical texts, in the works of Martin Luther.

This book will examine the mystical strand of thought that I believe exists in the writings of John Calvin. The topic might appear to be an unusual one. Indeed, the tendency in the secondary sources is to deny any kind of positive relationship between Calvin and the mystical tradition. For example, Georgia Harkness, in *Mysticism: Its Meaning and Message*, says of Calvin:

> If God ever designed him to be a mystic, the plan got mislaid along the way! This is not to say that it would have been impossible, for he was a sincere Christian with a powerful devotion to the God whom he sought to exalt and serve. Augustine . . . was a mystic and at the same time a great theologian and ecclesiastical statesman, but such a combination does not appear very often and it seems to have passed Calvin by.[1]

This negative verdict certainly receives some support when one looks at Calvin's writings. For example, in a letter to the Reformed congregation at Frankfurt, Calvin refers to the *Theologia Deutsch* only to exhort his readers "in the name of God to flee like the plague all those who try to infect you with such trash."[2] He also does not have much use for Pseudo-Dionysius, who has done nothing more than to "divert the ears with chatter," whereas the theologian's task is "to strengthen consciences by teaching things true, sure, and profitable."[3] Finally, his criticism of Osiander in the *Institutes* on "essential righteousness" can be taken as a critique of mystical notions of ontological "absorption" into God.[4]

However, other studies have shown that this negative relationship to the mystical tradition is only part of the story. No one, to my knowledge, has argued (nor will I) that Calvin was in any strict sense a mystic, however the term might be defined. Nevertheless, several scholars have pointed to mystical influences in Calvin's training, as well as references to mystical authors and themes in Calvin's works that appear to be more sympathetic to mystical theology than the ones noted above.[5] In short, this book is based on the premise that Calvin's relationship to the mystical tradition includes both positive and negative elements, each of which must be evaluated individually before any general statement can be made.

One area that has been largely neglected in this discussion is the relationship between Calvin's notion of "union with Christ," which he himself describes as "mystical union,"[6] and notions of mystical union that were prominent in the medieval period. Interestingly, Calvin quotes the medieval mystic Bernard of Clairvaux extensively in the *Institutes,* but only once does he cite Bernard in connection with a passage on union with Christ.[7] Yet a close look at their respective theologies on this theme yields striking parallels.

Building on the work of A. N. S. Lane,[8] Jill Raitt has analyzed Calvin's assessment of Bernard of Clairvaux in the *Institutes of the Christian Religion.* Raitt shows that quotes from Bernard in the *Institutes* fall under three main rubrics: the bondage of the will and grace, justification by faith, and election-reprobation. Although Calvin does not always interpret Bernard accurately or in context, the majority of his references (and in fact, *all* references added after the 1539 edition) contain favorable evaluations of Bernard's theology. It is worth noting that the mystical *Sermons on the Canticles* are the most frequently quoted works.[9]

This book takes its cue from a suggestion by Raitt: "A study which compared the theology of Bernard and Calvin, apart from the areas indicated by quotations, should prove interesting."[10] In the light of the facts noted above, the theme of "mystical union" suggests itself as a particularly fruitful avenue of study. I believe that the significant points of similarity that can be found between Bernard and Calvin on the theme of union with God or Christ make it appropriate to speak of a notion of "mystical" union in Calvin, as well as in Bernard.

It has already been noted that Calvin himself uses the term "mystical union" in reference to union with Christ. (Surprisingly, Bernard does *not* use the term.) However, much of the secondary literature takes great pains to exclude a mystical interpretation of Calvin's notion of union.

Usually this is done through the application of criteria that, if applied to Bernard, would rule out a mystical strand in his writings as well.

Clearly there is a problem here. At bottom, the difficulty is that there is no real consensus on the nature and meaning of mysticism. This book will not attempt to resolve that issue—indeed, it is questionable whether it *can* be resolved. However, there are understandings of mysticism that can embrace both Bernard's and Calvin's respective theologies.

It is indeed curious, considering the parallels that will be discussed in the following pages, that Calvin rarely cites Bernard directly in discussing union with Christ. One can only guess as to why. It certainly is not because Calvin did not have all Bernard's works available to him, for A. N. S. Lane has shown that Calvin unquestionably used an *Opera Omnia* of Bernard's at least as early as the 1543 edition of the *Institutes*.[11] The fact that the *Sermons on the Canticles* are the works most frequently quoted in the *Institutes* is especially puzzling, since they are always cited in reference to a theme other than mystical union. Similarly, Calvin quotes *De gratia et libero arbitrio*, but never in this connection. On the other hand, *De diligendo Deo*, Bernard's work on the stages of loving God, is not mentioned at all in the *Institutes*.

All these works of Bernard, and others, contain numerous parallels to Calvin's theology of "union with Christ." This book will attempt to explicate the parallels without trying to answer the question of why Calvin did not consciously exploit them in his writings.

Two things are necessary before we proceed: (1) Something must be said about the problematic nature of the word "mysticism," especially in relation to Protestant thought. (2) Some homage must be paid to the scholars who have paved the way for this book, in the form of a brief survey of the "state of the question" regarding Calvin and mysticism.

TOWARD A DEFINITION OF MYSTICISM

The relationship of John Calvin, or of any Protestant Reformer, to the medieval mystical tradition is a question that until recently was clouded by a set of prejudices that reached its most vivid expression in the writings of Albrecht Ritschl. In this view, the relationship between Protestant theology and mystical theology is virtually one of mutual exclusivity. More recent scholarship has shown this position to be highly debatable.

According to Ritschl, "wherever mysticism is found, the thought of justification no longer retains its true significance as the key to the whole domain of the Christian life." This statement is based on his belief that "whenever men give way to mystical states or aspirations, they imagine that the sphere of the preached Word and the promises of Grace, therefore the necessary subordination to the public Revelation in the Church, is transcended and may be forgotten."[12]

Certainly there have been some mystical authors in the history of the tradition for whom Ritschl's charges may ring true. However, a comment by Evelyn Underhill is important in this regard: "Those mystics, properly speaking, can only be studied in their works: works which are for the most part left unread by those who now talk much about mysticism."[13] Ritschl's judgment on mysticism quite simply does not hold up when measured against the writings of most of the classic Christian mystics. It will be seen that this is particularly true of Bernard of Clairvaux.

As a matter of fact, Ritschl pays a great deal of attention to Bernard in both *The Christian Doctrine of Justification and Reconciliation* and *The History of Pietism*. Unfortunately, his analysis leaves much to be desired. On the one hand, he is ready to say that in certain respects Bernard anticipates Reformation theology: for example, in his view of faith as a "believing confidence" and in his renunciations of merit.[14] On the other hand, he sees Bernard's references to the "exclusive value of grace" (e.g., in *De gratia*) as only a "temporary elevation" above the traditional Catholic notion of merit. Bernard inevitably "recurs" to the latter in his discussion of "fasts and vigils, continence and deeds of benevolence, and all the other exercises of virtue."[15] That Bernard upholds the concept of merit in any sense at all is, for Ritschl, cause for suspicion. He also criticizes Bernard for his stress on the monastery as the place where Christian perfection is attained through contemplation, a perfection that is not seen as being accessible to all Christians.[16]

But Ritschl reserves his most incisive critique for a discussion of Bernard's notion of mystical union. The fact that Bernard's conception centers on love makes it totally unacceptable:

> For love very distinctly implies the equality of the person loving with the beloved. St. Bernard, who gave to the world the pattern of this species of piety, expressly states that in intercourse with the Bridegroom awe ceases, majesty is laid aside, and immediate personal intercourse is carried on as between lovers or neighbors.

In contrast, the Reformers shifted to faith, which "denies the possibility of equality" with God.[17]

These criticisms of Ritschl's will be dealt with in due time. What is important at this point is to summarize his assumptions about mysticism in relation to justification: (1) It is inherently individualistic. A mystical conception of the scheme of salvation "completely isolates the individual from connection with the Church."[18] (2) It is quietistic, and therefore opposed to the ethical thrust of Reformation thought.[19] (3) It is elitist, because it tends to be a phenomenon restricted to the monastery. (4)

Mysticism is a form of works righteousness, particularly with respect to the various disciplines associated with the contemplative life. (5) It is the antithesis of evangelical doctrine in that it expressly speaks of a kind of "equality" with God. Thus Ritschl comes to his conclusion that mysticism and a sound theology of justification are totally incompatible.

The problem here is that Ritschl's understanding of the word "mysticism" (a flawed one, I will suggest) leads to an extremely one-sided assessment of Bernard, which is exacerbated by an obvious selectivity in the reading of the texts. I believe that Bernard can be defended against most of, if not all, Ritschl's charges. What is needed, however, is an understanding of mysticism that reflects a greater appreciation for the history of the tradition. In short, Ritschl often rejects positions that Bernard and most other mystics never held.

The denial of a mystical strand in Calvin proceeds along similar lines. Here the most perfect illustration of the problem is found in Wilhelm Kolfhaus's *Christusgemeinschaft bei Johannes Calvin*, the most complete study to date of Calvin's notion of union with Christ. Kolfhaus speaks of mysticism as "an extraordinary and multiform" phenomenon, but then goes on to say this:

> However, its main feature is everywhere the same: the effort on the part of the person for an unmediated communion with God, for a "sinking into" the divinity with its pleasures and pains, for the annihilation of the person through meditation, asceticism, prayer, or whatever other means, for reception into God, for an enjoyment of the fullness of salvation in the moment of the deepest "entering into" God, be this with or without connection with ecstasies or visions or with any other form of "being outside of oneself."[20]

Like Ritschl, Kolfhaus sees mysticism as a thinly veiled form of works righteousness. Mystical union is attained not by grace but by our own effort. (He later calls it a "relationship created by us.")[21] A few other things are significant in the citation above: (1) Kolfhaus sees all mystical experience as essentially the same, involving "annihilation" of the person or an absorption into God's essence. (2) He sees this union as "unmediated," suggesting that the grace of Christ and the sacraments of the church are inevitably bypassed. (3) He understands the mystics to claim the "enjoyment of the fullness of salvation," that is, seeing God as God really is. Interestingly, Kolfhaus does not think of the union of the mystic with God as *necessarily* related to ecstasies, visions, or other "esoteric" experiences.

After giving his definition of mysticism, Kolfhaus states, "Whoever approaches Calvin with the hope of finding one of the above-named characteristics in him will immediately encounter a strong resistance." He comes to the following conclusion: "Living and ardent witness to faith has been confused with mysticism, while in truth the two represent the sharpest imaginable opposites."[22] To accept these statements as true, however, would lead one who has read the works of Bernard to the conclusion that he was no more of a mystic than Calvin. The fact that even Bernard's works would be excluded as "mystical" by most of the criteria of Ritschl and Kolfhaus (even though these authors do not deny that he *was* a mystic) makes it clear that their definitions of mysticism are, at the very least, open to question.

Kolfhaus does take note of Calvin's frequent citation of Bernard and Augustine, and his use of similar vocabulary, but insists that "this does not mean that he himself subscribed to the range of ideas that grew out of their mysticism."[23] Calvin's attraction to Bernard, Kolfhaus suggests, was due to the latter's Pauline orientation and resolute affirmation of the *Ecce homo*, and perhaps also because of Bernard's being a perfect synthesis of the holy man and the statesman. But Calvin did not accept the claim— which Kolfhaus finds in Bernard, other medieval mystics, and the *Schwärmer* of the Reformation period—"that it is only to the *perfecti,* the perfect, that the full understanding of God's will is accessible, and that the believer attains to full communion with God through ecstatic vision." Rather, Calvin saw communion with Christ through faith as "the only and sure way to God's heart."[24]

Kolfhaus sums up the relationship between Bernard and Calvin as follows:

> Bernard's piety had two foci: the church and the investigation of the experiences of the pious soul. Calvin was in agreement with him on the first; the second he shunned, for to him it was not the pious soul with its experiences that was central, but rather Christ and the life that his members received from him.[25]

While there is some truth to Kolfhaus's observations on the differences between Bernard and Calvin, I believe that he presents the contrasts much too sharply and that his narrow definition of mysticism leads him ultimately to misrepresent their relationship. For example, in commenting on the second focus of Bernard's piety, the experiences of the pious soul, Kolfhaus insists that Calvin had a noteworthy lack of interest in himself, as evidenced in his *Reply to Sadolet,* in which he calls preoccupation with oneself "hardly theological."[26] However, we will see in our study of *De diligendo Deo* that Bernard understands the higher stages of love precisely as those in which selfishness has been overcome through the power of grace.

It is only in the last chapter of this book, after the textual evidence has been discussed, that a tentative conclusion can be drawn about a "mystical" strand in Calvin. (I say "tentative" because the lack of consensus about mysticism does not appear to be leading toward a resolution.) In the meantime, I believe that at least *some* specific way of understanding mysticism must be suggested before we proceed. Given the nature of this study as an exercise in historical theology, this understanding must above all be *historically* sound—that is, it should correspond as closely as possible to the way in which theologians of Bernard's time and Calvin's time would understand mysticism. Some of the philosophical issues must also be mentioned, but this work will make no pretense of being able to resolve them.

The *New Catholic Encyclopedia* appropriately begins its article on mysticism by describing it as "a term used to cover a literally bewildering variety of states of mind."[27] Jerald C. Brauer offers some examples of that bewildering variety:

> The term has been applied to everything from wild antinomian ecstasies to extreme quietism. It has been used to describe any longing of the soul for God, any first hand religious experience, various theosophical, occult, or magical speculations, or any vague mysterious esoteric systems. Often it has been equated with pantheism, romanticism, idealism, or any system of immanence.[28]

Nevertheless, there are certain characteristics that are rather consistently mentioned in definitions of mysticism by Christian theologians.[29] The focus in such definitions is often on the subjective ("felt") experience of being in intimate relation with God, the ground of reality. This intimate relation has been described in a number of different ways, including "direct contemplation or vision of God, rapture or ecstasy, deification, living in Christ, the birth of the Word in the soul, radical obedience to the directly-present will of God, *and especially union with God.*"[30]

This last category is underscored because it has been prominent since the twelfth century;[31] and indeed, some of the secondary literature in our own century has continued to describe mysticism in terms of an experience of union with God.[32] There are, however, broader definitions, such as that of Ernst Troeltsch, who states, "In the widest sense of the word, mysticism is simply the insistence upon a direct inward and present religious experience."[33] Very often these broader definitions would see mysticism as a phenomenon indigenous to all religiosity, rather than as a more restricted phenomenon that is only enjoyed by certain gifted or eccentric individuals.

The distinction between mysticism as a fundamental dimension of Christian life (so that a mystical element is present in every Christian's relationship to God) and mysticism as a unique kind of religious experience (usually with the implication that not everyone can be a mystic) is, I believe, an important one in evaluating the relationship between Bernard and Calvin. Therefore I would like to present a twofold understanding of mysticism: a broader, more "generic" conception (such as we find in Troeltsch) and a narrower, more specific conception (one taken from a medieval source and that describes mysticism, as Bernard and Calvin do, in terms of union with God).

Chapter 6 offers some tentative conclusions about Bernard and Calvin in relation to both categories of mysticism. I will attempt, in the light of the study of the texts, to clarify the question of the "scope" of mystical experience for Bernard and Calvin. Is mysticism a latent dimension of all Christian life, or a more peculiar phenomenon? Who is eligible for a mystical experience? Without going into detail, I should perhaps state here the conclusion to which I believe the evidence points: that, all things considered, Calvin's mysticism is broader in scope than Bernard's. Calvin presents a mysticism that can be enjoyed equally by all the elect, whereas Bernard tends to see the monastery as the unique environment where mysticism thrives. Calvin describes "union with Christ" using metaphors that are often virtually as powerful and graphic as Bernard's, yet with less emphasis on "esoteric" phenomena such as ecstasies or visions.

The broader understanding of Christian mysticism is very capably presented by Friedrich von Hügel in his work *The Mystical Element of Religion*. Von Hügel sees three elements that are everywhere and always present in religion. The first element is the Institutional, which would embrace the "external" aspects of religion: authority, history, tradition, and so on. "Religion is here, above all, a Fact and Thing." The second is the Speculative, which would embrace the "reasoning, argumentative, abstractive side of human nature. . . . Religion here becomes Thought, System, a Philosophy." Von Hügel characterizes the third element of religion as the Experimental and Mystical: "Here religion is rather felt than seen or reasoned about, is loved and lived rather than analyzed, is action and power, rather than either external fact or intellectual verification."[34]

Von Hügel insists that none of these elements ever stands totally apart from the others. Indeed, he sees the problems of religious persons as rooted in their attempts to eliminate or suppress one or more of the elements. It is tempting to live on the basis of a single element, for "the religious temper longs for simplification," but this unity for which we long will only be achieved when there is a balance and a harmonization of all three elements in our lives.[35]

Thus, von Hügel is less interested in a unique experience of union with God than in the integration of mysticism with the other dimensions of religious life. There is a unity *in* multiplicity, which he contrasts with the "impoverishing simplification" of one element's domination.[36] He wants nothing to do with "Pure Mysticism":

Is there, then, strictly speaking, such a thing as a specifically distinct, self-sufficing, purely Mystical mode of apprehending Reality? I take it, *distinctly not;* and that all the errors of the Exclusive Mystic proceed precisely from the contention that Mysticism does constitute such an entirely separate, completely self-supported kind of human experience.[37]

How, then, would von Hügel define this "mystical element"? He speaks of "the ontological presence of, and the operative penetration by the Infinite Spirit, within the human spirit," or of "*some,* however implicit, however slight, however intermittent, sense and experience of the Infinite" that is shared by all human beings.[38] The latter definition is not substantially different from the one given by Troeltsch above.

From a Christian point of view, there is one problematic aspect to this kind of understanding. Troeltsch speaks of a "*direct* inward and present religious experience"; von Hügel speaks of "ontological" presence and of "*penetration* by the Infinite Spirit." Similarly, Rufus Jones defines mysticism as "that type of religion which puts the emphasis on the *immediate* awareness of relation with God, on *direct* and intimate consciousness of the divine presence."[39] This claim of "immediacy," whether stated directly or indirectly, would seem to conflict with the doctrine of the mediation of grace. As Jerald Brauer notes, Christian mysticism "always has some relation to the person of Christ, the reality of the Church, the Christian ethic, and the Christian sacraments."[40]

This is one of the philosophical issues that this book will not attempt to resolve. A few comments, however, are in order. Certainly none of the authors mentioned in the previous paragraph would disagree with Brauer's criteria for Christian mysticism. This is especially clear in von Hügel's insistence on the Institutional and Speculative elements of religion, and in his rejection of a "purely Mystical" mode of apprehension.

Some authors have suggested a notion of "mediated immediacy," that is, that there is a sense of intimate relationship with God that is *experienced* subjectively as immediate, but that strictly speaking is a function of the mediation of grace or meaning. Thus, John Baillie writes:

> Though we are more directly and intimately confronted with the presence of God than with any other presence, it does not follow that He is ever present to us *apart* from all other presences. And, in fact, it is the witness of experience that only "in, with and under" other presences is the divine presence ever vouchsafed to us. . . . Clearly, then, the immediacy of God's presence to our souls is a mediated immediacy.[41]

For Baillie, this apparently self-contradictory phrase only makes sense in the light of a "conception of history as something that happens in the present." Baillie speaks of his knowledge of God as first coming to him from his parents and church community. He came to believe that God not only "used these media but that in using them He actually did reveal Himself to *my* soul." Thus he arrived at the conclusion: "God reveals Himself to me only through others who went before, yet in so doing reveals Himself to me now."[42]

Similarly, Bernard Lonergan asserts that except for infants, who live in a "world of immediacy," there is no experience that is not mediated by meaning. Even in the "prayerful mystic's cloud of unknowing," there is a "mediated return to immediacy."[43]

Whether or not one finds the notion of "mediated immediacy" helpful, it is clear that a "direct" experience of God that bypasses Christ or the church would be highly problematic from the standpoint of Christian dogmatics. One thing to keep in mind in this connection is that mystics do sometimes tend toward a paradoxical use of language. Thus it can be very misleading to put a great deal of stock in any single statement by a mystical author. Statements that seem to imply a total immediacy to God are often clearly qualified in other contexts. We shall see several examples of this in our study of the works of Bernard of Clairvaux.

It is interesting to see how von Hügel evaluates Bernard and Calvin in relation to his three elements of religion. Bernard is seen as a "great contemplative" who grasps the truth of the "multiplicity in unity" that is so central to von Hügel's thought.[44] Calvin, on the other hand, along with Luther and Huldreich Zwingli, is seen as falling back upon "some form and fragmentary continuation, or even in its way intensification, of Institutional Religion."[45]

This book will take issue with von Hügel's assessment of Calvin. Although it will not argue that Calvin had strong mystical leanings, it will suggest that there is a greater balance in Calvin's thought than has often been supposed. As William Siktberg puts it: "Calvin was not a heartless, coldly logical thinker. Behind his system of thought, so often foreboding and cruel, a piety burned which had been set ablaze by the Living Presence of divine mercy and love."[46]

Of course, Bernard's writings must also be scrutinized to see if his thought can be legitimately credited with the near-perfect balance attributed to it by von Hügel. To cite just one example of potential conflict, Bernard *does* seem to allow for a unique "mystical mode" of apprehending reality, although I will suggest that he qualifies this in such a way that he avoids the extreme of "pure mysticism" that von Hügel finds so objectionable.

It is interesting to note that von Hügel opposes Ritschl, whose aversion to "metaphysics of any kind" is "demonstrably excessive," an overreaction against the "contrary metaphysical excesses of the Hegelian school."[47] He takes issue especially with Wilhelm Herrmann, a member of the Ritschlian school, who, bent on a "will-o'-the-wisp quest of an exclusive objectivity . . . has to define Mysticism in terms of Exclusive Mysticism, and then to reject such an aberration."[48] This, in fact, is what Ritschl himself does, as we have already seen.

Having looked at a serviceable schema for a general understanding of mysticism, I now turn to a more specific conception. I would like to propose the definition given by Jean Gerson (1363–1429) as a guide for the present study:

> Mystical theology is experiential knowledge of God attained through the union of spiritual affection with Him. Through this union the words of the Apostle are fulfilled: "He who clings to God is one spirit with Him (1 Cor. 6:17)."[49]

The advantage of using Gerson's definition is that it represents not a modern scholarly construct, but a genuine medieval usage of the term, against which the mysticism of Bernard and Calvin can be compared. As we examine the texts, it should become clear that the definition is applicable to both Bernard and Calvin, although in somewhat different ways.

A few things are particularly noteworthy in Gerson's exposition of mystical theology. First, as is clear from the definition above, he exemplifies the focus on "union with God" that became prominent in the late medieval period. Second, he conceives of union as spiritual, not essential—a "union of will":

> The union with which we are concerned, namely that which unites the one who loves with the beloved, is touched upon by Aristotle in the *Ethics* when he says: "A friend is another self." The nature of this union becomes apparent when Aristotle says further: "Among friends there is a conformity of will." Thus, when our spirit clings to God through the most intimate love it is one spirit with Him through conformity of will (1 Cor. 6:17).[50]

A corollary to this statement is Gerson's rejection of any interpretation of mysticism that argues that "a soul loses itself and its creaturely being and receives true divine being, so that it is no longer a creature nor does it see and love God through creaturely existence." Thus, there is no question of an "essential union" or "equality with God." Gerson will accept the interpretation that "the unitive soul always remains in its own generic being and is said to be 'transformed' into God only in the sense of 'becoming like' God."[51]

A third point in Gerson's exposition is that *unio mystica* always has a cognitive component. The content of mystical union "will be in an experiential mode (*experimentalis*) but it will also be knowledge (*cognitio*)."[52] In this respect he is in continuity with a statement of Gregory the Great, which was also quoted by Bernard: "amor ipse notitia est" ("love itself is a form of knowing"). The relationship between love and knowledge in *unio mystica* was a significant concern in the medieval period and will therefore receive some attention in the following chapters.[53]

Finally, two points are made with reference to the church that have particular relevance for the present work: (1) Gerson's mysticism is not elitist. He specifically states that "mystical theology, although it is the highest and most perfect knowledge, can nevertheless be experienced by any of the faithful, even young girls or the uneducated."[54] (2) Gerson clearly affirms the necessity of church doctrine and the sacraments in the attainment of *unio mystica*.[55]

These five points drawn from Gerson yield a set of questions that will guide our comparative study of the theologies of Bernard and Calvin: (1) Granted that "union with God" (or Christ) is a dominant motif in Bernard and Calvin, how do they conceive the nature of this union? (2) What is the role of knowledge in their respective theologies of union? (3) Is mysticism seen as an experience accessible to all Christians or only to a few? (4) What is the relationship of mysticism to the institutional church? It is my thesis that the similarities between Bernard and Calvin on these points are much stronger than has been recognized by Calvin scholarship to date.

The third and fourth questions provide a link with the more "generic" understanding of mysticism discussed above, which, as we saw, wishes to conceive of mysticism as one of several components that are always and everywhere present in the Christian life. Gerson speaks at least of the possibility of any Christian enjoying mysticism as he defines it. We shall have to ask if the same is true of Bernard and Calvin and how they see mystical experience in relation to other aspects of the Christian life.

SCHOLARSHIP ON CALVIN
AND MYSTICISM: A BRIEF SURVEY

Research on Calvin's relationship to the mystical tradition has generally proceeded along three lines: (1) studies of direct references by Calvin to the writings of mystical authors; (2) studies of the influence of medieval and contemporary mystical movements on the life and works of Calvin; or (3) discussions of mystical themes that are present in Calvin's theology. This book is an attempt to contribute mainly to the third category of research.

Direct References to Mystical Authors
in Calvin's Writings

In the 1559 *Institutes*, Calvin refers to Bernard of Clairvaux, Pseudo-Dionysius, and (indirectly) Ignatius Loyola. The references to Pseudo-

Dionysius and Loyola are few and need not detain us here.[56] Bernard, however, is quoted extensively, and a number of recent studies have attempted to clarify the relationship between Calvin and Bernard.

A modest beginning is made by W. Stanford Reid in his article "Bernard of Clairvaux in the Thought of John Calvin."[57] Reid begins by noting that references to Bernard first appear in the second edition of the *Institutes* (1539), and constantly increase through the succeeding editions. The reason for this, Reid suggests, is not only that Bernard was "the only medieval Augustinian of whom Calvin had any great knowledge," but that Calvin may well have found in Bernard a "kindred spirit." Reid mentions similarities in their personalities, the fact that they were both "humanists," and similar preaching styles as parallels between the two men that may partially explain Calvin's attraction to Bernard's writings.[58] While this strikes me as a reasonable hypothesis, it would be difficult to establish definitively in the absence of direct statements in Calvin's works. For example, nowhere do we find Calvin referring to himself as having a personality similar to Bernard's.

Reid also speaks of doctrinal agreement between Calvin and Bernard, and of the possible influence on Calvin of Bernard's "mystical" conception of the knowledge of God (i.e., by revelation through grace).[59] However, a more complete textual analysis has since appeared. A.N.S. Lane laid the groundwork in his article, "Calvin's Sources of St. Bernard." This was followed by Jill Raitt's "Calvin's Use of Bernard of Clairvaux."[60] Raitt undertakes a systematic study of almost all of Calvin's direct references to Bernard in the *Institutes*. Her findings are worth summarizing here.

In answer to the question, Why did Calvin use Bernard? Raitt points to a statement in the *Institutes* in which Calvin cites Bernard in defense of the orthodoxy of his own positions. She further surmises, prescinding from Reid's hypotheses, that Calvin simply came to have an increasing appreciation for Bernard's work. This can be seen in an examination of the successive editions of the *Institutes*. For example, there are three instances where a quotation from Bernard is the only new material added in the 1559 edition. Furthermore, there are only two passages where Calvin explicitly disagrees with Bernard, both in the 1539 edition. While Calvin does not remove these negative references from the later editions, all his subsequent citations express a positive assessment of Bernard's theology, as evidenced by the laudatory phrases he uses when referring to Bernard.[61]

Raitt proceeds to discuss the references to Bernard in the *Institutes*. These fall under three "theological loci": the bondage of the will and grace, justification by faith, and election-reprobation. There are direct references to eight works by Bernard, the majority being from the *Sermons on the Canticles*. Raitt's concern is to show how accurately Calvin quotes texts from Bernard, whether his interpretations are true to Bernard's contexts, and whether he agrees or disagrees with Bernard in each case.[62]

In the 1539 edition of the *Institutes,* there are only three references to Bernard, all from *De gratia,* and two of them contain negative judgments. But one quote from *De gratia* is inaccurate, which leads Raitt to the conclusion that in the 1539 edition "Calvin was working from memory, not from a text, and probably his memory was based on the reading of isolated passages of *De gratia* only." This was to change in the later editions, where Calvin began to quote Bernard more extensively. From 1543 on, "Calvin clearly has a text before him and . . . all his quotations are preceded by laudatory comments."[63]

Raitt concludes that Calvin came to see Bernard not as a "representative of the corrupt medieval church" (Peter Lombard was increasingly mentioned in this capacity by Calvin), but as the "'last of the Fathers' and an ally." Bernard provided a "nearer link" than Augustine in passages where Calvin was trying to prove his continuity with the tradition. Perhaps because Bernard was a "friendly" source, Calvin quoted him with greater care than he did many of his opponents.[64]

It is clear from Raitt's thorough analysis of the texts that Calvin looked to Bernard mostly for support of his doctrinal positions, and not for help to clarify his understanding of "mystical union." Nevertheless, the doctrinal agreement that exists certainly invites a comparison of other aspects of their thought.[65]

Calvin and Mystical Movements

Any discussion of the "influence" of mystical movements on Calvin's thought is necessarily tentative, since the connections made are usually based on inference and not on direct quotations from Calvin's works. The secondary literature has examined Calvin's relationship to Platonism and the Brethren of the Common Life, as well as Calvin's view of some of his contemporaries who, according to some commentators, had affinities to mysticism (e.g., the Libertines).[66]

Numerous references to Plato appear in the 1559 edition of the *Institutes.* Jean Boisset, in his *Sagesse et sainteté dans la pensée de Jean Calvin,* analyzes several Platonist themes that can be found in Calvin's works. Boisset is careful to point out that Calvin was not a Platonist in any strict sense, but that he sometimes borrowed Platonic formulas and patterns of expression, adapting them to his purpose of clarifying biblical revelation. He stresses that Plato was motivated by the concerns of the philosopher, Calvin by the concerns of the biblical theologian. Nevertheless, they both wished to understand human and divine realities with a view toward the common good.[67]

Boisset proceeds to discuss seven Platonic themes found in Calvin: the body as "prison" and the immortality of the soul; tranquillity in the face of death; the existence of "two worlds"; contemplation; the longing for a return to a state of "purity"; political concerns; and the use of similar images and points of view (even when Plato is not directly cited by Calvin).[68]

A look at just one of these themes, body and soul, will suffice to provide a context for understanding Boisset's conclusions. Calvin sees Plato as the only philosopher having "a proper view of the soul, its essence and its destiny," particularly because he recognizes it as immortal.[69] However, Plato is praised by Calvin in this instance precisely because he agrees with scripture. Similarly, Calvin will sometimes speak, like Plato, of the body as a prison.[70]

But Calvin draws quite different conclusions from the affirmation of the soul's immortality than those of Plato: "Plato draws the conclusion that the philosopher must hate the body and despise it; Calvin concludes that the Christian must use the body for the ends desired by the soul."[71] For Calvin, it is *sin*, not the body per se, that is to be hated. Furthermore, Plato does not affirm bodily resurrection, which is of capital importance to Calvin.[72] There is a final difference with respect to people's eternal destiny: Plato sees the fullness of life after death as enjoyed only by the "pure philosopher," while others must return to another life in order to complete their purification. Calvin recognizes no such "degrees" of purification—one is either saved or damned.[73]

Boisset's analysis of texts leads him to the following conclusion:

> How then are we to understand the expression: "the Platonism of John Calvin"?
>
> Certainly not as a "doctrine" or a "philosophy" which the Reformer might have appropriated and whose contents he might have adopted in order to diffuse it throughout the different parts of his system. But as the application to a doctrine of the thought of a philosopher; the application of a philosophy to theology, expressing itself in an extremely flexible manner, by an orientation, an adoption of points of view, images, experiences, terms, expressions, themes, by a method which amounts to a "Christian Socratism," so that humanity might discover the truths which God has revealed and manifested in his Word. Plato furnished Calvin with a language that was fitting for the expression of revelation and its symbols in their deepest profundity.[74]

Charles Partee, in a later article, takes a more cautious stance, stopping short of any reference to a "Christian Socratism." He concedes that Calvin speaks of Plato as being part of the "sounder class" of philosophers, "but this approval and a few common themes does not make Calvin a Platonist in any 'strong' sense. Calvin was aware of the possibility of a Christian

Platonism and rejected it in the strongest possible terms." In support of this conclusion, he cites Calvin's *Excuse de Iehan Calvin à Messieurs les Nicodémites*.[75]

More significant for the present study would be a connection between Calvin and Neoplatonism, since much medieval mysticism was built upon Neoplatonic foundations.[76] Apart from the reference to Pseudo-Dionysius noted above, Calvin makes no mention of Neoplatonism. Historically, his main contact with later Platonism was through Renaissance Florence, particularly in his acquaintance with Jacques Lefèvre d'Etaples. Calvin also was probably exposed to Platonist mysticism during the years in which he was in the circle of Marguerite of Navarre.[77]

Another movement with which Calvin had contact was the Brethren of the Common Life. This group was central to the *Devotio Moderna* of the late medieval period. The spirit of the Brethren had been introduced at the College of Montaigu, which Calvin entered in 1523. The college had a library filled with mystical treatises by Gerhard Groote and his followers.[78]

The extent of the Brethren's influence on Calvin has been variously described. Alexandre Ganoczy suggests that "Calvin's pessimistic attitude toward theological speculation and temporal power in the church, as well as his keen sense of transcendence, certainly reflect the mentality of the mystics." By "the mystics" he specifically means the tradition of German mysticism that includes Groote and the Brethren.[79] In an earlier work, Albert Hyma goes further, declaring that at Montaigu Calvin "found at least some of the material for his 'Institutes.' It is now apparent that this remarkable work is at least in part one of the last fruits of the 'New Devotion.' "[80] This latter statement is much more problematic, since it claims direct influence of the *Devotio Moderna* on Calvin. Although this is not totally implausible, the fact is that Calvin does not once mention Groote or his associates in the *Institutes*.

Two more recent studies have looked at Calvin's relationship to the *Devotio Moderna*. Lucien Richard presents a theological analysis in *The Spirituality of John Calvin*. Regarding the influence of the Brethren, Richard makes a more modest claim than Hyma:

> How deeply Calvin was influenced by his stay in Montaigu is difficult to assess. But there is no doubt that the spirituality of John Calvin shows a marked resemblance to the vocabulary, and to a lesser extent to the ideas, of the *De Imitatio Christi* and the writings of Groote.[81]

Richard acknowledges that Calvin's spirituality follows the "same impulse" as the *Devotio Moderna*, that is, a stress on the transcendence of God. This is exemplified by his "preoccupation with the concepts of election, of holiness, and of the glory of God," as well as the idea of order.

However, Calvin also departs in significant ways from the movement. For example, he substitutes *pietas* for *devotio,* since the latter word had the "pejorative connotation of exteriority." His advocacy of "contempt for the world" does not express itself in an attempt to "pattern life in the world on life in the cloister," as in the *Devotio;* rather, it is expressed as an apostolic and humanistic spirituality of service to God in the world.[82]

Finally, like the *Devotio Moderna,* Calvin's spirituality is individualistic. But in the *Devotio* this individualism is always subordinate to the church. According to Richard, such is not the case with Calvin, who develops a new epistemology of the correlation of Word and Spirit. For Calvin, no external authority can be the ultimate criterion of truth. Instead, the truth of God's word is validated by the action of the Holy Spirit in the life of the individual believer. As Richard puts it:

> Through the action of the Spirit, the believer is made capable of distinguishing the reality of God from the products of his own mind. . . . The Holy Spirit creates within man a *sensus divinitatis* which becomes the source of new understanding, spiritual discernment in the things of God and man, and certainty.

Thus, for Calvin, "the action of the Holy Spirit occurs principally in the individual and not in the Church. The Spirit acts toward the individual independent of the community." This is not to say that the church is unimportant—indeed Calvin refers to the church as "mother." But the church is mother "only in the measure that the Holy Spirit acts in her." That Spirit "cannot be institutionalized."[83]

Richard concludes that Calvin's spirituality differed radically from that of the *Devotio Moderna* on three points:

> It was a spirituality of service within the world; it was accompanied by a new religious epistemology which made possible a reinterpretation of ecclesiological models and laid sound foundations for individualism in spirituality; and it asserted the inner unity of Christian life and theology.[84]

Kenneth Strand's examination of John Calvin and the Brethren, in contrast to Richard's, is more historical than theological in its emphasis. Strand notes at the outset that evidence of "direct contact" with the Brethren is lacking in Calvin, but that he "came in touch with the ideals and practices fostered by the Brethren" through three avenues: his education at Montaigu, his contact with the "Fabrisian Reformers," and his association with Sturm and Bucer in Strassburg.[85]

At Montaigu, Calvin studied under Noel Béda, who in turn had been a student of John Standonck. Standonck had been trained by the Brethren of the Common Life in Gouda. When he came to Montaigu in 1483, he brought with him many of the Brethren's ideals for reform. By 1503 Standonck had managed to secure the adoption of a new constitution for Montaigu, a "plan of reorganization" that contained many parallels to life in Brethren houses.[86]

Béda himself, although he did not attempt to dismantle Standonck's program, was much more interested in scholastic theology. Thus, it is reasonable to assume that Béda and Calvin shared the ideals of the Brethren and Standonck "in only a somewhat diminished way." But Strand hastens to add:

> However, the influence of the Montaigu was not limited to Béda personally. The daily schedule and other aspects of the program which reflected the innovations of Standonck could not but have touched the life of young Calvin. Moreover, Standonck had provided the Montaigu with a library containing writings of pioneer leaders of the Devotio Moderna, such as those of Gerard Zerbolt. With this literature Calvin must certainly have become acquainted.

Similarly, Strand suggests that Calvin's reputation for correcting his student colleagues may have been partly motivated by a desire to live up to Standonck's constitution, which encouraged students "to reprove one another in cases of wrongdoing."[87]

A second line of contact with the Brethren came through the so-called Fabrisian Reform movement, whose leader was Jacques Lefèvre d'Etaples. Some of Lefèvre's disciples became Calvin's teachers when he returned to Paris after studying law, and Calvin visited Lefèvre himself in 1534. Guillaume Farel was also in this circle. Strand reminds his readers that most of the Fabrisians (Farel was one exception) did not leave the Catholic Church. Nevertheless, many of Lefèvre's ideas anticipated Protestantism, such as the emphasis on *sola scriptura* and justification by faith in his 1512 *Commentary on the Epistles of Paul*.[88]

Strand takes special note of a fact that has often been overlooked: Lefèvre's indebtedness to the *Devotio Moderna*. Lefèvre had not only visited the Brethren but was instrumental in the publication of some works related to the movement. Strand cites an important study by C. Louise Salley that compares Lefèvre's *Commentary on the Four Gospels* with *The Imitation of Christ* and the writings of Wessel Gansfort (both of which he quoted). Important parallels include

> statements regarding *sola scriptura*, justification by faith, imitation of Christ in the life, contempt for the present world (in the sense that "the Christian should desire to be unknown in this world in order that he may receive glory in the next," to use Lefèvre's words), mystical union between God and the Christian individual, distaste for empty formalism, critical attitude toward excessive veneration of saints and of the

Virgin Mary, and appraisal of education as worthwhile only as it is placed within the context of the love of Christ.[89]

Strand sees Lefèvre, then, as a possible link between the religious thought of the "Northern Reformers" (i.e., the Brethren) and the theology of John Calvin. The parallels are particularly strong in such areas as justification by faith, the use of the vernacular, the role of good works, and the sacraments.[90] However, Strand hastens to point out, in concluding this first part of his study, that

> care must be taken not to overemphasize these links to the extent that Lefèvre is considered to be truly a "Protestant before his time" or that Calvin is considered to be a direct spiritual descendent of either the Fabrisian Reformers or the Devotio Moderna.

It is important to recall that Lefèvre never officially left Roman Catholicism and that many of his views could not be considered "Protestant." Furthermore, "both Lefèvre and Calvin were certainly influenced by factors from more than one direction, and the latter's religious development was especially complex." Nevertheless, "although influence from the reformers to the North should not be overemphasized, neither should it be overlooked."[91]

In a second article, Strand examines a third point of contact with the Brethren, through the educational reforms of Johann Sturm in Strassburg, where Calvin lived from 1538 to 1541. Sturm had been trained by the Brethren of the Common Life in Liège, and explicitly set up the Strassburg curriculum according to the "Liège pattern." This reform was implemented the very year Calvin arrived, and it included the addition of Greek and theology to the curriculum. Calvin paid a return visit to Strassburg in 1556, shortly before establishing the Geneva Academy. The resulting curriculum in Geneva bears a striking resemblance to the one in Strassburg, both "in organizational scheme and in curricular content."[92] In addition to this there was Calvin's relationship to Martin Bucer, who had been deeply influenced by the writings of Gansfort, a humanist who was closely associated with the Brethren. It has been suggested that Bucer's influence is significant in Calvin's views on the Eucharist, justification, and predestination.[93]

Strand comes to the following conclusion regarding the "influence" of the Brethren on Calvin: "Perhaps the most striking, as well as the most clearly demonstrable, line of influence from this Brotherhood to him was that pertaining to educational reforms."[94] He reiterates his caution about overemphasizing the links between Calvin and the Brethren; nevertheless, his study has shown that this connection is not insignificant.

In an "Additional Note on Calvin and the Influence of the Brethren of

the Common Life in France," Strand takes issue as a historian with some
of Richard's theological conclusions in *The Spirituality of John Calvin*. He
sees Richard's treatment of the *Devotio* as "somewhat imbalanced,"
especially in his stress on the "anti-intellectualism" and "asceticism" of
the movement.[95] This may be true of *The Imitation of Christ*, he concedes,
but there is a great deal of evidence regarding "educational work" (as in
Sturm's reforms in Strassburg) and "book-copying and printing activities" on the part of the Brethren.[96]

Strand takes issue with Richard's further claim that the *Devotio* had
separated theology and spirituality. Richard sees the integration of the
two in French humanism (e.g., by Lefèvre) as owing to an "Erasmian"
influence. But Strand points out (again referring to C. Louise Salley) that
the *Devotio* nourished Lefèvre's thought "in *much the same way* in which
Richard declares that Erasmus did." Furthermore, "if the kinds of books
used and disseminated by the Brethren may be used as any sort of
criterion in this regard," the Brethren showed more openness to scholastic
theology than the humanists, even though both groups "tended to decry
finespun scholastic argumentation."[97]

Thus, Strand cannot agree with Richard's conclusions regarding the
three essential differences between Calvin and the Brethren.[98] He states,
"On all three counts, Calvin's spirituality was more similar to, than
different from, the emphases of the Devotio Moderna."[99] It is important to
emphasize that Strand is not taking issue with Richard's interpretation of
Calvin (as I will), but rather of the *Devotio*. For Strand, then, there is more
than just a superficial "resemblance" of vocabulary and ideas between
Calvin and the Brethren.[100]

There is one other, relatively untouched, area of research regarding
Calvin and mystical movements, and that is his relationship to some of his
contemporaries who might be seen as having affinities to mysticism.
William Siktberg gives a brief introduction to this area without providing
much detail. These individuals and groups would include Sebastian
Castellio, Michael Servetus, Bernardino Ochino, the Anabaptists (!), and
the Libertines.

Siktberg takes note of Calvin's admiration of the piety of Bernardino
Ochino, a piety encouraged by Jean de Valdes, an Italian mystic. But when
Ochino wrote his *Dialogues*, in which he repudiated predestination, the
Trinity, and free will, Calvin expressed disapproval. Similarly, Siktberg
points to Calvin's letter to the Queen of Navarre, in which Calvin explains
his objections to the Libertines (also well documented in the *Institutes*).[101]

Siktberg's treatment of the Anabaptists suffers from his adoption of
Jules Bonnet's mistaken view that the *Theologia Deutsch* was an Anabaptist
document.[102] Calvin's problems with the Anabaptists were rooted in
issues other than mysticism. The key study on this topic has been done by

Willem Balke, in *Calvin and the Anabaptist Radicals*. Balke catalogs several areas of disagreement with the Anabaptists, which Calvin puts in writing as early as the 1536 *Institutes*. These would include the notions of law and the community of goods (directed against the Münster Anabaptists), the doctrine of the church, the role of church discipline, the sacraments, and attitudes toward civil government.[103]

Siktberg's assessment of Calvin's relationship to mysticism (in the light of Calvin's opinions of these various persons and groups) is worth quoting:

> When mysticism led to theological heresy, Calvin no longer tolerated it. But just so long as it stayed within the bounds of what he considered to be orthodox Christianity and peaceful living, he seemed to give it his hearty support. For Calvin, mysticism was evidently legitimate and useful as long as it subjected itself to proper religious and institutional authority.[104]

The remainder of Siktberg's study looks at mystical elements found in Calvin's theology. His contributions to this discussion will be noted in the appropriate places below.

Mystical Themes in Calvin

A number of scholars have suggested the presence of mystical themes and terminology in the writings of Calvin. Stanford Reid, for example, points to Calvin's notion of the knowledge of God as coming "only by revelation understood through the grace of God. This is exactly the position of Bernard in his mystical writings."[105] John T. McNeill and Ford Lewis Battles take note of terms used by Calvin in the *Institutes* that parallel the language of the mystics, but they think "the parallels are often more verbal than substantial."[106] Siktberg sees mystical elements in Calvin's anthropology, his doctrine of the Spirit, his notions of repentance and faith, his understanding of prayer, and his teachings on the Lord's Supper. At the same time, Siktberg holds to his thesis that the mystical element is always bound by the authoritative.[107]

Most of these areas will be treated in the remainder of the book as part of the background for a discussion of *unio mystica* in Bernard and Calvin. The theme of mystical union itself has received some measure of attention in the secondary sources, but usually only by way of a denial of a mystical strand in Calvin. For example, in a note on Calvin's use of the term *unio mystica* in *Institutes* 3.11.10, McNeill and Battles quote Wilhelm Niesel's remark that Calvin's notion of union with Christ "has nothing whatever to do with the absorption of the pious mystic into the sphere of the divine being."[108] While this statement is true as it stands, it implies that "absorption into the divine being" is the only way of understanding mystical union. On the contrary, Calvin's description of the union as a "spiritual" one has much in common with the understanding of mystics like Gerson and Bernard.[109]

Before proceeding with a study of the texts, I would like to reiterate a point that is of some importance: John Calvin apparently did not see himself as a mystic, nor was mysticism a major focus of concern in his works. Nevertheless, as the preceding survey of secondary literature has shown, there is a relationship between Calvin and the mystical tradition. The clearest historical evidence for this is his extensive and laudatory use of the writings of Bernard of Clairvaux, but there also seems to be a fairly significant relationship to the Brethren of the Common Life. This book attempts to evaluate the presence of mystical themes in Calvin, particularly in relation to his teaching on union with Christ.

Chapter 2 discusses the anthropological underpinnings of Bernard's and Calvin's respective theologies, with particular emphasis on the notion of *sensus divinitatis*. Chapter 3 compares Bernard's and Calvin's overall theologies of justification. These chapters lay the groundwork for a discussion of *unio mystica* in chapters 4 and 5. A final chapter presents a summary and draws some tentative conclusions about Calvin and mysticism.

A NOTE ON THE USE OF SOURCES

I have attempted to incorporate as wide a variety of works as possible in the following chapters. Thus, I make reference to Bernard's major treatises, such as *De gratia* and *De diligendo Deo*, and to the *Sermones super Cantica*, but I also consider other sermons (e.g., those on conversion and others from the liturgical year) and letters of Bernard. Similarly, the treatment of Calvin includes relevant material not only from the *Institutes* but also from his scripture commentaries and a sampling of letters and sermons.

Chapters 2 and 3 do not pretend to give exhaustive treatments of Bernard and Calvin on anthropology and justification, but rather to survey the main outlines of their thought on these questions through a general sampling of texts, and to focus specifically on direct citations of Bernard by Calvin or parallels in their theologies. Chapters 4 and 5, as the main focus of this work, *do* strive for a more exhaustive treatment of texts.

2

THE CHRISTIAN ANTHROPOLOGY
OF BERNARD AND CALVIN

In order to discuss adequately the notion of mystical union in Bernard and Calvin, one must first have an understanding of their anthropologies, that is, how they conceive of the human being's status in relation to God. In Christianity, mysticism has always been inseparable from the question of salvation. Thus, before Bernard and Calvin could ask about the nature of union with God, they first had to discuss how union is even possible, in the light of the sinful condition of humanity. This chapter will examine their respective views on the need for salvation. Of particular importance is the question, Do Bernard and Calvin see a "point of contact" with God's redeeming grace? Having answered this, we can then turn to the questions of how that grace is received (chap. 3) and experienced (chaps. 4 and 5) by the Christian believer.

BERNARD'S ANTHROPOLOGY

When discussing the structure of the soul, Bernard does no more than to repeat the "official" formula that dates from the time of Augustine, as in his sermon *Ad clericos de conversione*, where he states, "The soul is nothing but reason, memory, and will."[1] However, according to Endre von Ivánka, "Bernard attributes no importance to this tripartite distinction. On the contrary, he insists on the indivisibility of the soul, on its fundamental unity, notwithstanding the plurality of its different functions."[2] Indeed, Bernard is more interested precisely in the functions rather than in the structure of the soul. This is clear in statements like the following:

> There are two places in the rational soul, the lower which it rules, and the higher in which it rests. The lower, which it rules, the body; the

higher, in which it rests, God. . . . Indeed, the soul has three things to do
in the body: to live, to sense, and to rule.[3]

Rather than a concern with the structure of the soul per se, we see here a
concern with the structure of the "domain in which the soul exercises its
power and displays its activity: the diversity is in the objects towards
which it can orient itself."[4]

This emphasis allows Bernard to employ several different schemas in
speaking of the soul that are not contradictory but also not entirely
consistent with one another. A good example will be what we will see
regarding image and likeness. Von Ivánka also contrasts the three levels
of liberty in De gratia with the four levels of loving God in De diligendo Deo.
Thus, he concludes, "the schemas utilized by Bernard never cease to
vary."[5]

It is important to note that when Bernard discusses the structure of the
soul, he never speaks of distinct faculties as though one or more of them
had some *active* capacity to receive the gift of God's presence. As we have
seen, the soul rules in relation to the body, but rests in relation to God. Von
Ivánka is emphatic that Bernard does not "localize" the presence of God
in a distinct part of the soul (which would open him to the charge of
"ontologizing" grace). Rather, he preserves the totally graced nature of
God's presence:

> As soon as one refuses to admit different levels, distinct faculties of the
> soul, in accordance with the different degrees of knowledge and love, as
> soon as one refuses to see anything there but different *states* of the soul,
> to which the soul submits, different kinds of divine action upon it, owing
> to God's prerogative to insert himself immediately into the spiritual
> being, this divine visit, this "divina inspectio," retains entirely its
> supernatural and gratuitous character.[6]

As Bernard says in one place, God "communicates himself directly to the
mind, he makes himself known directly." The soul is not active, but
passive in its reception of this presence.[7]

Thus, there is no trace in Bernard's anthropology of an ontological
"mixture" of divine and human substance. This is especially clear in
passages like the following, from Sermons on the Canticles 71:

> The Father and Son cannot be said to be one person, because the Father
> is one and the Son is one. Yet they are said to be, and they are, one,
> because they have and are one substance, since they have not each
> separate substance. On the contrary, since God and man do not share the
> same nature or substance, they cannot be said to be a unity, yet they are
> with complete truth and accuracy, said to be one spirit, if they cohere
> with the bond of love.[8]

This point is of no small importance in relation to Calvin, who attacks Osiander on precisely this ground.

Probably the best place to begin a discussion of the application of Bernard's anthropology is his work *De gratia et libero arbitrio*.[9] In this treatise, Bernard was attempting to deal with the problem of grace and freedom posed by the text of Paul's letter to the Romans (which he cites, explicitly or implicitly, forty-three times in the course of the treatise). "Free choice" and not "free will" was the issue, that is, a person's ability to perform free acts. It was from scholasticism that treatises on the will would later emerge.[10]

Bernard begins by mentioning a conversation in which he referred to his experience of grace, "how I recognized myself as being impelled to good by its prevenient action . . . and helped, with its help, to find perfection." A "bystander" then asked, "What part do *you* play, then, . . . or what reward or prize do you hope for, if it is all God's work?"

Bernard answered by first insisting that we are saved not by good works but by the mercy of God. Then he rephrased the bystander's question and answered it directly:

> Maybe you are saying: "What part, then, does free choice play?" I shall answer you in one word: it is saved. Take away free choice and there is nothing to be saved. Take away grace and there is no means of saving. Without the two combined, this work cannot be done: the one as operative principle, the other as object toward which, or in which, it is accomplished. . . . Consequently, free choice is said to co-operate with operating grace in its act of consent, or, in other words, in its process of being saved.[11]

Bernard's point in this section is crucial to the present study: in his view (and, we shall see, in Calvin's as well), one cannot speak of the influx of grace without recognizing some kind of "opening," or capacity, for the reception of grace. That "opening," for Bernard, is free choice, and its role is nothing more than consent to God's act of salvation. Bernard insists that this

> voluntary consent . . . is neither forced nor extorted. It stems from the will and not from necessity, denying or giving itself on no issue except by way of the will. But if it is compelled in spite of itself, then there is violent, not voluntary, consent. Where the will is absent, so is consent; for only what is voluntary may be called consent. Hence, where you have consent, there also is the will. But where the will is, there is freedom. And this is what I understand by the term "free choice."[12]

To Bernard, it is impossible to speak of a creature's being made just or unjust without its being capable of consent (i.e., having a will). Otherwise, we could speak of trees and animals experiencing beatitude, which is patently "out of the question." Bernard is emphatic that there is no way in which the will can be "deprived of its freedom." This is true even in the present sinful state of humanity.[13]

Does this mean, then, that we are free to choose the good apart from grace? Bernard's answer is an unequivocal no. His approach to resolving this apparent contradiction is to make a distinction between three kinds of freedom. There is "freedom from necessity," which belongs to our "natural condition," and is another way of speaking of "free choice." Even sin does not change this, for in free choice lies the unerasable imprint of the image of God.[14] "Freedom from sin," on the other hand (more properly called "free counsel") was lost by sin and is restored only through grace. Similarly, "freedom from sorrow" (or "free pleasure") was lost by sin and will be enjoyed only in heaven.[15]

More specifically, freedom from necessity is "that freedom alone by which the will is free either to judge itself good if it has consented to good, or bad, if to evil."[16] However, the will cannot, in the present state of human sinfulness, go beyond this:

> Now to the "judgment" is added a "choice," and this act of choosing (*eligere*) is itself the result of a deliberation (*consilium*). However, as a result of original sin, we are not inevitably capable of choosing good or avoiding evil, even when they are judged as such by our reason.[17]

Thus, freedom remains, but it is only freedom to choose among evil options. As Bernard himself says:

> To will lies in our power indeed as a result of free choice, but not to carry out what we will. I am not saying to will the good or to will the bad, but simply to will. For to will the good indicates an achievement; and to will the bad, a defect; whereas simply to will denotes the subject itself which does either the achieving or the failing.[18]

Therefore, even *willing* the good, let alone carrying it out, is out of the question.

Bernard clarifies his position by discussing his understanding of pre- and postlapsarian anthropology. Adam, he claims, possessed the lower of two degrees of the freedoms of counsel and pleasure, that is, "being able not to sin or be disturbed." (*Not to be able* to sin or be disturbed is reserved to God, the angels, and the blessed in heaven.) By his abuse of freedom of choice, however, "he deprived himself of the others."[19] Bernard explains:

> The sinner's fall, therefore, was not due to the gift of being able to, but to the vice of willing to. However, if he fell by the power of his will, this does not mean that he was equally free to rise again by that same power. The ability to remain standing lest he fall was indeed given to his will,

but not to get up again once he fell. It is not as easy to climb out of a pit as to fall into one. By his will alone, man fell into the pit of sin; but he cannot climb out of his will alone, since now, even if he wishes he cannot not sin.

Bernard insists that this does not compromise his position on free choice:

> If he finds himself unable simply to will the good, this is a sign that he lacks free counsel, not free choice. And if he finds himself powerless, not indeed to will the good, but to accomplish that good which he already wills, let him recognize that it is not free choice that is wanting to him, but free pleasure.[20]

Later, Bernard describes a situation where the will can be forced (Peter's denial of Christ, where his love of self outstripped his desire not to deny the Lord), but he continues to hold his ground. Free choice would indeed be compromised if the will could "be forced by some cause other than itself." But when the will itself does the forcing, it becomes both the cause and the recipient of the coercion. Thus, "just when it seemed to lose its freedom, it actually received it."[21]

In summary, Bernard's anthropology holds that after the fall, freedom of choice remains but is rendered impotent by sin, since it is able neither to will nor to carry out the good. As he puts it, "Free choice . . . constitutes us willers; grace, willers of the good."[22]

Throughout this discussion, Bernard is implicitly reflecting on the nature of the soul. Free choice, by his own definition, is "a self-determining habit of the soul." It is important to note that he does not mean "habit" in a Thomistic sense, but simply as a "way of acting."[23] In any event, we must ask, What is it about the soul that makes free choice its permanent possession?

Etienne Gilson describes "free choice" as the "voice of conscience" which can never be extinguished in a person.[24] It was noted above that Bernard sees in free choice a vestige of the *image* of God. In one of the *Sermones super Cantica canticorum*, on the other hand, Bernard asks, "What can be a clearer sign of her [the soul's] heavenly origin than that she retains a natural *likeness* to it in the land of unlikeness [in regione dissimilitudinis retinere similitudinem]?"[25] The difference between Bernard's expression in the two works merits a closer look.

In Sermon 81, Bernard speaks of the soul having "a great affinity [affinitatem] with the Word, the Bridegroom of the Church, Jesus Christ our Lord," because of a threefold "likeness" (*similitudine*) to the Word: its simplicity, immortality, and freedom (i.e., free choice).[26] However, there is also a distinction to be made between Christ (described here as the "image" of God) and the soul: "For the soul receives according to its capacity, but the image receives in equal measure with God."[27]

The soul, too, is in the image of God, possessing "greatness" and "uprightness," but it is not identical to these qualities, for they are God's gifts. After sin, the greatness of the soul remains, but its uprightness is lost.[28] In other words, the *image* of God is partially lost by sin. In contrast to *De gratia*, Bernard here insists that the *likeness* is preserved, although it has been

> concealed by something else which has been laid over it. The soul has not in fact put off its original form but has put on one foreign to it. The latter is an addition; the former has not been lost. This addition can hide the original form, but it cannot blot it out.

Thus, Bernard holds that "duplicity of heart does not wipe out essential simplicity," that death (whether the spiritual death which comes from sin or bodily death) does not "destroy the immortality of nature," and that "the compulsion of voluntary servitude does not extinguish free will." In other words, the three likenesses to the Word remain intact, although defiled and confused.[29]

Bernard, then, is not consistent in maintaining either the "image" or the "likeness" as that which is not lost after sin. However, it is important to note that he does not see this as a crucial point.[30] For the purposes of this study, what is important is that he recognizes some kind of openness for the reception of grace as remaining after sin. This is where Bernard locates what he calls free choice. His understanding of the *role* of free choice (prescinding from its relation to the "image" or "likeness") is the same in the Sermons on the Song of Songs as it is in *De gratia*, that is, consent:

> The soul seeks the Word, and consents to receive correction [Quaerit anima Verbum, cui consentiat ad correptionem], by which she may be enlightened to recognize him, strengthened to attain virtue, moulded to wisdom, conformed to his likeness, made fruitful by him, and enjoy him in bliss.[31]

Corneille Halflants, in his Introduction to the *Sermones super Cantica*, comments on Bernard's anthropology as follows:

> To know God, man must know himself, and between these two extremes there must be some resemblance, since all knowledge supposes likeness: *iam in aliquo similis.* Christ made himself known and loved by becoming like unto man. The tiny spark which always glows in the depths of the soul, the indelible image of God which lost so much of its likeness to him, is the ontological point of departure which opens to every human creature the possibility of a return to his Father's house.[32]

Thus, to use a term that has been very controversial in Calvin studies, we can definitely speak of a "point of contact" for redeeming grace in the anthropology of Bernard.

There is one other aspect of Bernard's anthropology that is crucial to the shape of his mystical theology: his preference for will over essence or intellect when discussing the relation of human beings to God. For example, we have already seen in *De gratia* that Bernard looks to the will as what is most distinctive about the human person.[33] Later we will see, in our discussion of *De diligendo Deo*, that Bernard conceives of union with God primarily in terms of love, the highest degree of which is a union of wills, the *unus spiritus* of 1 Cor. 6:17.[34] We will find a similar emphasis in Calvin.

CALVIN'S ANTHROPOLOGY

Calvin's anthropology is most fully developed in the 1559 edition of the *Institutes*, to which we now turn. Calvin defines the soul as "an immortal yet created essence," adding that "something divine has been engraved upon it."[35] Calvin makes it clear that this latter statement is not meant to imply that the soul is somehow a "derivative" of God's substance. For example, against the doctrines of both the Manicheans and Osiander, he states, "Souls, although the image of God be engraved upon them, are just as much created as angels are. But creation is not inpouring, but the beginning of essence out of nothing."[36]

Unlike Bernard, Calvin does not accept the traditional Augustinian formula regarding the three "faculties" of the soul.[37] Rather, he wishes to speak of only two faculties, understanding and will. Why he omits memory is unclear; apparently, he does not see it as important for his purposes. The mind and the will, however, are crucial to his understanding of anthropology:

> Therefore God provided man's soul with a mind, by which to distinguish good from evil, right from wrong; and, with the light of reason as guide, to distinguish what should be followed from what should be avoided. . . . To this he joined the will, under whose control is choice.[38]

In the state of original integrity, Adam had the power, by free choice, to attain eternal life. However, like Bernard, Calvin sees the possibility of the fall as intrinsic to human nature. Recall that Bernard makes a distinction between "being able not to sin" and "not being able to sin," the latter being reserved to God, the angels, and the blessed in heaven. Nevertheless, "the sinner's fall . . . was not due to the gift of being able to, but to the vice of willing to."[39] Calvin's argument is similar, with one notable difference:

> Adam could have stood if he wished, seeing that he fell solely by his own will. But it was because his will was *capable of being bent to one side or the other*, and *was not given the constancy to persevere*, that he fell so easily.

Yet his choice of good and evil was free, and not that alone, but the highest rectitude was in his mind and will, and all the organic parts were rightly composed to obedience, until in destroying himself he corrupted his own blessings.[40]

Thus, for both Bernard and Calvin, the will in its original state of integrity was capable of choosing either good or evil. Since the fall is a matter of free choice, Adam is therefore responsible. Calvin, however, adds a note about his not being given the grace of perseverance. The reason for this, Calvin declares, lies hidden in God's plan. He concedes that a nature which "could not or would not sin . . . would, indeed, have been more excellent." But God was free to give us any kind of nature that he pleased. This leads naturally into a discussion of providence, which immediately follows in the *Institutes*.[41] Bernard, on the other hand, does not ask in *De gratia* why God allowed Adam to fall, apart from the fact that he gave him a free will.

Calvin also has much to say about the terms "image" and "likeness." He speaks of a "nonexistent difference between these two words, except that 'likeness' has been added by way of explanation." Therefore, although he does not explicitly single Bernard out in this connection, Calvin would reject Bernard's distinctions regarding these terms (which, as we have seen, Bernard did not use consistently in any case). On the positive side, he does, like Bernard, see the soul as the "seat" of the *imago Dei*.[42]

A closer look at Calvin's understanding of "free choice" (*liberum arbitrium*) reveals some interesting similarities to Bernard, as well as some contrasts.[43] In one of two explicit disagreements with Bernard in the *Institutes* (both dating from the 1539 edition, but not removed from the later ones), Calvin accuses Bernard of "obscurity" and "subtlety" in defining free choice as consent.[44] Calvin's second disagreement with Bernard is on the question of a natural human ability to seek the good, which Calvin discusses under the rubric of "operating" and "co-operating" grace. His main opponent in this section is Peter Lombard, but he associates Bernard with Lombard's position:

> The Master of the Sentences meant to settle this point when he taught: "We need two kinds of grace to render us capable of good works." He calls the first kind "operating," which ensures that we effectively will to do good. The second he calls "co-operating," which follows the good will as a help. The thing that displeases me about this division is that, while he attributes the effective desire for good to the grace of God, yet he hints that man by his very own nature somehow seeks after the good—though ineffectively. Thus Bernard declares the good will is God's work, yet concedes to man that of his own impulse he seeks this sort of good will. But this is far from Augustine's thought, from whom Peter Lombard pretended to have taken this distinction.[45]

Jill Raitt points out that if Calvin had read *De gratia* carefully, "he would have found Bernard laying the foundations for Lombard," especially in 1.2, where Bernard says that "free choice is said to co-operate with operating grace in its act of consent, or, in other words, in its process of being saved." On the other hand, this passage might have been less "alarming" to Calvin than Lombard's statement, since it does speak of "one operating grace under the influence of which consent is given."[46]

Unfortunately, Calvin apparently had only an incomplete knowledge of Bernard's treatise. This fact, along with the inaccuracy of some of Calvin's quotations of Bernard in the 1539 *Institutes*, leads Raitt to conclude that in the 1539 edition, "Calvin was working from memory, not from a text, and probably his memory was based on the reading of isolated passages of *De gratia* only." From 1543 on, Calvin quotes Bernard more accurately, and always approvingly.[47]

In any case, we must ask where Calvin finds in Bernard the idea that "man . . . of his own impulse . . . seeks this sort of good will." Again, Raitt's analysis is particularly helpful here. She points to Bernard's statement in *De gratia* 14.46 (B.O. 3:199) that "good will suffices on its own at times." However, Bernard has already asserted that the "good" will is an effect of grace, and that consent itself does not originate with us, but with God. "Bernard nowhere speaks of cooperating grace that comes to the fallen will; only to the will already inspired, healed, and empowered by operating grace."[48] In short, Calvin is mistaken in his interpretation of Bernard in this instance.

On the other hand, Calvin's own view of the conversion of the will is not all that different. In *Institutes* 2.3.6 (O.S. 3:280), he insists that "everything good in the will is the work of grace alone," a statement with which Bernard would agree. In this same section, he quotes 2 Cor. 3:5 ("we are not even capable of thinking"), the same text Bernard quotes in *De gratia* 14.46 in support of his belief that consent is not "its own doing."

The difference, as Raitt aptly notes, is that Calvin does not want to allow for the term *liberum arbitrium*. He is uncomfortable with the idea that free choice cooperates with operating grace in *any* sense, for it seems to him to compromise his rock-steady conviction that God himself is "wholly the Author of good works." Yet even in rejecting this, he recognizes that some of his forebears were not too far removed from his own position:

> In so far as it is anticipated by grace, to that degree I concede that you may call your will an "attendant." But because the will reformed is the Lord's work, it is wrongly attributed to man that he obeys prevenient grace with his will as attendant.

As we have seen, it is precisely as "anticipated by grace" that Bernard wishes to discuss the converted will. However, as this quotation dates from the 1539 *Institutes*, it is not surprising that Calvin does not take note of this. He does, at least, recognize that Augustine agrees with him on God's authorship of all good works.[49]

Having isolated the explicit points of disagreement between Calvin and Bernard, let us return to the more general question of what happens to the *imago Dei* after the Fall, to see how Calvin's treatment relates to Bernard's. Calvin succinctly describes Adam's state after sin as follows, "Even though we grant that God's image was not totally annihilated and destroyed in him, yet it was so corrupted that whatever remains is frightful deformity."[50] Later, he clarifies his position by returning to a discussion of the two faculties of the soul, understanding (or reason) and will:

> Since reason, therefore, by which man distinguishes between good and evil, and by which he understands and judges, is a natural gift, it could not be completely wiped out; but it was partly weakened and partly corrupted, so that its misshapen ruins appear. . . . In man's perverted and degenerate nature some sparks [*scintillas*] still gleam. . . . Similarly the will, because it is inseparable from man's nature, did not perish, but was so bound to wicked desires that it cannot strive after the right.[51]

What remains of our natural endowment with respect to reason includes the *sensus divinitatis* and the conscience. These are so important that they will be treated in a separate section below. For now, let us note that Calvin does recognize a soundness of understanding with respect to "earthly things," that is,

> those which do not pertain to God or his Kingdom, to true justice, or to the blessedness of the future life; but which have their significance and relationship with regard to the present life and are, in a sense, confined within its bounds.

These are distinguished from "heavenly things," in which Calvin includes "the pure knowledge of God, the nature of true righteousness, and the mysteries of the Heavenly Kingdom." Thus, Calvin can speak positively of a "natural instinct to foster and preserve society" which results in government, and of art and science, always insisting that at bottom, all these things are gifts of God's spirit.[52]

However, *spiritual* insight, which consists in knowing God and his benefits, and how we should live according to his law, is beyond fallen humanity's capability. To be sure, a "taste" of God's divinity remains (as well as a sense of our responsibility to God, as we shall see below), but because of sin we are left in utter confusion.[53]

As far as the will is concerned, we are also left utterly unable to choose the good. Indeed, in describing the state of the fallen will, Calvin directly quotes *De gratia* 6.16, where Bernard says that "to will the good indicates an achievement; and to will the bad, a defect. . . . Because of our willing faculty, we are able to will; but because of grace, to will the good." Calvin's quotation of this passage is not entirely accurate (not surprisingly, as it dates from the 1539 edition); as Raitt points out, it is really "mixed comment and quotation":

> Not inappropriately Bernard teaches that to will is in us all: but to will good is gain; to will evil, loss. Therefore simply to will is of man; to will ill, of a corrupt nature; to will well, of grace.[54]

This passage is an accurate interpretation of Bernard. Nevertheless, a close look at this section of the *Institutes*, in which Calvin later quotes Bernard's *Sermons on the Canticles* 81 (a reference added in 1559), reveals a subtle but real difference between their respective anthropologies.

Calvin finds support in this sermon of Bernard's for his doctrine of "willing necessity." He quotes a number of sentences, interspersed with his own comments, from sections 7 and 9 of the sermon. We need not examine every one of these.[55] The key passage for our purposes is quoted (quite accurately) as follows by Calvin:

> In some base and strange way the will itself, changed for the worse by sin, makes a necessity for itself. Hence, neither does necessity, although it is of the will, avail to excuse the will, nor does the will, although it is led astray, avail to exclude necessity. For this necessity is as it were voluntary.[56]

Even apart from Calvin's interpretation, this passage would seem to conflict with what we have already seen in *De gratia*, where Bernard speaks of *freedom* from necessity.[57] However, as Jill Raitt carefully points out, what Bernard means by "freedom from necessity" is only freedom from extrinsic "coercion." True freedom (which would include the freedoms of sin and sorrow) is only possible in Christ. It is *this* kind of freedom (i.e., the freedom that comes from victory over sin), and not merely freedom from coercion, that is at issue in Sermon 81 on the Song. Thus he can speak in this context of a "willing necessity,"[58] which fits right into Calvin's argument in *Institutes* 2.3.5.

Nevertheless, a genuine difference remains. Bernard sees "spontaneity" (freedom from extrinsic coercion) as something worth designating as "freedom." Calvin, while not denying that spontaneity exists, does not wish to call it "freedom" since its object is inevitably evil. As Raitt puts it, "Calvin is practical and sees the action of the will as it is able to accomplish, to obtain, a true good; the fallen will is incapable of accomplishing the truly good, and so is not truly free."[59]

There is one other quotation that has particular relevance to this work. In *Institutes* 2.3.12 (O.S. 3:288), Calvin appeals to Bernard in support of his belief that the fallen will can add nothing to God's grace. This appeal comes at the end of an extended discussion (in sections 10–12) in which Calvin rejects Chrysostom's phrase, "Whom he draws he draws willing." Bernard's statement, added in 1559 and quoted with perfect accuracy, is from *Sermons on the Canticles* 21.9: "Draw me, however unwilling, to make me willing; draw me, slow-footed, to make me run."[60] However, Calvin takes this statement out of context. His own concern in this section is to stress the fallen will's utter dependency on God. Bernard's concern, on the other hand, is with the perseverance of the graced will (this section is an exhortation to persevere in prayer). Calvin does, in another place, address this concern, and admits to a "weariness" that exists in the elect as long as they inhabit the "prison" of the body. This would have been an appropriate place to quote *Sermons on the Canticles* 21; however, Calvin does not refer to Bernard here.[61]

Apart from the places where Calvin specifically quotes Bernard with respect to anthropology, one other parallel is worth mentioning: Calvin's discussion of the continuity of the faculty of the will in the transition from sin to justification. For example, speaking of our conversion to righteousness, Calvin says:

> What takes place is wholly from God. I say that the will is effaced; not in so far as it is will, for in man's conversion what belongs to his primal nature remains entire. I also say that it is created anew; not meaning that the will now begins to exist, but that it is changed from an evil to a good will. . . . From this, one may easily infer, as I have said, that everything good in the will is the work of grace alone.

This statement can be compared to Bernard's in *De gratia*, where he says, "Free choice . . . constitutes us willers; grace, willers of the good."[62] Although Calvin does not like the language of consent or cooperation, he nevertheless asks in the *Institutes:*

> For who is such a fool as to assert that God moves man just as we throw a stone? And nothing like this follows from our teaching. To man's natural faculties we refer the acts of approving and rejecting, willing and not willing, striving and resisting. That is, approving vanity and rejecting perfect good; willing evil and not willing good; striving toward wickedness and resisting righteousness. What does the Lord do in this? . . . When the Lord establishes his Kingdom in [the righteous], he restrains their will by his Spirit that it may not according to its natural inclination be dragged to and fro by wandering lusts. That the will may be disposed to holiness and righteousness, He bends, shapes, forms, and directs, it to the rule of his righteousness.

What Calvin describes in the first part of this passage is precisely what Bernard means when he refers to the fallen will apart from grace: its horizon is *cupiditas*. Indeed, at the end of this section of the *Institutes*, Calvin quotes the phrase that I just mentioned from *De gratia* 6.16: "To will is of nature, but to will aright is of grace." He does not mention Bernard here, however.[63]

It is clear that both Calvin and Bernard wish to attribute salvation to God's grace and not to human striving. Bernard, as we have seen, at least speaks of what we may call a "point of contact" with redeeming grace. We might expect, given Calvin's strong aversion to the term "free choice," that he would deny any "point of contact." On the contrary, a careful look at his teaching on the *sensus divinitatis* and the conscience will reveal strong parallels with Bernard's theology.

SPECIAL QUESTIONS IN CALVIN'S ANTHROPOLOGY

In this section, we will deal with elements of Calvin's anthropology in which he does not explicitly take note of any parallels with Bernard. These elements, however, have much in common with the "building blocks" of Bernard's mystical theology, and represent part of the "mystical strand" that I see running through Calvin's works. They are (1) the *sensus divinitatis* and *conscientia*, distinct yet related notions, and (2) the primacy of "will" over "intellect" in Calvin's understanding of God.

The *Sensus Divinitatis* and *Conscientia*

For though the Son of God sheds His light upon [sinful people], they are so dull that they do not comprehend the source of that light; carried away by doting and perverse fantasies they end up in madness. There are two main parts in that light which yet remains in corrupt nature. Some seed of religion is sown in all: and also, the distinction between good and evil is engraven in their consciences. But what is the fruition at last, save that religion comes to monstrous birth in a thousand superstitions, and conscience corrupts all judgment, confounding vice with virtue? In short, natural reason will never direct men to Christ.[64]

The above quotation from Calvin's Commentary on the Gospel of John summarizes Calvin's understanding of the *sensus divinitatis* and the *conscientia* as "endowments" of human nature that are unerasable even by sin. However, apart from grace, they give birth only to superstition and corrupt judgment. This, in a nutshell, is Calvin's rationale for pronouncing "natural theology" (i.e., a theology that speculates on a divine revelation apart from the revelation in Christ) an enterprise doomed to failure. Some commentators in our own century, most notably Karl Barth, have appealed to such passages in Calvin in order to support a total bypassing of natural theology in favor of a strict adherence to *sola scriptura*.[65] A corollary of this is the rejection of any "point of contact" for revelation.

Whatever may be the merits of such an argument from a philosophical-theological point of view (an issue on which I will not focus attention here), I maintain that the appeal to Calvin on this point is quite simply misguided. Indeed, Calvin speaks of the natural endowments of the *sensus divinitatis* (sometimes also called the *semen religionis*, as in the quotation above) and the *conscientia* as functioning in a way similar to what we have seen in our discussion of the *imago* in Bernard: as a point of contact with redeeming grace.

Let us take a closer look at these "natural endowments." In the *Institutes*, Calvin first speaks of an "awareness of divinity" that exists "by natural instinct" within the human mind. This awareness can never be effaced, not even by sin; it can, however, be "smothered" by those who, "after they have become hardened in insolvent and habitual sinning, furiously repel all remembrance of God," or corrupted by "vanity joined with pride," which leads people to "fly off into empty speculations." This is similar to Bernard's discussion of the "likeness" of God being preserved after sin, but defiled and confused.[66]

Edward Dowey notes that "if this *sensus* is a knowledge of God's existence, it is also an overwhelming and ineludible apprehension of his awfulness and majesty. It is the *mysterium tremendum*." This is clear in passages like the following:

> You may see now and again how . . . he who is the boldest despiser of God is of all men the most startled at the rustle of a falling leaf. Whence does this arise but from the vengeance of divine majesty, which strikes their consciences all the more violently the more they try to flee from it? Indeed, they seek out every subterfuge to hide themselves from the Lord's presence, and to efface it again from their minds. But in spite of themselves they are always entrapped. Although it may sometimes seem to vanish for a moment, it returns at once and rushes in with new force. . . . The impious themselves therefore exemplify the fact that some conception of God is ever alive in all men's minds.[67]

True knowledge of God, however, comes only with piety, which Calvin defines as "that reverence joined with love of God which the knowledge of his benefits induces."[68] This knowledge comes through the scriptures, described by Calvin as analogous to "spectacles":

> Just as old or bleary-eyed men and those with weak vision . . . with the aid of spectacles will begin to read distinctly; so Scripture, gathering up

the otherwise confused knowledge of God in our minds, having dispersed our dullness, clearly shows us the true God.[69]

The use of this image by Calvin is a crucial one, for it makes clear that he implicitly recognizes a "point of contact" with redeeming grace. Brian A. Gerrish argues this point simply and forcefully:

> It seems clear that the saving knowledge, when it comes, attaches itself to a remnant of the natural knowledge; otherwise, Calvin's famous comparison of the Word to a pair of spectacles, which bring to clear focus a confusa alioqui Dei notitia, would make no sense. . . . Consequently, I do not see how those for whom a "christocentric" theology entails denial of a point of contact for the gospel can cite Calvin in their support.[70]

Thus, Karl Barth's claim that God comes and creates his own point of contact with grace is not, as he seems to think, compatible with Calvin's thought.[71] This misunderstanding of Calvin is an unfortunate by-product of Barth's insistence (correct in itself) that Calvin did not intend to promote a "natural" theology, that is, one that speculates on a divine revelation apart from the revelation in Christ. Indeed, Calvin himself says when he discusses natural knowledge of God, "I speak only of the primal and simple knowledge to which the very order of nature would have led us *if Adam had remained upright.*"[72]

But this is not to say that Calvin refuses to admit natural theology as, to use Barth's phrase, a "separate problem." In fact, Calvin *does* give "systematic attention" to natural theology in Book 1, chapters 3–5 of the *Institutes.* Of course, Calvin reaches the conclusion that natural theology serves to render us inexcusable before God.[73] Edward Dowey appropriately refers to this as Calvin's "sin-negated natural theology." However, he hastens to point out, "While it is true that a negative sign stands over the whole revelation in creation in Calvin's theology, we must not allow this sign to erase from our minds the magnitude of the sum thus negated." He further notes that although "sin has blinded man to the revelation in creation . . . the revelation itself is not harmed. Man's *receiving apparatus* functions wrongly."[74]

For our purposes, the important thing to notice here is that the negation of natural theology by sin does *not* mean that natural knowledge of God has no positive function whatsoever. On the contrary, it is precisely this knowledge which is affected by scripture, as noted above. Thus, the *sensus divinitatis* can indeed be seen as a "point of contact" with redeeming grace.

Is there a *sensus divinitatis* in Bernard? Although he does not express it in so many words, Bernard does speak of a revelation in creation that triggers an awareness of God's existence. In one of the Sermons on the Song of

Songs, referring to the "countless species of creatures" that exist, he states, "Though not seeing himself but what comes from him, you are made aware beyond all doubt that he exists, and that you must seek him."[75]

The *sensus* and the *conscientia* together can be seen as approximating Bernard's anthropological point of contact. Let us now turn to the latter notion.

Speaking of Adam, in his Commentary on Genesis, Calvin notes:

> His sin proceeded from an evil conscience; whence it follows, that a judgment had been given him, by which he might discriminate between virtues and vices. Nor could what Moses relates be otherwise true, namely, that he was created in the image of God; since the image of God comprises in itself the knowledge of him who is the chief good.[76]

Dowey infers from this passage that "conscience is an element of the subjective revelation of God the Creator, given in the created order itself, not in Scripture. It is a universal endowment, part of man as man, an element of the *imago Dei*."[77]

Conscience represents the "moral" element of this subjective revelation, having as its content "the proposition that the will of God is to be obeyed," while the *sensus divinitatis* represents the intellectual, having as its content "the proposition that One God is."[78] Thus, *conscientia* is understood by Calvin as a *sensus*, as when he calls it a "sense of God's judgment."[79]

However, Calvin also defines conscience in many other ways. Dowey speaks of his "baffling variety of expressions" in this regard.[80] The most important of these for our purposes is that it *is* a genuine kind of knowledge, particularly of the law of nature. For example, in *Institutes* 2.8.1 (O.S. 3:344), Calvin speaks of the content of the "inward law" (here identified with conscience) as being the same as the laws written in the Ten Commandments. But just as the *sensus divinitatis* is smothered or corrupted by sin, and is therefore unable by itself to lead us to a saving knowledge of God, so too is the conscience powerless to do anything more than "holding before us the difference between good and evil and thus accusing us when we fail in our duty."[81] As Dowey so aptly summarizes it, conscience "shows man his responsibility, but only the will can carry it out."[82]

To summarize, it appears that both the *sensus divinitatis* and the *conscientia* belong to the soul's faculty of understanding.[83] I would suggest that taken together, these two notions have approximately the same function vis-à-vis grace as free choice does in Bernard.

Let us recall how Bernard develops his understanding of "free choice," otherwise known as "freedom from necessity." Bernard calls it a freedom by which "the will is free either to judge itself good if it has consented to good, or bad, if to evil."[84] Interestingly, Etienne Gilson speaks of this as the "voice of conscience," which is inextinguishable even in the sinner.[85] Similarly, Calvin understands the conscience as a judgment given to Adam "by which he might discriminate between virtues and vices."[86] It appears, then, that with respect to their function, Calvin's understanding of conscience is parallel to Bernard's understanding of freedom from necessity, that is, they bring us to an awareness of good and evil.

There is another similarity here: for both Bernard and Calvin, the ability to *distinguish* between good and evil is not accompanied by the ability to *will* good instead of evil. It is clear that in Bernard, the horizon of the will has changed in the state of sin, so that whereas before the fall the will was able to choose good *or* evil, it is now free only to choose among evil options.[87] This is not substantially different from Calvin's position, as was already noted above.[88]

A significant difference does exist, however, because Bernard will at least go so far as to give the fallen will the role of "consent" to God's grace. Thus, Bernard's "point of contact" with grace is assessed positively as a kind of "cooperation."[89] Calvin, on the other hand, wants nothing to do with any notion of "cooperative" grace, as we have seen.[90] He assures this anthropologically in placing the *sensus divinitatis* and the *conscientia* both under the soul's faculty of understanding rather than will. Fallen human beings can see their need for saving grace, but are absolutely powerless to do anything about it.

On the other hand, this difference itself needs to be qualified. Bernard himself makes clear that consent is not "its own doing." Even our yes to grace is an effect of grace.[91] Thus, this "consent" of which Bernard speaks belongs, strictly speaking, under the rubric of justification by grace, and not as some kind of capacity for grace that resides in our fallen state. Calvin, in turn, does not wish to speak in terms of consent but he does wish to speak of *faith* as a gift of the Holy Spirit who unites us to Christ.[92] The difference between the two approaches may be more verbal than substantial. This can only be decided after we look at Bernard and Calvin's respective understandings of faith in chapter 3.

It seems evident to me that it is primarily in Calvin's treatment of *conscientia* that he comes closest to Bernard's idea of "free choice." Yet, as we have seen, we can also find parallels in Bernard for the *sensus divinitatis*.[93] It is worth noting again that for Calvin, the two notions are distinct but inseparable.

The Primacy of "Will" over "Intellect" in Calvin

Bernard's primary motif in discussing divine-human relations is that of love. For example, in *De gratia*, Bernard makes it clear that grace is given so that we may know "how to will the good, and how to fear God, and how to love God."[94] This is not to say that knowledge is unimportant, but it appears to be subsumed under love in Bernard's thought. The goal of the Christian life is to experience a union with God's will.[95]

Calvin, too, is more concerned about the will of God than about theoretical knowledge. Indeed, Calvin has no use for a desire to know God *in essentia*. People who seek such theoretical knowledge of God

> are merely toying with idle speculations. It is more important for us to know of what sort he is and what is consistent with his nature. . . . What help is it, in short, to know a God with whom we have nothing to do?[96]

In other words, really to know God is to know his goodness. This kind of knowledge only comes in the context of piety, which, as we have seen, Calvin defines as "that reverence joined with love of God which the knowledge of his benefits induces."[97] It is significant that the word "love" is included in Calvin's definition. While we shall see later that Calvin does not characteristically speak of union with God explicitly in terms of love, piety is always the context of our relationship to God, and love can therefore be seen as being at the heart of the Christian life, just as it is for Bernard.

This stress on will in both Bernard and Calvin is important because it undergirds anthropologically their conceptions of mystical union as a union of spirit (or will) and not of essences. The latter notion, that is, of some kind of ontological "absorption" into the divine, is explicitly rejected by both authors.

CONCLUSION

The evidence presented here suggests that, in the main, Bernard and Calvin's respective anthropologies are quite compatible. Calvin was even aware of the compatibility to a great extent. Although he rejected the notion of consent to cooperative grace, it remains to be seen whether his understanding of faith has essentially the same function in the life of the believer. It is now time to turn precisely to the question of how God's grace is received in justification.

3

THE THEOLOGY OF JUSTIFICATION
IN BERNARD AND CALVIN

One major task remains before we can move to a discussion of mystical union in Bernard and Calvin: namely, an examination of their respective theologies of justification, which of course is always the foundation and context for an experience of union with God. On this topic, as on anthropology, Calvin quotes Bernard directly on several occasions. Four issues will be of particular concern in this chapter: (1) the primacy of grace in Bernard and Calvin; (2) their respective notions of faith; (3) the question of merit; and (4) the relationship between justification and sanctification as conceived by both authors.

BERNARD'S THEOLOGY OF JUSTIFICATION

For Bernard, the justification of the sinner is attributed entirely to God's grace, but without a denial of some form of human cooperation with that grace, usually discussed in terms of "consent" or "merit." We have already discussed the notion of consent in chapter 2; here we will take a closer look at his use of the term "merit."[1] What is most interesting is that Calvin, who is so vigorously opposed to the concept of merit, nevertheless is willing to tolerate its use by Bernard.

Justification and the Primacy of Grace

Unlike some later medieval thinkers, Bernard does not veer in the direction of semi-Pelagianism when discussing the beginning of justification. He clearly states—both in his dogmatic and in his mystical writings—that all begins and ends with grace. At the same time, he insists on the element of human response to that grace. For example, in *De gratia*, he asserts:

> There can be no doubt . . . that the beginning of our salvation rests with God, and is enacted neither through us nor with us. The consent and the work, however, though not originating from us, nevertheless are not without us. . . . What was begun by grace alone, is completed by grace and free choice together, in such a way that they contribute to each new achievement not singly but jointly; not by turns, but simultaneously. It is not as if grace did one half of the work and free choice the other; but each does the whole work, according to its own peculiar contribution. Grace does the whole work, and so does free choice—with this one qualification: that whereas the whole is done *in* free choice, so is the whole done *of* grace.[2]

The emphasis on God's initiation and the primacy of grace is equally strong in the mystical writings. For example, in *De diligendo Deo* it is made clear at the outset that God is to be loved because "He loved us first" (1 John 4:10), and that all we have is a gift from God:

> The Apostle says to him who glorifies himself: "What have you that you have not received? And if you have received it, how can you boast of it as if you had not received it? . . . It is pride, the greatest of sins, to use gifts as if they were one's by natural right and while receiving benefits to usurp the benefactor's glory."[3]

A similar emphasis is found in the *Sermones super Cantica*. In Sermon 82, Bernard baldly declares that the soul in its fallen state can approach God *only* "by grace, not by nature, nor even by effort."[4] In Sermon 67, Bernard reflects on Canticle 2:16, "My beloved is mine, and I am his." He notes that the bride "does not pretend to any merit [meritum], but mentions first the kindness she has received, acknowledging that the grace of the Beloved goes before her." He goes on to quote the same passage we saw above (1 John 4:10), that we love because God loved us first. He then cites Canticle 6:2, where the bride declares, "I am my Beloved's and he is mine," with the following comment:

> Why this? Surely that she may show herself more full of grace when she surrenders wholly to grace, attributing to him both the beginning and the ending. How indeed could she be full of grace if there were any part of her which did not itself spring from grace? There is no way for grace to enter, if [a sense of] merit has taken residence in the soul. A full acknowledgement of grace then is a sign of the fullness of grace. Indeed if the soul possesses anything of its own, to that extent grace must give place to it; whatever you impute to merit you steal from grace. I want nothing to do with the sort of merit which excludes grace [Deest gratiae quidquid meritis deputas].[5]

The positive sense in which Bernard understands "merit" will be discussed below. What I wish to stress here is that Bernard's teaching on the primacy of grace runs consistently through all his writings. His sermons on the theme of conversion provide some of the most striking examples. In his *Sermon to Clerics on Conversion*, Bernard speaks of the power of God's word in relation to human discourse:

> For who would dare to compare human discourse to what God is said to have spoken? Indeed, the word of God is living and active and his voice is powerful and majestic. For he spoke and they were created. He said "let there be light" and there was light. He said "be converted" and the children of men were converted. Clearly, then, the conversion of souls is the working of the divine, not the human, voice.[6]

Speaking of our deliverance from sin in Sermon 8 on Psalm 90, Bernard cautions against attributing virtue to our own goodness, "Do not say, 'our hand is triumphant,' but truly and salutarily confess that it is the Lord who has done all these things."[7]

It is clear, then, that for Bernard we are justified by grace. What is effected by this grace? As Bernard puts it in *De gratia*, "Free choice . . . constitutes us willers; grace, willers of the good."[8] Grace restores both "free counsel," which allows us to will the good, and "free pleasure," which allows us to carry out the good that we will.[9] In other words, grace gives human beings the possibility to be the creatures God intended them to be.

Justification includes the notion of the nonimputation of sins, as in one of the *Sermons on the Canticles* where Bernard states, "I ask no further pledge of righteousness if he is on my side whom alone I have offended. If he decrees that a sin is not to be imputed to me, it is as if it never existed."[10] This, as we shall see, is a passage of which Calvin will approve. Bernard also seems to include sanctification under the rubric of justification. Although he does not conceive of their relationship in quite the same way as Calvin (who sees sanctification as distinct but related), he develops his understanding of what sanctification is along very similar lines, as we shall see below.

Finally, Bernard is emphatic that the grace of justification comes to us through Christ. In *De gratia*, he states:

> In him, man possesses the necessary "power of God and the wisdom of God," who, inasmuch as he is wisdom, pours back into man true wisdom, and so restores to him his free counsel; and, inasmuch as he is power, renews his full power, and so restores to him his free pleasure.[11]

Although we never lost the "image" of God (represented in this text by free choice), it is Christ who restores the "likeness" of free counsel and free pleasure, the perfection of which, however, must wait until the next life.[12]

In the *Sermones super Cantica*, Bernard asserts that it is only in Christ that we can "ascend the hill of the Lord":

> Therefore anyone who stands and does not wish to fall, should not place his trust in himself, but lean on the Word. The Word says, "without me you can do nothing." And so it is. We can neither rise to the good nor stand in the good without the Word.[13]

In this connection, Bernard notes that our prayer should be Christ-centered, for Christ can offer us everything we need in order to approach God:

> You will not pray aright, if in your prayers you seek anything but the Word, or seek him for the sake of anything but the Word; for in him are all things. In him is healing for your wounds, help in your need, restoration for your faults, resources for your further growth; in him is all that men should ask or desire, all they need, all that will profit them. There is no reason therefore to ask anything else of the Word, for he is all.[14]

In another passage, Bernard speaks of the desirability of our weakness before Christ: "Let me not be merely weak, then, but entirely resourceless, utterly helpless, that I may enjoy the support of the power of the Lord of hosts."[15] The centrality of Christ will be a crucial point in our discussion of mystical union in Bernard and Calvin.

Justification and Faith

It is significant that Bernard sees faith as the point of departure for the return of the soul to God. As he puts it in one of his *Sermones super Cantica*:

> By "the righteousness that comes of faith," he [Jesus] loosed the bonds of sin, justifying the sinners by his free gift. By this twofold favor he fulfilled those words of David: "The Lord sets the prisoners free; the Lord opens the eyes of the blind."[16]

A second passage is worth quoting because it makes a connection between faith and the primacy of grace:

> For you have not chosen me, but I have chosen you; not for any merits that I found in you did I choose you, but I went before you. Thus have I betrothed you to myself *in faith, not in the works of the law.*[17]

A closer look at Bernard's references to faith reveals some striking similarities to Calvin's theology. A parallel that becomes immediately evident is Bernard's connection of faith with the Holy Spirit. For example, in reflecting on verse 9 of Psalm 90 ("You, O Lord, are my hope"), Bernard notes:

> Brothers, to savor this is to live by faith. No one can pronounce the sentence, "because you, O Lord, are my hope," except the person who is inwardly persuaded by the Spirit that, as a prophet admonishes, he casts his burden upon the Lord, knowing that he will be cared for by him, as in keeping with what the apostle Peter said, "Cast all your anxieties on him, for he cares about you."[18]

In his Third Sermon for Christmas Eve, Bernard makes a similar connection:

> Just as iron and clay cannot be welded together, so it is equally impossible to conjoin so mighty a force of faith with the weakness and inconstancy of the human heart, without the solder of the Holy Spirit.[19]

According to Bernard, then, it is the Holy Spirit who enables us to hear the Word in faith. This Spirit does what no created spirit can do: it acts "directly on our minds," not requiring "an ear to hear him or a mouth to speak."[20]

Another parallel, which I would say is of equal importance, is Bernard's notion of faith as a certain kind of knowledge. This has already been hinted at above in chapter 2;[21] it is now time to take a closer look.

In Sermon 28 on the Song of Songs, Bernard declares, "With the power to understand invisible truths, faith does not know the poverty of the senses; it transcends even the limits of human reason, the capacity of nature, the bounds of experience."[22] Thus, faith is a kind of knowledge that surpasses human understanding. This is an idea with which Calvin will wholeheartedly agree.

What is the nature of the knowledge that is faith? Here again, Bernard gives an answer that is remarkably similar to Calvin's. Bernard speaks in one of the Sermons on the Song of Songs of those who knew God but refused to honor him. These people, he claims, did not have

> a revelation of the Holy Spirit; for even though they possessed knowledge they did not love. . . . They were content with the knowledge that gives self-importance, but ignorant of the love that makes the building grow. . . . For if their knowledge had been complete, they would not have been blind to that goodness by which he willed to be born a human being, and to die for their sins.[23]

Clearly, then, Bernard believes that truly to know God is to know his goodness. Indeed, Bernard recommends that contemplation of God's goodness should take precedence over the recollection of our sins:

> Sorrow for sin is indeed necessary, but it should not be an endless preoccupation. You must also dwell on the glad remembrance of God's

loving kindness, otherwise sadness will harden the heart and lead it more deeply into despair.[24]

To sum up, the knowledge that comes from faith is not a purely intellectual, but an *experiential* knowledge. This will be important later when we discuss the cognitive component of mystical union.

For Bernard, faith does not stand alone. In a Sermon on the Song of Songs, he asks, "Why should there be a division between your faith and your conduct? It is a wrong division, it destroys your faith, for 'faith without good works is dead.' "[25] This leads us to the problem of merit, which deserves special attention.

The Question of Merit

Although Bernard never shrinks from speaking of both faith *and* good works, there is no question that he gives priority to faith.

> Faith ought to come before good works. Without faith, moreover, it is impossible to please God, as Paul attests. And he even teaches that "whatever does not proceed from faith is sin." Hence there is neither fruit without a flower nor a good work without faith. But then, faith without good works is dead, just as a flower seems vain where no fruit follows.[26]

When Bernard speaks specifically of merit, he usually takes pains to stress that merit is not our own. In the dogmatic treatise *De gratia*, Bernard does wish to speak of merit, but strictly in the Augustinian sense of God's choosing to crown as merits what in fact are God's own gifts: "God, therefore, kindly gives man the credit, as often as he deigns to perform some good act through him and with him." God is "the author of merit, who both applies the will to the work, and supplies the work to the will."[27]

This emphasis is equally present in Bernard's pastoral and mystical writings. In one of his sermons on Psalm 90, Bernard reflects on the meaning of "the arrow that flies by day" (Ps. 90:6 [Vulgate]), identifying the "arrow" as "vain glory." The opposite of vanity is truth, of which a person's soul should be conscious:

> Surely if he thinks about his own condition, he will say to himself, "How can you, who are but dust and ashes, be proud?" Surely, if he considers his own corruption, he must necessarily admit that there is no good in him. Or, if he does perhaps seem to find some good, he will not, I think, be able to argue against the apostle when he says, "What do you have that you have not received?" and elsewhere, "Let him who stands look out lest he fall."[28]

Thus, any "merit" that might exist is to be attributed to God. In one of his seasonal sermons, Bernard speaks of the "water pots" of the wedding feast of Cana as representing the grace that will purify the church: "For grace not only washes out sin, but it bestows merit [Gratia enim non solum peccata lavat, sed et merita donat]." He goes on to state that this merit is Christ's.[29]

In a later sermon on Psalm 90, Bernard speaks of fear of the Lord as containing "the soundest and most effectual grounds for hope." He goes on to assert that God "never fails those who hope in him. Man's whole merit consists in placing all his hope in him who has saved the whole man."[30]

To sum up, it is clear that merit is rooted in God and is bestowed on the believer through the grace of Christ. Bernard does at times speak of a merit of "our own," but he never wishes this to be understood as apart from Christ's. In his trying to explain this, his terminology gets a little precarious, as in the following passage:

> It is enough for merit to know that merit is not enough. But as merit must not presume on merit, so lack of merit must bring judgment. Furthermore, children re-born in baptism are not without merit, but possess the merits of Christ; but they make themselves unworthy of these if they do not add their own—not because of inability, but because of neglect; this is the danger of maturity. Henceforward, take care that you possess merit; when you possess it, you will know it as a gift. Hope for its fruit, the mercy of God, and you will escape all danger of poverty, ingratitude, and presumption. The lack of merit is a poverty which destroys, but presumption of spirit is false riches.[31]

The key to understanding Bernard's use of the term "merit," in this passage and others, is to keep in mind that he sees it as nothing more than *consent* to God's grace.[32] Bernard speaks in *De gratia* of the merits of "fasting, watchings, continence, works of mercy and other virtuous practices, by means of which, as is evident, our inner nature is renewed every day." He goes on to say, "Since it is clearly the divine Spirit who activates these things in us, they are God's gifts; yet because they come about *by the assent of our will* [cum nostrae voluntatis assensu], they are our merits."[33]

One might expect that Calvin would attack Bernard for the amount of attention he gave to talking about merit. On the contrary, Calvin will single out Bernard's theology as an exception to what he perceives as the otherwise wrongheaded thinking on this topic during the late Middle Ages.

Justification and Sanctification

Bernard generally does not make the sharp distinction between justification and sanctification that will become a trademark of reformers like

Luther and Calvin. Nevertheless, there are passages in Bernard that are suggestive of Calvin's language of the "twofold grace of Christ." For example, in one of the early sermons on the Song of Songs, Bernard distinguishes the grace of repentance from the grace of perseverance:

> He, however, who gave me the grace to repent, must also give me the power to persevere, lest by repeating my sins I should end up being worse than I was before. Woe to me then, repentant though I be, if he without whom I can do nothing should suddenly withdraw his supporting hand. I really mean nothing; of myself I can achieve neither repentance nor perseverance. . . . For these various reasons I must confess that I am not entirely satisfied with the first grace by which I am enabled to repent of my sins; I must have the second as well, and so bear fruits that befit repentance, that I may not return like the dog to its vomit.[34]

The theme of perseverance is a strong one in Bernard, which comes to expression largely in his discussion of the Christian life as process. This theme also relates to the question of election or predestination. Let us take a closer look at both of these areas.

For Bernard, sanctification in our present existence is always partial. This is especially clear in *De diligendo Deo*, where Bernard develops his theology of love. He insists that we will never be able to love God enough:

> My love is less than is your due, yet not less than I am able, for even if I cannot love you as much as I should, still I cannot love you more than I can. I shall only be able to love you more when you give me more, although you can never find my love worthy of you.[35]

Bernard goes on to speak of four stages or "degrees" of love: where people love themselves for their own sake, love God for their own sake, love God for God's sake, and finally, love even themselves for God's sake.[36]

Bernard's own belief is that the highest degree of love is not achieved in this life, although he does suggest that the martyrs may receive a taste of it while still in their bodies, and that a momentary rapture may be possible for some.[37] Ordinarily, the fourth degree of love takes place in a "spiritual" body; in fact, it must await the final resurrection, because only then will the soul not be held back by a desire to reunite with the flesh.[38]

What kind of progress in sanctification can be expected in our present existence? In *De diligendo Deo*, Bernard asserts that at the third stage of loving God (i.e., loving God for God's sake), a person "will not have trouble in fulfilling the commandment to love his neighbor."[39] In another place, Bernard mentions that righteous deeds are an indication of a righteous soul, "I shall judge you to be righteous if your opinions are correct and your deeds do not contradict them. For the state of the invisible soul is made known by one's belief and practice."[40] In other words, Bernard expects that righteousness will become evident through certain visible, discernible signs, just as we will see Calvin recognizing some external criteria of righteousness.

There remains the question of perseverance. At times, Bernard uses language suggestive of Calvin's double predestination, as in the following passage from one of the Sermons on the Song of Songs. Commenting on Canticle 1:3 [Vulgate] ("The king has brought me into his rooms"), Bernard speaks of one room from which God watches over the world as a judge:

> The awe-struck contemplative sees how, in this place, God's just but hidden judgment neither washes away the evil deeds of the wicked nor is placated by their good deeds. He even hardens their hearts lest they should repent, take stock of themselves, and be converted and he would heal them. And he does this in virtue of a certain and eternal decree, all the more frightening from its being unchangeably and eternally determined.[41]

Yet Bernard does not consistently speak in this way. In an earlier Sermon on the Song, Bernard speaks of the kindness and patience of God, noting that

> to this very end he postpones his punishment of the contumacious [contemnente], awaiting a favorable moment to bestow on them the grace of repentance and forgiveness. He does not wish the death of the wicked man, but that he turn back and live.[42]

It should be noted that the context for the passage on Canticle 1:3 is the importance of the contemplative learning the fear of the Lord. Since fear is the beginning of wisdom, a contemplation of the Lord's justice is a fitting preparation for the one who is about to enter the bridal chamber (where God will be encountered as Bridegroom).

Bernard does not believe that it is possible to be certain of one's election. In a sermon for Septuagesima on John 8:47, he asks:

> Which of us can say, "I belong to the elect, I am one of those predestinated to life, I am of the number of God's children"? . . . Absolute certitude we cannot have [Certitudinem utique non habemus]. But still we may find comfort in the confidence of hope, lest otherwise the anxiety occasioned by this doubt should become an insufferable torment.

He goes on to say that there are "indications which minister to our confidence and furnish a solid basis for hope." He gives an example of those who genuinely hear God's word.[43]

The foregoing is only intended as a brief sketch of Bernard's theology of justification and not an exhaustive treatment. My main purpose is to focus on points of comparison with Calvin, to whom we now turn.

CALVIN'S THEOLOGY OF JUSTIFICATION

Calvin begins Book 3 of the *Institutes* with a discussion of the notion of faith, follows with a discussion of regeneration (sanctification), and finally moves to unpack the meaning of justification by faith. I will discuss them in a different order, following the outline given at the beginning of this chapter.

Justification and the Primacy of Grace

Christ was given to us by God's generosity, to be grasped and possessed by us in faith. By partaking of him, we principally receive a double grace: namely, that being reconciled to God through Christ's blameless-ness, we may have in heaven instead of a Judge a gracious Father; and secondly, that sanctified by Christ's spirit we may cultivate blameless-ness and purity of life.[44]

At the outset, Calvin lays out what for him is a fundamental point: that justification and sanctification are distinct yet inseparable. Thus, he speaks of a "double grace" of Christ. By keeping sanctification distinct, he maintains an understanding of justification as totally the work of God.

Calvin defines justification "simply as the acceptance with which God receives us into his favor as righteous men. And we say that it consists of the remission of sins and the imputation of Christ's righteousness."[45] It is important to note the terms that Calvin uses in discussing justification. He speaks of "acceptance," of being acquitted *"as if* his innocence were confirmed," of being *"considered* as a just man in God's sight."[46] In other words, justification is *forensic*. The sinner is "declared" just. In ourselves, we remain sinners. God does not impute guilt to us, however, but rather imputes to us the righteousness of Christ.

Calvin proceeds at this point in the *Institutes* to launch into an extended tirade against Osiander, whose doctrine of "essential righteousness" he regards as diametrically opposed to the proper understanding of justifica-tion. Osiander believed that Christ imparted to sinners something of his very essence in justification, so that sinners literally had a share in Christ's substance. Calvin insists that our union with Christ takes place "by the secret power of the Holy Spirit," and not by "the infusion both of his [Christ's] essence and quality."[47] His aim here, as noted by McNeill and Battles, is to safeguard the idea that righteousness is imparted solely through Christ's sacrifice on the cross.[48]

There is another problem with Osiander's conception: it mixes up justification and sanctification. Here Calvin becomes very clear in his insistence that the two must be distinguished: "to be justified means something different from being made new creatures."[49] Calvin will see the Roman Church as also suffering a misunderstanding of this truth, as we shall see below.

Calvin is unequivocal in his insistence that humans can offer nothing to justification. It is totally God's work. Calvin is willing to take on no less a personage than Augustine in driving home this point.[50] When one looks to scripture to teach about faith righteousness, Calvin notes, it leads us "to turn aside from the contemplation of our own works and look solely upon God's mercy and Christ's perfection." Calvin later quotes Bernard's 68th Sermon on the Song of Songs in support of this precise point. There Bernard asks, "Why . . . should the church concern itself with merits when it has a firmer and more secure reason to glory in God's purpose? God cannot deny himself; he will do what he has promised."[51]

When Calvin turns in *Institutes* 3.11.22 to the question of how righteousness is obtained, he refers to statements in Paul that speak of God's not imputing, or counting, our sins against us—in other words, of God's free acceptance. For example, he quotes 2 Cor. 5:19: "God was in Christ reconciling the world to himself, not counting men's trespasses against them, and has entrusted to us the word of reconciliation." In this connection, he also quotes two passages from Bernard's *Sermons on the Canticles:*

> And this ought not to seem an unusual expression, that believers are made righteous before God not by works but by free acceptance, since it occurs so often in Scripture, and ancient writers also sometimes speak thus. . . . Bernard's famous sentences correspond to this: "Not to sin is the righteousness of God; but the righteousness of man is the grace of God." And he had previously declared: "Christ is our righteousness in absolution, and therefore those alone are righteous who obtain pardon from his mercy."[52]

Jill Raitt notes, however, that Calvin, while not misinterpreting the meaning of these passages of Bernard, is merely using them as proof texts.[53] Bernard's broader context in this sermon is not the nonimputation of sin, but rather a discussion of virtue.

In the very next section, we see that Calvin, like Bernard, ties justification to Christ:

> From this it is also evident that we are justified before God solely by the intercession of Christ's righteousness. This is equivalent to saying that man is not righteous in himself but because the righteousness of Christ is communicated to him by imputation—something worth carefully noting.[54]

This is similar to what we saw in Bernard, who notes that Christ, "inasmuch as he is wisdom, pours back into man true wisdom, . . . and inasmuch as he is power, renews his full power."[55] Also one instance occurs where Calvin quotes Bernard on the subject of seeking salvation in Christ alone:

> Accordingly, the moment we turn away even slightly from him, our salvation, which rests firmly in him, gradually vanishes away. As a result, all those who do not repose in him voluntarily deprive themselves of all grace. Bernard's admonition is worth remembering: "The name of Jesus is not only light but also food; it is also oil, without which all food of the soul is dry; it is salt, without whose seasoning whatever is set before us is insipid; finally, it is honey in the mouth, melody in the ear, rejoicing in the heart, and at the same time medicine. Every discourse in which his name is not spoken is without savor."[56]

In short, for both authors, there is no such thing as justification apart from Christ. There are, however, some differences in their description of the role of Christ, which will be discussed under the rubric of *unio mystica*.

Justification and Faith

Calvin's definition of faith is given in *Institutes* 3.2.7:

> Now we shall possess a right definition of faith if we call it a firm and certain knowledge of God's benevolence toward us [divinae erga nos benevolentiae firmam certamque cognitionem], founded upon the truth of the freely given promise in Christ [quae gratuitae in Christo promissionis veritate fundata], both revealed to our minds and sealed upon our hearts through the Holy Spirit.

Thus, faith goes beyond the knowledge of the *sensus divinitatis* and the *conscientia*, which were discussed in chapter 2. Those faculties only give one the most basic knowledge of God's existence and the awareness of God's judgment.[57]

In *Institutes* 3.2.6 Calvin speaks of faith as a "knowledge of God's will toward us," but in 3.2.7 he decides that he actually prefers to speak of God's "benevolence" rather than simply his "will." He states, "What if we were to substitute his benevolence or his mercy [benevolentiam seu misericordiam] in place of his will [voluntatis], the tidings of which are often sad and the proclamation frightening? Thus, surely, we shall more closely approach the nature of faith; for it is after we have learned that our salvation rests with God that we are attracted to seek him."[58]

Calvin goes on to say that "faith can in no wise be separated from a devout disposition."[59] In other words, faith is the *saving* knowledge of God that corresponds to piety.

One direct parallel to Bernard is that Calvin understands faith as a "higher knowledge" that surpasses human understanding:

> When we call faith "knowledge" we do not mean comprehension of the sort that is commonly concerned with those things which fall under human sense perception. For faith is so far above sense that man's mind has to go beyond and rise above itself in order to attain it. Even where the mind has attained, it does not comprehend what it feels. But while it is persuaded of what it does not grasp, by the very certainty of its persuasion it understands more than if it perceived anything human by its own capacity.[60]

Bernard makes a similar statement in *Sermons on the Canticles* 28, where he speaks of faith transcending "the limits of human reason."[61]

Calvin continues by saying that what our mind embraces in faith is the "secret of his will." He concludes that "the knowledge of faith consists in assurance rather than in comprehension [fidei notitiam certitudine magis quam apprehensione contineri]."[62] Again, this is similar to the conclusion we arrived at regarding Bernard's notion of faith: that it is an experiential knowledge, a knowledge of God's goodness.[63] Thus, we see in Calvin's treatment of faith the same stress on God's will rather than intellect as we saw in his anthropology.[64]

Another important parallel to note here is the *source* of faith as conceived by both Calvin and Bernard. We saw that Calvin, after describing faith as a "knowledge of God's will toward us," went on to say, "But the foundation of this is a preconceived conviction of God's truth." Whence comes this conviction? Calvin's answer is precisely the same as Bernard's: the Holy Spirit. After clarifying his understanding of God's "will" as benevolence and mercy, he declares that our mind and heart are incapable of themselves to make us rely confidently on this merciful God. The definition of faith that follows is emphatic about the role of the Holy Spirit:

> Therefore our mind must be otherwise illumined and our heart strengthened, that the *Word of God* may obtain full faith among us. Now we shall possess a right definition of faith if we call it a firm and certain knowledge of God's benevolence toward us, founded upon the truth of the freely given promise in Christ, *both revealed to our minds and sealed upon our hearts through the Holy Spirit.*[65]

In addition to the reference to the Spirit, I wish to call attention to the connection between faith and the *Word of God*, which Calvin's definition of faith mentions. In chapter 5, I will say more about the intimate connection between faith, the Word of God, and the Holy Spirit, but at least a brief comment is in order here. In his commentary on 1 Cor. 1:9, Calvin speaks of our being "brought into fellowship with Christ through the Gospel, which you have received by faith." But this faith, Calvin notes in his comment on 1:8, is effected by the Spirit. This compares favorably to the way we described the Holy Spirit in Bernard, as enabling us to hear the Word in faith.[66]

At the end of chapter 2, I asked whether faith might be considered functionally equivalent to Bernard's "consent." We saw how Calvin disagreed explicitly with Bernard (which he did not do very often) on the use of the term "consent," accusing Bernard of "obscurity" and "subtlety" in defining free choice as such.[67] We know, too, that Calvin preferred to leave behind what he called the "worn distinction" between operative and cooperative grace.[68] Bernard insists that consent is a gift of God; nevertheless he assesses it positively as a kind of "cooperation."[69] Calvin avoids even a hint of "cooperation" by locating both the *sensus divinitatis* and *conscientia* under the soul's faculty of understanding rather than will.

The closest Calvin seems to come in his understanding of faith to Bernard's notion of consent is where he speaks of faith as a "vessel" in *Institutes* 3.11.7, "We compare faith to a kind of vessel; for unless we come empty and with the mouth of our soul open to seek Christ's grace, we are not capable of receiving Christ."[70] It seems to me that Bernard's understanding of consent is not far from an "openness to Christ's grace"; however, I would not want to press a comparison here, especially since Bernard himself does not identify consent with faith.

Calvin refers explicitly to Bernard in his teaching on faith three times in the *Institutes*. The first instance appears in 3.2.25 and refers to *In dedicatione ecclesiae*.[71] As Jill Raitt points out, this passage first appeared in the 1543 edition of the *Institutes* and remains unchanged in the 1559 edition.[72] Calvin's context in this section is the union with Christ that is the result of faith. In 3.2.24, which deals with the certitude of faith, he recognizes that "certain interruptions of faith" occur; however, faith "ceases not its earnest quest for God."[73] He moves directly in 3.2.25 to the quotation from Bernard.

Bernard's concern in this sermon is to juxtapose the misery of the soul contemplating its sins with the great mercy of God. Calvin's quotation is appropriate; in ourselves we are nothing, but in God we are "magnified," therefore, we *can* have the certitude of faith that he describes in 3.2.24.[74]

A second direct citation, which deals with the same theme and quotes from the same work of Bernard, is found in *Institutes* 3.13.4.[75] Again, Calvin is concerned about our having faith in God's promises, and not trusting in our own righteousness. He quotes Bernard on the confidence that comes through faith. However, we must return later to the question of the certitude of election, for Calvin and Bernard do not entirely agree on this.

The final direct citation of Bernard relating to faith is found in *Institutes* 3.2.41 (1559 edition only). Here the text quoted is *In annunciatione* I:1, 3. Calvin's context is the relation of faith and love. He rejects the "teaching of the Schoolmen, that love is prior to faith and hope" and continues:

> How much more rightly Bernard states: "I believe that the testimony of the conscience, which Paul calls 'the glory of the pious,' consists of three things. First of all, it is necessary to believe that you cannot have forgiveness of sins apart from God's mercy. Second, you can have no good work at all unless he gives it. Finally, you cannot merit eternal life by any works unless that is also given free." Shortly thereafter he adds that *these things are not enough, but are a beginning of faith;* because in believing that sins cannot be forgiven except by God, we ought at the same time to believe that they are forgiven, so long as we are persuaded also by the testimony of the Holy Spirit that salvation is stored up for us. And because God himself forgives sins, gives merits, and gives back rewards, we must also believe that we cannot take a firm stand in this beginning.[76]

Jill Raitt provides an excellent analysis of this quotation. The first thing that is evident is that Calvin seems to take "love" as a "good work," and on this basis sees Bernard as advocating the primacy of faith. Certainly "Calvin has warrant for claiming Bernard for justification by faith" in *In annunciatione,* as Raitt points out, for in I:1, Bernard speaks of merits as God's gifts. However, when he moves into the citation of *In annunciatione* I:3, Calvin "omits a phrase that could upset the neatness of his use of Bernard." Raitt explains:

> Bernard wrote: "Truly these things about which we have just spoken, do not in any way suffice, but should be taken as the beginning and as a foundation of faith." Calvin omits "as a foundation" since that could indicate that faith stands upon something other than God's election.[77]

Thus, Calvin is not entirely in harmony with Bernard on this point, as he himself perhaps implicitly recognized.

To summarize, it appears that Calvin and Bernard do have very similar notions of faith. The parallels would include: (1) faith as a knowledge that is "higher" than ordinary human knowledge; (2) faith as primarily a knowledge of God's *goodness*—that is, *experiential* knowledge; (3) faith as a gift of the Holy Spirit; and (4) faith as bringing a certain kind of confidence. However, this fourth parallel must be qualified, since we will see that Bernard does not go so far as to speak of certitude of salvation.

The Question of Merit

Ordinarily, when Calvin speaks of merit, sparks fly. In Book 3, chapter 14 of the *Institutes,* Calvin has gone to great lengths to make clear that justification in *no* sense includes works. In chapter 15, he confronts directly the issue of merit. He asks, "Though works may by no means suffice for justification, should they not yet deserve favor with God?"[78]

Calvin begins by lamenting the use of the term "merit" as dangerous and unscriptural:

> Of course, I would like to avoid verbal battles, but I wish that Christian writers had always exercised such restraint as not to take it into their heads needlessly to use terms foreign to Scripture that would produce great offense and very little fruit. Why, I ask, was there need to drag in the term "merit" when the value of good works could without offense have been meaningfully explained by another term? How much offense this term contains is clear from the great damage it has done to the world. Surely, as it is a most prideful term, it can do nothing but obscure God's favor and imbue men with perverse haughtiness.[79]

Calvin is well aware that some of his "heroes" from the past, including Augustine and Bernard, had used the term. Indeed, he appeals to them almost immediately in 3.15.2. First he mentions Augustine and Chrysostom, referring to texts that attribute all (including works) to God's grace. Calvin goes on to suggest, "But laying aside the term [merit], let us rather look at the thing itself." He cites Bernard's 68th Sermon on the Song of Songs (which he also quotes earlier in the *Institutes*), speaking of the "godly sense" in which Bernard used the word "merit":

> "For why," he asks, "should the church concern itself with merits when it has a firmer and more secure reason to glory in God's purpose? God cannot deny himself; he will do what he has promised. Thus you have no reason to ask, 'By what merits may we hope for benefits?' Especially since you hear: 'It is not for your sake . . . but for mine.' For merit, it suffices to know that merits do not suffice."[80]

Thus, although Calvin dislikes the *term*, he has no quarrel with Bernard's *concept*.[81]

Calvin continues by acknowledging that "those good works which he has bestowed upon us the Lord calls 'ours,' and testifies they not only are acceptable to him but also will have their reward."[82] To underline the fact that God *calls* the works ours, Calvin adds, "There is no doubt that whatever is praiseworthy in works is God's grace; there is not a drop that we ought by rights to ascribe to ourselves." If we understand merit in this way, Calvin concludes, "not only will all confidence in merit vanish, but the very notion."[83] Bernard, too, attributes all merit to God in this Augustinian sense; he does not see anything wrong with the term itself when properly understood.[84]

In general, Calvin has no use for the scholastic view of merit. First, he opposes the connection of "merit" and "free choice." Speaking of the schools' view of justification, he notes, "And they do not deny that the principal cause, indeed, lies in grace. But they still contend that in this, free choice [liberum arbitrium] is not ruled out, through which all merit exists."[85] We have seen that Bernard too makes this connection. In *De gratia*, he speaks of "free choice" as consent; and later adds that it is in consent that all merit consists.[86] Calvin's main target in the passage just quoted is Peter Lombard (along with the "schools of the Sorbonne"), but elsewhere he does criticize Bernard directly on this point, as we have already seen.[87]

Another development in theology that Calvin attacks is the idea that election is the result of God's "foreknowledge" of merit: in other words, the idea that God knows who will prove themselves worthy of grace, and that this is the basis of their election. Calvin's response is that "God chooses some and passes over others according to his own decision" and not because of a foreknowledge of good works.[88] Indeed, the latter *follow* election, they do not precede it:

> For when it is said that believers were chosen that they might be holy, at the same time it is suggested that the holiness that was to be in them originated from election. What consistency is there in saying that the things derived from election gave cause to election?[89]

There is one person in connection with whom we can legitimately use the word "merit," and that person is Christ. As Calvin puts it: "By his obedience . . . Christ truly acquired and merited [promeritus] grace for us with his Father."[90] It is *not* legitimate, Calvin insists, to speak of the superfluous "merits" of saints and martyrs being applied to us; for any "merits" they may have had were properly Christ's.[91] Again, Bernard also often refers all merit to Christ.[92]

Two other instances occur in the *Institutes* where Calvin refers directly to Bernard on the question of merit. The first is in 3.12.3, where Calvin cites five passages from the *Sermons on the Canticles* and one from Sermon 15 on Psalm 90.[93] Calvin's concern in this section is to stress the proper understanding of true righteousness, which consists in glorifying God's mercy and not trusting in our own works. Bernard's concern in the quoted sermons, as Jill Raitt points out, is different: rather than juxtaposing grace and merit in these passages, he wishes to speak of the peace that comes to Christians who *do* give God all the glory. In any case, Calvin is certainly on the mark in citing Bernard, as an example of "all devout writers" (referred to in the beginning of this section, 3.12.3), in his defense.[94]

The fifth citation from Bernard in this section, from *Sermons on the Canticles* 68.6, is of particular interest. Calvin quotes Bernard as follows:

> "Why should the church be concerned about merits, since it has in God's purpose a surer reason for glorying? Thus there is no reason why you

should ask by what merits we may hope for benefits, especially since
you hear in the prophet: 'It is not for your sake . . . that I am about to act,
but for mine . . . says the Lord.' Merit enough it is to know that merits are
not enough; but as it is merit enough not to presume upon merits, so to
be without merits is enough for judgment."

Calvin comments, "The fact that he uses the term 'merits' freely for good
works, we must excuse as the custom of the time." Here Jill Raitt disagrees
with Calvin's interpretation, insisting that Bernard does mean "merit"
since he often couples it with "reward." However, she herself recognizes
that this objection does not have great force, since every "truly good
work" (that is, one that proceeds from God and is recognized as such) *is*
meritorious for Bernard and Calvin (again, in the sense that God is the
author of merit). What our authors object to is rather "the presumption of
those who take merits to be a claim on God, a 'right' which they
themselves possess as though God were not the source and giver of both
works and merit."[95]

The final quotation of Bernard on merit in the *Institutes* is found in
3.12.8. The context is the same as it was in 3.12.3 (glorifying God and not
our own merits). The Bernard citation is again from the *Sermones super
Cantica* 13.5. Here Bernard assails the proud,

> who claim even the slightest thing for their own merits because they
> wrongfully retain the credit for grace that passes through them, as if a
> wall should say that it gave birth to a sunbeam that it received through
> a window.[96]

Calvin's use of Bernard here is not inappropriate, as Raitt points out that
earlier in the same sermon Bernard reflects on the Pharisee who in his
heart "pays tribute to himself."[97] However, Bernard's *immediate* context,
Raitt adds, "is that only those who truly honor God are at peace."[98]

In short, Calvin judges the word "merit" to be applied legitimately
only to the work of God or Christ. Although he is aware that Bernard
sometimes uses the word to refer to Christians, he is generally willing to
excuse this, because he sees Bernard as being substantially in agreement
with his own position. His only explicit disagreement is on Bernard's
definition of "free choice" as "consent."

Justification and Sanctification

Earlier, we saw Bernard speaking of two graces, "the first grace by
which I am enabled to repent of my sins," and the second by which one
can "bear fruits that befit repentance." This is certainly suggestive of
Calvin's "twofold grace of Christ," since for Calvin, the grace that makes
repentance possible is the grace of justification. However, I would not

want to press a comparison here, since Bernard does not ordinarily distinguish the graces in the way that Calvin does.[99]

Let us now take a closer look at the way Calvin relates the two graces. A good place to start would be Calvin's statement in *Institutes* 3.16.1:

> Do you wish . . . to attain righteousness in Christ? You must first possess Christ; but you cannot possess him without being made partaker in his sanctification, because he cannot be divided into pieces. Since, therefore, it is solely by expending himself that the Lord gives us these benefits to enjoy, he bestows both of them at the same time, the one never without the other. Thus it is clear how true it is that we are justified not without works yet not through works, since in our sharing in Christ, which justifies us, sanctification is just as much included as righteousness.[100]

Thus, justification and sanctification are bestowed simultaneously; it is impossible to have one without the other. At the same time, Calvin never departs from the conviction that they are distinct. He criticizes the schoolmen because "they include under the term 'justification' a renewal, by which through the Spirit of God we are remade to obedience to the Law."[101]

We saw that justification means God's acceptance of us as righteous by imputing to us the righteousness of Christ.[102] Sanctification, in turn, means regeneration, so that "we become new creatures."[103] This gift is bestowed along with faith.[104]

Calvin characteristically describes the process of sanctification under the rubric of "repentance," which he defines as "the true turning of our life to God, a turning that arises from a pure and earnest fear of him; and it consists in the mortification of our flesh and of the old man, and in the vivification of the Spirit."[105] Calvin is emphatic that repentance is the *fruit* of, not the prerequisite for, faith: for "a man cannot apply himself seriously to repentance without knowing himself to belong to God. But no one is truly persuaded that he belongs to God unless he has first recognized God's grace."[106] He is even willing to take on John the Evangelist in pressing home this point. In his comment on John 1:13 (where he understands John to say that "faith . . . is the fruit of spiritual regeneration"), he declares:

> It seems as if the Evangelist puts things back to front by making regeneration prior to faith, since it is rather the result of faith and therefore follows it. . . . When the Lord breathes faith into us He regenerates us in a hidden and secret way that is unknown to us.[107]

This reflects a theme that we will see again in our treatment of *unio mystica:* that "there is no sanctification apart from union with Christ."[108]

In a rare autobiographical passage found in the Preface to his *Commentary on the Psalms,* Calvin speaks of his "conversion" (which I understand as being under the rubric of "justification") as sudden:

> When I was too firmly addicted to the papal superstitions to be drawn
> easily out of such a deep mire, by a sudden conversion He [God] brought
> my mind (already more rigid than suited my age) to submission.[109]

However, Calvin does not characteristically speak of *repentance* (which I
take as related to "sanctification") as sudden. On the contrary, he often
insists that it is a lifelong process. Herein lies a major parallel with Bernard
of Clairvaux.

> And indeed, this restoration does not take place in one moment or one
> day or one year; but through continual and sometimes even slow
> advances God wipes out in his elect the corruptions of the flesh, cleanses
> them of guilt, consecrates them to himself as temples renewing all their
> minds to true purity that they may practice repentance throughout their
> lives and know that this warfare will end only at death.[110]

Similarly, we saw Bernard insisting that our sanctification is not com-
pleted in this life; for example, in *De diligendo Deo* he speaks of the highest
degree of love taking place after the final resurrection.[111]

What is the goal of sanctification in our present existence? Calvin's
answer is contained in part in his treatment of the Christian life as
self-denial. The gifts that we have received from God in our sanctification
are to be shared with one another. God is not "enriched" by this sharing,
although it is essential that we "dedicate" all gifts to God as their
author.[112]

Similarly, we saw in Bernard's *De diligendo Deo* that insofar as earthly
existence is concerned, we can progress in sanctification to the point
where we will be able to fulfill God's command to love our neighbor.
Bernard goes on to say that "this love is pleasing because it is free." In
other words, it is given totally for God's sake and not for our own. The
context here is the third stage of love, "loving God for God's sake."[113] This
brings us to another important parallel with Calvin: that the goal of the
Christian life is to give glory to God, not to be preoccupied with one's own
salvation. Such preoccupation, for Bernard, would fall under the second
stage of loving God, loving God for one's own sake. The classic text to
illustrate this is Calvin's famous *Reply to Sadolet*, where he chides Sadolet
for appealing to the Genevans to return to union with Rome on the
grounds of concern for their personal salvation:

> It is not very sound theology to confine a man's thoughts so much to
> himself, and not to set before him as the prime motive of his existence
> zeal to show forth the glory of God. . . . I therefore believe that there is no
> man imbued with true piety, who will not regard as in poor taste that
> long and detailed exhortation to a zeal for heavenly life, which occupies
> a man entirely concerned with himself, and does not, even by one
> expression, arouse him to sanctify the name of God.[114]

Calvin makes one specific reference to Bernard when discussing sanctification. The reference is specifically to the notion of repentance. Calvin is reflecting on Paul's catalog of seven characteristics of repentance in 2 Cor. 7:11, one of which is "avenging." Calvin describes this as "shame, confusion, groaning, displeasure with self, and other emotions that arise out of a lively recognition of sin." However, Calvin cautions against carrying this to extremes, lest we fall into despair:

> That fear cannot, indeed, be too great which ends in humility, and does not depart from the hope of pardon. Nevertheless, in accordance with the apostle's injunction the sinner ought always to beware lest, while he worries himself into dissatisfaction weighed down by excessive fear, he becomes faint. For in this way we flee from God, who calls us to himself through repentance. On this matter Bernard's admonition is also useful: "Sorrow for sins is necessary if it be not unremitting. I beg you to turn your steps back sometimes from troubled and anxious remembering of your ways, and to go forth to the tableland of serene remembrance of God's benefits. . . . If you take thought upon yourselves in your humility, take thought likewise upon the Lord in his goodness."[115]

Jill Raitt comments that Calvin's use of this passage is accurate and true to Bernard's own context.[116]

One other topic relating to justification and sanctification that I wish to explore before closing this chapter is Calvin's notion of election.[117] In three instances Calvin directly cites Bernard in support of his own theology.

First, let us review Calvin's general understanding of election or "predestination":

> We call predestination God's eternal decree, by which he compacted with himself what he willed to become of each man. For all are not created in equal condition; rather, eternal life is foreordained for some, eternal damnation for others.[118]

Calvin later adds that God's free election "has been only half explained until we come to individual persons, to whom God not only offers salvation but so assigns it that the certainty of its effect is not in doubt."[119] Here is where a definite difference with Bernard emerges, for Bernard denies that we can have absolute certitude of our own election. However, in the sermon that we looked at earlier, he also adds that there are "indications which minister to our confidence and furnish a solid basis for hope," among which he includes the genuine hearing of God's word.[120]

Although Bernard claims that absolute certitude of one's personal election is impossible to have, like Calvin he expects that justification will become evident to others in the good deeds of the sanctified believer. In

Sermon 24 on the Song of Songs he declares that "the state of the invisible soul is made known by one's belief and practice."[121]

Let us now proceed to the texts where Calvin quotes Bernard on election. The first appears in *Institutes* 3.21.1. Calvin argues that the doctrine of election, which he has just introduced in this section, brings comfort, for "all those who do not know that they are God's own will be miserable through constant fear." He turns to Bernard in support of this, saying that "Bernard rightly teaches" that the church "could not otherwise be found or recognized among creatures, since it lies marvelously hidden . . . *both within the bosom of a blessed predestination and within the mass of a miserable condemnation.*"[122]

Jill Raitt points out that only the italicized text above is a direct quote from Bernard; the rest is paraphrased. Furthermore, Bernard's context is somewhat different: he is speaking of the salvation of the "bride" (the church) and the "cooperation" of both God and humans in this salvation (God's cooperation always precedes). Only one person is known to have entered this world with integrity, and that is Christ. As for the rest, all have sinned, both the saved and the damned. The church "lies hidden" within the two.[123]

The second quotation is in *Institutes* 3.22.10. Here Calvin is speaking of the universality of God's invitation (through preaching) but the particularity of election: "although the voice of the gospel addresses all in general, yet the gift of faith is rare." He goes on to quote Bernard's Letter 107 to Thomas of Beverly, in which the key passage is this: "[God] does not vouchsafe to others participation in so great a mystery [God's plan], save to those whom he has foreknown and predestined to become his own [Nec alios sane dignatur tanti participatione mysterii, nisi eos ipsos, quos fore suos praescivit et praedestinavit]." As Raitt confirms, Calvin has used this passage appropriately.[124]

The final quotation is found in *Institutes* 3.24.4, and it includes a quotation from a Bernard passage that Calvin earlier cited in 3.11.22 (*Sermons on the Canticles* 23:15).[125] In this section, Calvin is speaking of the proper way of attaining certainty of election, that is, through God's word. Calvin refers to Bernard in explaining the peace that comes from knowing one's adoption by God.

However, as Raitt shows, Calvin omits portions of Bernard's text, where Bernard speaks of but a *momentary* certainty of his election. Bernard's context, according to Raitt, is a recounting "of the ultimate mystical experience, of his brief visit to the bridal chamber where peace reigns."[126] Calvin's context is a discussion of *all believers* enjoying this peace, not just the mystic "transported in prayer." Therefore Raitt suggests that "Bernard would feel his words had been misused." Although it is true that "both aspire to this ravishing vision of peace,"[127] the difference between Bernard and Calvin here is significant. It will be taken up again under the question of the scope of mysticism in chapters 4 and 5. We shall see that Calvin's mysticism is in some senses more "inclusive" than Bernard's.

To sum up: Calvin sees Bernard as an ally who reinforces his own doctrine of election. To some extent, he is right; however, Bernard does not hold to a personal certitude of election, nor does he imply that election will yield a mystical experience for all believers.

CONCLUSION

With Jill Raitt, we can summarize the common ground between Bernard and Calvin on justification as follows: (1) righteousness is of God and God alone; (2) justification consists of the free acceptance of God, that is, the nonimputation of sins; (3) it is absurd to claim merits for ourselves when all we have received is from God; and (4) we should turn from contemplation of sin and judgment (or of our own works) to a considera-tion of God's benefits.

I would also include the following points not noted by Raitt: (5) faith is a "higher knowledge" that is primarily experiential rather than theoreti-cal;[128] (6) regeneration is a lifelong process, in which a genuine growth in holiness is achieved and expressed in love of neighbor; (7) justification is visibly evident in the life of the believer through the process of sanctifica-tion; and (8) there is a certain confidence one can have in election. Calvin speaks of an "absolute" certitude, however, which Bernard denies.

4

BERNARD OF CLAIRVAUX ON MYSTICAL UNION

In chapters 2 and 3, I showed that many parallels exist between Bernard and Calvin in their discussions of anthropology and the theology of justification. On both of these subjects, Calvin explicitly quotes Bernard, and is usually in agreement with him. In fact, we saw that the only *stated* disagreements with Bernard are in the area of anthropology: in his rejection of Bernard's definition of free choice as consent, and in his criticism of Bernard on a natural human ability to seek the good.[1] Whenever Calvin quotes Bernard on other aspects of his anthropology and on the topic of justification, he always does so approvingly (if not always appropriately to Bernard's context).

Now that I have laid the groundwork, it is time to look directly at Bernard and Calvin's respective views on *unio mystica*. This is a subject on which Calvin rarely quotes Bernard directly;[2] nevertheless, I hope to show that many parallels exist in this area as well. This chapter and the next will treat the following questions for Bernard and Calvin respectively: (1) the nature of mystical union, including the question of divine and human components, the images used, the cognitive dimensions of union, and most especially the role of Christ; (2) the scope of mystical union, that is, who can or cannot be a mystic; and (3) the relationship of mystical union to each author's ecclesiology, that is, to the church and to Christian life in general, particularly the issue of sanctification.

Before proceeding, I think it is appropriate to recall the medieval definition against which both Bernard and Calvin's mystical theologies are to be compared:

> Mystical theology is experiential knowledge of God attained through the union of spiritual affection with Him. Through this union the words of the Apostle are fulfilled: "He who clings to God is one spirit with Him (1 Cor. 6:17)."[3]

Each of our authors, in his own way, conforms to this definition by Gerson.

THE NATURE OF MYSTICAL UNION

In his Introduction to the text of Bernard's Sermons on the Song of Songs, Corneille Halflants asserts:

> St. Bernard is, above all, an affective genius. Love is his proper domain and it is through love that he attains his loftiest experiences. Here there is no need to search out isolated passages. There is an unlimited supply of them. The abundance of his heart simply pours itself forth.[4]

Indeed, it would be both tedious and unnecessary to cite every example of Bernard's love-based mysticism. My goal is to outline the main features of this mysticism, with reference to the most relevant major works, particularly the *Sermones super Cantica* and *De diligendo Deo*.

At the outset it is important to note that in discussing union, as when he discusses justification, Bernard is emphatic about attributing all to grace. For example, in one description of the contemplative experience, Bernard says:

> When the Word therefore tells the soul, "You are beautiful," and calls it friend, he infuses into it the power to love, to know it is loved in return. And when the soul addresses him as beloved and praises his beauty, she is filled with admiration for his goodness and attributes to him without subterfuge or deceit the grace by which she loves and is loved.[5]

For Bernard, divine love triggers a process that makes its recipient want to love God as much as possible in return.[6] On one occasion, Bernard speaks of the early days of his own conversion, when he experienced "coldness and hardness of heart." Echoing Augustine, he says:

> I could not yet love him [God] since I had not yet really found him; at best my love was less than it should have been, and for that very reason I sought to increase it, for I would not have sought him if I did not already love him in some degree.[7]

Bernard makes it clear on several occasions that only those who seek God's glory, and not their own, will be led to contemplation. Such persons *experience* the glory of which God is the source.[8] It must be mentioned that there are times when Bernard speaks of good works as preceding contemplation. For example, speaking of the "marriage bed" (*lectulum sponsae*) of contemplation, Bernard states:

> Therefore you must take care to surround yours [i.e., your bed] with the flowers of good works, with the practice of virtues, that precede holy contemplation as the flower precedes the fruit. . . . It is a perversion of

order to demand the reward before it is earned, to take food and not to
work.[9]

This might be interpreted as a kind of works righteousness on Bernard's
part. Indeed, it is precisely the kind of statement that Ritschl points to as
an example of what makes Bernard's mysticism unacceptable. However, I
trust that by now it is clear that Bernard never wishes to speak of "good
works" that are not effected by grace. Calvin himself, as we have seen in
chapter 3, recognizes this. Other statements in Bernard serve to under-
score his fundamental point of view. For example, in another Sermon on
the Song, he asks in reference to the soul, "How could she be full of grace
if there were any part of her which did not itself spring from grace? There
is no way for grace to enter, if . . . merit has taken residence in the soul."[10]
In a word, the soul's relationship with God begins and ends with grace.

Turning now to the nature of mystical union, let us begin by reviewing
the stages of loving God that Bernard outlines in *De diligendo Deo*. Bernard
speaks of the following "degrees" of love: where people (1) love themselves for their own sake, (2) love God for their own sake, (3) love God for
God's sake, and (4) love even themselves for God's sake.[11] It is the second
two stages that especially interest us here, for at these two stages one
moves beyond selfishness to a love that glorifies God. However, Bernard
does not totally disparage the earlier degrees of love. In the first degree
(*amor carnalis*), for example, one can begin to love one's neighbor as
oneself, but this love is imperfect since it is not rooted in God. It is only in
the third degree that one loves with "perfect justice."[12]

Of the second degree of love, Bernard has little to say. Here people love
God for their own advantage, particularly because God frees them from
sin. Bernard believes that after a while, these oft-forgiven sinners cannot
help but be transformed to a higher degree of love, for God's love melts
even the hardest of hearts:

> If man's tribulations, however, grow in frequency and as a result he
> frequently turns to God and is frequently freed by God, must he not end,
> even though he had a heart of stone in a breast of iron, by realizing that
> it is God's grace which frees him and come to love God not for his own
> advantage but for the sake of God?

Bernard goes on to say, "Tasting God's sweetness entices us more to pure
love than does the urgency of our own needs."[13]

At the third stage of love, one begins to experience the kind of unity
with God that is Bernard's goal. A person whose love of God is unselfish
(and indeed, only God can be the source of such love) "will not have
trouble in fulfilling the commandment to love his neighbor." Such a
person "loves with justice and freely embraces the just commandment."
Finally, Bernard notes that "this love is pleasing because it is free [Amor

iste merito gratus, quia gratuitus]." It is pleasing because its sole motivation is the glory of God; it is a love that says, "Confess to the Lord for he is
good."[14]

Bernard is convinced that the third degree of love is the highest that one
can attain in this life:

> No doubt man remains a long time in this degree, and I doubt if he ever
> attains the fourth degree during this life, that is, if he ever loves only for
> God's sake. Let those who have had the experience make a statement; to
> me, I confess, it seems impossible.

However, in other sections of *De diligendo Deo*, he suggests that martyrs
may receive a taste of it while still in their bodies, and that some may
experience a momentary rapture of this degree of love.[15] For Bernard, the
fullness of love is *permanently* enjoyed in a "spiritual" body, which one
acquires in the final resurrection. Only then will the soul not be distracted
by a desire to reunite with the flesh.[16]

What is the nature of this highest degree of love that defines mystical
union? In *De diligendo Deo*, Bernard describes it as follows:

> It is therefore necessary for our souls to reach a similar state in which,
> just as God willed everything to exist for himself, so we wish that neither
> ourselves nor other beings to have been nor to be except for his will
> alone, not for our pleasure. The satisfaction of our wants, chance
> happiness, delights us less than to see his will done in us and for us,
> which we implore every day in prayer saying ". . . your will be done on
> earth as it is in heaven . . ." . . . It is deifying to go through such an
> experience. As a drop of water seems to disappear completely in a big
> quantity of wine, even assuming the wine's taste and color; just as red,
> molten iron becomes so much like fire it seems to lose its primary state;
> just as the air on a sunny day seems transformed into sunshine instead of
> being lit up; so it is necessary for the saints that all human feelings melt
> in a mysterious way and flow into the will of God. Otherwise, how will
> God be all in all if something human survives in man? No doubt, the
> substance remains though under another form, another glory, another
> power [Manebit quidem substantia, sed in alia forma, alia gloria, alia
> potentia].[17]

This quotation embraces a number of important elements in Bernard's
concept of mystical union. For example, it stresses that the mystic is one
with the *will* of God. This corresponds to the stress on will over intellect in
Bernard, which we have seen throughout this study. Second, Bernard is
careful to exclude a "substantive" understanding of union. Although he
uses a number of familiar images for union (e.g., the drop of water in a vat
of wine, molten iron taking on the properties of fire, etc.) that are
suggestive of an annihilation of the self, Bernard explicitly rejects such an

interpretation. Rather, "human feelings melt in a mysterious way and flow into the *will* of God" (emphasis added); the substance of humanity, on the other hand, somehow remains, albeit transformed by the experience.[18]

These insights are echoed in the Sermons on the Song of Songs. In Sermon 62, Bernard declares that the bride should not scrutinize God's majesty (although it is appropriate to admire it) but rather his will:

> Scrutinizing God's majesty is then a thing to fear; but scrutinizing his will is as safe as it is dutiful [Ergo formidolosa scrutatio maiestatis; at voluntatis, tam tuta quam pia]. Why should I not tirelessly concentrate on searching into the mystery of his glorious will, which I know I must obey in all things?

He goes on to say that contemplation of God's "goodness and the multitude of his mercies" is the sweetest glory one can have.[19]

Bernard clearly states that the union between the Word and the soul is a spiritual union:

> Be careful, however, not to conclude that I see something corporeal or perceptible to the senses in this union between the Word and the soul. My opinion is that of the Apostle, who said that "he who is united to the Lord becomes one spirit with him."[20]

An even clearer statement of Bernard's meaning is found in Sermon 71:

> The Father and Son cannot be said to be one person, because the Father is one and the Son is one. Yet they are said to be, and they are, one, because they have and are one substance, since they have not each separate substance. On the contrary, since God and man do not share the same nature or substance, they cannot be said to be a unity, yet they are with complete truth and accuracy, said to be one spirit, if they cohere with the bond of love [sibi glutino amoris]. But that unity is caused not so much by the identity of essences [essentiarum cohaerentia] as by the concurrence of wills [conniventia voluntatum].[21]

The notion of *unus spiritus* is one of the most frequently mentioned explanations of mystical union in the Sermons on the Song of Songs. The reference is to Paul in 1 Cor. 6:17. Bernard correlates it with the notion of the spiritual marriage, a primary image in the Sermons. For example, in Sermon 61, speaking of the bride (i.e., the soul) drawing near the "wine of love," Bernard states:

> When she will have attained to it and become perfect she will celebrate a spiritual marriage [spirituale coniungium]; and they shall be two, not in one flesh but in one spirit [non in carne una, sed in uno spiritu], as the apostle says: "He who is united to the Lord becomes one spirit with him."[22]

Bernard also correlates the *unus spiritus* theme in these sermons with his stress on love, as shown in the citation from Sermon 71 above. To give another example: reflecting in the context of the death of his brother Gerard, Bernard states:

"He who is united to the Lord becomes one spirit with him," his whole being somehow changed into a movement of divine love. . . . But God is love, and the deeper one's union with God, the more full one is of love [Deus autem caritas est, et quanto quis coniunctior Deo, tanto plenior caritate].[23]

It bears repeating that for Bernard, this union with God in love is *God's* doing. In the long passage from *De diligendo Deo* cited above, Bernard has this to say about reaching the highest degree of love: "sic *affici*, deificari est" (to be so affected is to be deified). By using the passive voice, Bernard makes it clear that God is doing the transforming. Similarly, in the Sermons on the Song of Songs, Bernard frequently refers to the Bride surrendering wholly to grace.[24]

Another characteristic of Bernard's notion of mystical union is that it is not a union of equals. As we saw in chapter 1, this is the most severe charge that Ritschl makes against Bernard's mysticism. He bases his objection precisely on the fact that Bernard's conception centers on love. His words bear repeating here:

For love very distinctly implies the equality of the person loving with the beloved. St. Bernard, who gave to the world the pattern of this species of piety, expressly states that in intercourse with the Bridegroom awe ceases, majesty is laid aside, and immediate personal intercourse is carried on as between lovers or neighbors.[25]

Before defending Bernard, I think it is only fair to note that there are times when he uses language that is suggestive of a relationship of equals. However, a careful look at the Latin text will invariably exonerate him. For example, in Sermon 43, when commenting on Canticle 1:12 ("My beloved is to me a little bundle of myrrh that lies between my breasts"), Bernard states:

Recently he [God] was king, now he is the beloved; recently he was on his royal couch, now he lies between the breasts of the bride. This illustrates the great power of humility, to which the God of majesty will so gladly yield. In a moment reverence has given way to friendship, and he who seemed so distant has been quickly brought close [Cito reverentiae nomen in vocabulum amicitiae mutatum est; et qui longe erat, factus est in brevi prope].[26]

Furthermore, Bernard makes it clear in other places that what is experienced as intimate "friendship" is not in fact a relationship of equality. In Sermon 64, for example, he quotes God as speaking the verse of Canticle 2:15 to the bride: "Catch us the little foxes that spoil the vines, for our vines are in flower." Bernard clarifies as follows:

> He who speaks is indeed God, yet it is not as God that he speaks, but as a Bridegroom.
> "Catch us the foxes." You see how he speaks, *as though to equals*—he who has no equal [Vides quam socialiter loquitur qui socium non habet?]. He could have said "me," but he preferred to say "us," for he delights in companionship. What sweetness! What grace! What mighty love! Can it be that the Highest of all is made one with all?[27]

It is not that God is in any sense the Bride's equal; rather, God, whose majesty is absolute, condescends in an act of great humility (as noted also in the quotation from Sermon 43 above) to share an experience of his love with the Bride. Bernard speaks with great awe of this act of condescension:

> I cannot restrain my joy that this majesty did not disdain to bend down to our weakness in a companionship so familiar and sweet, that the supreme Godhead did not scorn to enter into wedlock with the soul in exile and to reveal to her with the most ardent love how affectionate was this bridegroom whom she had won.[28]

In a later sermon on the Song, Bernard makes an unequivocal statement about the nature of the love relationship. Commenting on Canticle 2:16 ("My beloved is mine, and I am his"), he asserts:

> There is no doubt that in this passage a shared love blazes up, but a love in which one of them experiences the highest felicity, while the other shows marvellous condescension. *There is no betrothal or union of equals here* [Neque enim inter pares est consensio seu complexio haec].[29]

However, while there is no union of equals, Bernard does wish to speak of a perfectly *mutual* relationship between the Bride and the Bridegroom. This is especially clear in Sermon 83, where Bernard distinguishes equality and mutuality:

> Although the creature loves less, being a lesser being, yet if it loves with its whole heart nothing is lacking, for it has given all. . . . For it is nothing other than love, holy and chaste, full of sweetness and delight, love utterly serene and true, mutual and deep, which joins two beings, not in one flesh, but in one spirit, making them no longer two but one.[30]

As we saw in chapter 1, some Reformation scholars would have a problem not only with the language of "equality" in mystical union but also with the language of "likeness." For example, Steven Ozment criticizes Gerson for accepting the idea that in mystical union the soul "becomes like" God:

Gerson . . . preserves the distance between God and man in the mystical union. But it is a distance and otherness of two generic "likes." The radical opposition between a righteous God and a sinful man disappears in the union of likes.[31]

I will refrain from discussing the legitimacy of this criticism in relation to Gerson, but would like to comment on its applicability to Bernard.

Bernard does speak of the soul being "glorified by its likeness to the Word," adding, "yet because of its distinction between them it will always have to say 'Lord, who is like you?' "[32] However, I understand Bernard to mean that the soul is transported in the experience of mystical union not by any innate merit of its own, but insofar as it has been transformed by *grace*.[33] He insists on this often enough that we can assume that it is presupposed in a passage such as this. Thus, it is *not* a question, to use Ozment's term, of "generic" likes—except in the sense of the natural likeness (or image, depending upon which work of Bernard one is reading!) that remains in the soul after sin. Even Calvin recognizes that there is a vestige of the *imago Dei* that was not eradicated by the fall, which is found in the *sensus divinitatis* and *conscientia*. As we have seen, these become a point of contact with grace.[34]

A further quality of mystical union in Bernard is that the experience of union with God in our present existence is both incomplete and brief. Bernard often mentions that even the contemplative does not see God "as he is":

Those who contemplate him without ceasing are short of nothing, those whose wills are fixed on him have nothing more to desire.

But this vision is not for the present life; it is reserved for the next. . . . Even now he appears to whom he pleases, but as he pleases, not as he is [Et nunc quidem apparet quibus vult, sed sicuti vult, non sicuti est]. Neither sage nor saint nor prophet can nor could ever see him as he is, while still in this mortal body; but whoever is found worthy will be able to do so when the body becomes immortal.[35]

On the other hand, later in the same sermon Bernard says that God "does not reveal himself as altogether different from what he is" either. Thus, the contemplative gets an "authentic" taste of the sweetness of the Lord. Bernard often qualifies this by speaking of God's being experienced "in relation to your power to enjoy [certe prout tuum sapere est]."[36]

The full experience of love, then, whether contemplative (*affectus*) or active (a distinction that will be expounded below), cannot be had in this life: "We do not deny that the present life, by divine grace, can also experience its beginning and progress, but we unreservedly maintain that its consummation is in the happiness of the life to come."[37]

Those who do enjoy an experience of affective union find that it is a fleeting one. Bernard states that he has himself been blessed by the experience:

> But there is a place where God is seen in tranquil rest, where he is neither Judge nor Teacher but Bridegroom. To me—for I do not speak for others—this is truly the bedroom to which I have sometimes gained happy entrance. Alas! How rare the time, and how short the stay![38]

The person who enjoys this vision of the Bridegroom experiences happiness, "but it is a happiness that is never complete because the joy of the visit is followed by the pain at his departure."[39] Indeed, the person who has received "this mystical kiss from the mouth of Christ at least once, seeks again that intimate experience, and eagerly looks for its frequent renewal."[40]

What about those who never have such an experience of union? Bernard's answer is that all people, contemplative or not, are saved by grace through faith, and not through mystical visions. "It is living faith," Bernard says, "which obtains for us the most exalted graces."[41] Indeed, it is faith that brings us true knowledge of God, for it "does not know the poverty of the senses," and "transcends even the limits of human reason, the capacity of nature, *the bounds of experience*."[42] Bernard will even suggest that those whose faith is strong have no need to experience such visions: "What they do not know from experience, let them believe, so that one day, by virtue of their faith, they may reap the harvest of experience."[43]

Before proceeding to the questions of knowledge and the role of Christ, I would like to summarize some of the images used in Bernard's mystical writing. We have already seen several examples above. Bernard is comfortable with using images of absorption/identity (drop of water in a vat of wine, molten iron taking on the qualities of fire, air transformed into sunshine) as long as these images are not taken in the literal sense of a substantive or essential union.[44] But his most famous and often-used images revolve around the notion of a "spiritual marriage." The *Sermones super Cantica canticorum*, indeed, are centered on this notion.

One image in this cluster is that of the kiss (*osculum*). Bernard expounds on the text "Let him kiss me with the kiss of his mouth" as follows: "A fertile kiss, therefore, a marvel of stupendous self-abasement that is not a mere pressing of mouth upon mouth, it is the uniting of God with man."[45] Other images of contemplation include the garden, the chamber, and the marriage bed.[46] All images converge in the notion of *unus spiritus*, which was discussed above.

What role does knowledge play in mystical union? In chapter 3, I noted that for Bernard, faith is a certain kind of knowledge: experiential rather than purely cognitive. To know God is to know his goodness; a knowledge unaccompanied by love is a paltry knowledge indeed, leading to nothing but pride.[47]

When speaking of the spiritual union of the contemplative, Bernard also refers to knowledge. Consistently with his general preference for the will over the intellect, he will at times explicitly downplay the latter, as in the following comment on Canticle 2:16 ("My beloved is mine, and I am his"): "It is the *affectus*, not the intellect, which has spoken, and it is not for the intellect to grasp."[48]

However, Bernard explicitly speaks of a cognitive element in mystical union:

> For as holy contemplation has two forms of ecstasy, one in the intellect, the other in the will [in intellectu unus et alter in affectu]; one of enlightenment, the other of fervor; one of knowledge, the other of devotion: so a tender affection, a heart glowing with love, the infusion of holy ardor, and the vigor of a spirit filled with zeal, are obviously not acquired from any place other than the wine-cellar.[49]

In contemplation, then, love and knowledge go hand in hand. As Bernard says in another place: "Felicitous . . . is this kiss of participation that enables us not only to know God but to love the Father, who is never fully known until he is perfectly loved."[50]

Bernard never really explains exactly how love and knowledge are related in the experience of *unus spiritus*; he does, however, refer in one place to the old dictum of Gregory the Great, that "love itself is a form of knowing [amor ipse notitia est]." Bernard McGinn expresses the crucial point succinctly, "The powers of knowing as well as those of loving are fulfilled in the marital embrace."[51]

An important question about mystical union, especially in relation to Calvin, is the role of Christ. Despite some variety in his use of language, Bernard presents a consistent view. In the Sermons on the Song of Songs, Bernard at times speaks of God as the Bridegroom (*sponsus*);[52] more characteristically, however, he speaks of Christ. The vast majority of the *Sermones super Cantica* end with a praise of Christ as the Bridegroom (this pattern becomes especially consistent after Sermon 20).[53] In *De diligendo Deo*, on the other hand, Bernard refers, more "generically," to union with God, but not without reference to Christ.

To flesh out Bernard's view on this matter, let us first recall what he says about Christ in *De gratia*. A passage quoted in chapter 3 is worth repeating here:

> In him, man possesses the necessary "power of God and the wisdom of God," who, inasmuch as he is wisdom, pours back into man true wisdom, and so restores to him his free counsel; and, inasmuch as he is power, renews his full power, and so restores to him his free pleasure.[54]

Bernard also notes in *De gratia* that while we never lost the "image" of God (i.e., free choice), it is Christ who restores the "likeness" of free counsel and free pleasure, which will only be perfectly enjoyed in the next life.[55]

In *De diligendo Deo*, Bernard refers to Christ as absolutely essential in the process of loving God. "The faithful," he says, "know how totally they need Jesus and him crucified." Christ not only shows us a "charity which surpasses all knowledge," but spurs us on to greater love by "wounding" us with his own.[56]

In the *Sermones super Cantica canticorum*, references to Christ are legion. Bernard frequently reminds his readers that the whole enterprise of approaching God is rooted in Christ, who is the "ultimate source of all virtue and knowledge. . . . Hence from him as from a well-head comes the power to be pure in body, diligent in affection and upright in will."[57]

A common theme in these Sermons is that of Christ "drawing" his Bride (who can be understood as either the church or the soul, as we shall see below) to God:

> But those whom the Father draws are drawn also by you, for whatever works the Father does the Son does too. There is a more intimate note however about her [i.e., the Bride's] request to be drawn by the Son, for he is her Bridegroom, sent before her by the Father as leader and teacher.[58]

In describing the experience of union in the *Sermones super Cantica canticorum*, Bernard uses the image of a spiritual marriage between the soul and the Word:

> When she loves perfectly, the soul is wedded to the Word. . . . Truly this is a spiritual contract, a holy marriage [Vere spiritualis sanctique connubii contractus est iste]. . . . What other bond or compulsion do you look for between those who are betrothed, except to love and be loved?[59]

However, union with Christ does not begin at this level. It is preceded by a carnal love of the humanity of Christ. Although Bernard is emphatic that the proper interpretation of the Song of Songs is spiritual and not carnal,[60] there is one kind of carnal love that is a necessary stage on the path to union. As Bernard puts it in Sermon 20:

> Notice that the love of the heart is, in a certain sense, carnal, because our hearts are attracted most toward the humanity of Christ and the things he did or commanded while in the flesh. . . . I think this is the principal reason why the invisible God willed to be seen in the flesh and to converse with men as a man. He wanted to recapture the affections of carnal men who were unable to love in any other way, by first drawing them to the salutary love of his own humanity, and then gradually to raise them to a spiritual love.[61]

I would suggest that this carnal love of Christ would fit most neatly into Bernard's second stage in *De diligendo Deo*, although Bernard himself does not make this connection. This emphasis on love for the body of Christ is historically significant, in that it "made Bernard a crucial figure in the medieval development of affective devotion to Christ the man, which centers particularly on his Passion."[62]

It should be noted that Bernard speaks in his writings of union not only with Christ but also with the Father and, in a certain sense, with the Holy Spirit. We have already seen examples of how Bernard alternates between Christ and the Spirit in his mystical imagery: for example, in his discussion of being "drawn" to God.[63] Let us take a closer look at how Bernard conceives of mystical union in relation to the Trinity.

In the *Sermones super Cantica*, Bernard clarifies the role of the Father and the Son in mystical union:

> What does it mean for the Word to come into a soul? It means that he will instruct it in wisdom. What does it mean for the Father to come? . . . It is the Father's nature to love, and therefore the coming of the Father is marked by an infusion of love.[64]

What, then, is the role of the Holy Spirit? In an earlier sermon, *Sermons on the Canticles* 8.2, Bernard says, "It is no mean or contemptible thing to be kissed by the kiss, because it is nothing less than the gift of the Holy Spirit." He goes on to say that the bride "dares to ask for this kiss, actually for that Spirit *in whom* both the Father and the Son will reveal themselves to her."[65] In this section, Bernard refers to several passages from the scripture about knowing both the Father and the Son, particularly John 17:3 ("Eternal life is this: to know you, the only true God, and Jesus Christ whom you have sent"). He anticipates an objection that the Holy Spirit is irrelevant:

> But one of you may interpose and say: "Therefore knowledge of the Holy Spirit is not necessary, because when he said eternal life consisted of the knowledge of the Father and the Son, he did not mention the Holy Spirit." True enough; but where there is perfect knowledge of the Father and the Son, how can there be ignorance of the goodness of both, which is the Holy Spirit? . . . The Holy Spirit is indeed nothing else but the love and the benign goodness of them both.[66]

He goes on to clarify again the precise role of the Spirit: that God reveals himself "through the kiss, that is, through the Holy Spirit. . . . It is by giving the Spirit, through whom he reveals, that he shows us himself; he reveals in the gift, his gift is in the revealing."[67] Thus, union with God takes place "in" or "through" the Spirit. This will be important in relation to Calvin.

Typical of Bernard, he does not follow this same schema in other writings. In *De gradibus*, he offers another way of distinguishing the operation of the persons of the Trinity on the soul in contemplation. He begins by distinguishing "three degrees in the perception of truth": truth in ourselves, in our neighbors, and in itself. He continues, "We look for truth in ourselves when we judge ourselves; in our neighbors when we have sympathy for their sufferings; in itself when we contemplate it with a clean heart."[68]

Later in the treatise, Bernard correlates these degrees with the Trinity:

> These are the three steps of truth. We climb to the first by the toil of humility, to the second by a deep feeling of compassion, and to the third by the ecstasy of contemplation. . . . It occurs to me here that it is possible to allot each of these three works to one of the Persons of the Undivided Trinity, that is, in so far as a man sitting in darkness can make distinction in the work of the Three Persons who always work as One. There would seem to be something characteristic of the Son in the first stage, of the Holy Spirit in the second, of the Father in the third.

Thus, Jesus, "the Master of truth gave his disciples an example of humility and opened to them the first stage of truth." Charity, in turn, "is a gift of the Holy Spirit," which leads to compassion for one's neighbor. Finally, the Father bestows glory.[69]

Having said all this, Bernard adds:

> However, Truth is the proper title, not of the Son alone but of the Spirit and the Father too, so that it must be made quite clear, while giving full acknowledgement to the properties of Persons that it is the one Truth who works at all these stages: in the first teaching as a Master, in the second consoling as a Friend and Brother, in the third embracing as a Father.[70]

In short, Bernard is emphatic that all three divine persons are "involved" in a human's attaining to the highest realm of truth, which Bernard identifies with contemplation. I would summarize by saying that Bernard's mysticism is certainly Christ-centered (like Calvin's), but it can also be described as having a trinitarian element, although this is not really developed in Bernard's thought.

THE SCOPE OF MYSTICAL UNION

To whom is an experience of mystical union granted? Gerson, as we saw in chapter 1, thinks it is possible for any Christian to be a contemplative.[71] At times, Bernard seems to suggest the same thing. For example, commenting on Canticle 2:16 (which he understands as "the Lord has inclined to me"), he asks to whom this passage applies. His answer:

> I think myself that any inquiry would show that there is no member of the church to whom it may not be applied in some degree. . . . It was not

for one soul, but for many who should be gathered up into the one church, his only Bride, that God wrought so great a work at so great a cost, "working salvation in the midst of the earth."[72]

However, the key words here are "in some degree." In several places, Bernard makes it clear that he does not think that contemplation is an experience that can be enjoyed by any Christian: "For it is not within the power of everybody in the Church to examine the mysteries of the divine will or of themselves to pierce the depths of God."[73] In Sermon 32, Bernard speaks of how Christ adapts his graces in a way that is appropriate for each person. As for a visit from the Bridegroom (i.e., mystical contemplation), he says, "He will not reveal himself in this way to every person, even momentarily, but only to the one who is proved to be a worthy bride by intense devotion, vehement desire and the sweetest affection."[74]

Bernard does not hesitate to say that it is in the monastery where such an experience is most likely to happen. I do not know of any passage where he absolutely rules it out for one who is not a monk, but he clearly sees the monastery as the natural and perfect environment for contemplation. Reflecting on Canticle 1:15 ("Our bed is covered with flowers"), Bernard states, "And indeed in the Church, the 'bed' where one reposes is, in my opinion, the cloisters and monasteries, where one lives undisturbed by the cares of the world and the anxieties of life."[75]

This preference for the monastic life is a bias that pervades many of the Abbot's writings. As Marie-Bernard Saïd notes in his Introduction to the English translation of *De conversione*, Bernard clearly understands "conversion" in the sense of "becoming a monk." To use Bernard's own words:

> Spare your souls, brothers, I beg you, spare, spare the blood which has been poured out for you. . . . Flee from the midst of Babylon. Flee and save your souls! Flock to the city of refuge [urbes refugii], where you can do penance for the past, obtain grace in the present, and confidently wait for future glory.[76]

It is clear from the context that the "city of refuge" is the monastery.

Similarly, in *De gradibus*, Bernard notes that ten out of the twelve steps of humility are taken within the monastery, beginning with submitting to superiors. Conversely, the last two steps of pride "take place outside the cloister."[77] In one of the *Sermones super Cantica*, Bernard goes so far as to speak of a monk leaving the monastery by analogy to a "dog returning to his vomit."[78]

Such passages prompt Saïd to remark, "We would be tempted to say, if we did not know better, that for St. Bernard there could be no salvation except within monastery walls."[79] We have already seen that Bernard does not claim that the contemplative experience of union is necessary (even in the monastery). Faith in Jesus ranks above all else in importance.[80] Indeed, even though Bernard favors the contemplative life, he does recognize that those who are married can ultimately attain the fruits of faith:

> Those [who marry] will indeed have trials of the flesh; but we do not deny that on the last day they will attain to the fruits of faith if they shall have made a last good confession, and especially if they compensate by almsgiving for their worldliness.[81]

One might remark that Bernard is damning the married with faint praise in this passage; nevertheless, his reference to their salvation is clear.

In chapter 1, I noted that one of Ritschl's charges against Bernard's mysticism is that it is "elitist," precisely because it is a phenomenon restricted to the monastery.[82] Frankly, this is one charge that seems to hold some weight. However, there is a sense in which Bernard can be defended, insofar as he balances his valuing of the contemplative life with that of the active. This brings us to the question, What, finally, is the relationship of mysticism to the church and to the Christian life in general (particularly the active life)? It is to this question that we now turn.

MYSTICISM, ECCLESIOLOGY, AND THE CHRISTIAN LIFE

One of the charges Reformation scholars have leveled against the medieval mystics is that they promote an individualism that, to use Ritschl's phrase, "completely isolates the individual from connection with the Church."[83] Wilhelm Kolfhaus specifically singles out Bernard in this connection. His words are worth repeating here:

> Bernard's piety had two foci: the church and the investigation of the experiences of the pious soul. Calvin was in agreement with him on the first; the second he shunned, for to him it was not the pious soul with its experiences that was central, but rather Christ and the life that his members received from him.[84]

It is my view that both Ritschl and Kolfhaus are not entirely fair to Bernard in these statements. In spite of his preference for the contemplative life, in practice Bernard does not advocate isolation from the community of the church. Quite the contrary—Bernard sees the church as the necessary context for the contemplative life, and believes that a true contemplative is not always absorbed in private prayer, but is more often engaged in active service and participation in the general life of the church.

When Bernard speaks of the "Bride" in the *Sermones super Cantica*, he makes it clear that his referent can be either the church or the individual soul. For example, speaking of the "lovers" in the poem, he says:

And when you consider the lovers themselves, think not of a man and a woman but of the Word and the soul. And if I should say Christ and the Church the same applies, except that the word Church signifies not one soul but the unity or rather unanimity of many.[85]

However, Bernard also states that the church is the *primary* referent of the title of Bride. The individual shares in the title in virtue of participation in the church:

Although none of us will dare arrogate for his own soul the title of bride of the Lord, nevertheless we are members of the Church which rightly boasts of this title and of the reality that it signifies, and hence may justifiably assume a share in this honor.[86]

Thus, we can say with James Wimsatt that for Bernard, "on one level of apprehension Canticles deals with the Church, the whole body of Christian souls. . . . The meaning of the kiss for the individual soul is derived from, and parallel to, this ecclesiological significance."[87]

Dom Jean Leclercq makes a further point that is especially relevant: that Bernard's chief concern is "to highlight the mysterious love which unites Christ to the Church."[88] As we saw above, Bernard speaks of Christ and the church as "lovers." In different places he speaks of God's love for the church, and of the church's love for God.[89] Thus, "the Church is the meeting place of two loves: the charity of God towards man and that of man towards God."[90]

In this world, the church is made up of sinners; nevertheless, "each of us, and all together, are the Church."[91] Therefore, as Leclercq points out, "there is no individualism. The essence of the Church, and her very definition, is to be the communion of all with Christ and among all in Christ."[92] Contrary to Ritschl's statement, promoting individualism is the farthest thing from Bernard's intention, and I hope to show that his mystical theology is true to this intention.

I believe that one key to understanding the ecclesial dimension of Bernard's mysticism is his distinction between active and affective love. This distinction is especially prominent in Sermon 50, where Bernard says, "Love exists in action [actus] and in feeling [affectus]."[93] In expounding this distinction, Bernard does not hesitate to say that affective love is to be more highly valued:

Now the active prefers what is lowly, the affective what is lofty. For example, there is no doubt that in a mind that loves rightly, the love of God is valued more than love of men, and among men themselves the more perfect [is esteemed] more than the weaker, heaven more than earth, eternity more than the flesh.

However, Bernard *immediately* goes on to qualify this statement, telling the reader that active love usually (if not always!) takes precedence. His argument is worth quoting at length:

In well-regulated action, on the other hand, the opposite order frequently or even always prevails. For we are more strongly impelled toward and more often occupied with the welfare of our neighbor; we attend our weaker brothers with more exacting care; by human right and very necessity we concentrate more on peace on earth than on the glory of heaven; by worrying about temporal cares we are not permitted to think of eternal things; in attending almost continually to the ills of our body we lay aside the care of our soul; and finally, in accord with the saying of the Apostle, we invest our weaker members with greater honor, so fulfilling in a sense the word of the Lord: "the last shall be first and the first last." Who will doubt that in prayer a man is speaking with God? But how often, at the call of charity, we are drawn away, torn away, for the sake of those who need to speak to us or be helped! How often does dutiful repose yield dutifully to the uproar of business! . . . A preposterous order; but necessity knows no law.

Bernard goes on to say that "love in action devises its own order," which is "swayed not by worldly values but by human needs."[94] He summarizes his argument as follows, "Now true love is found in this, that those whose need is greater receive first."[95]

Having said all this, Bernard still speaks of active love as a "step" (*gradus*) to affective love. However, in no sense does he wish to devalue the former. On the contrary, he insists that the active person is also a better contemplative:

After a good work one rests more securely in contemplation, and the more a man is conscious that he has not failed in works of charity through love of his own ease, the more faithfully will he contemplate things sublime and make bold to study them.[96]

Bernard is well aware that many people would say that the contemplative life is to be valued *less* than the active. In an earlier sermon on the Song of Songs, Bernard, after exhorting his readers to "do good to all," even enemies, remarks:

There have been times, if I may digress a little, when as I sat down sadly at the feet of Jesus, offering up my distressed spirit in sacrifice, recalling my sins, or again, at the rare moments when I stood by his head, filled with happiness at the memory of his favors, I could hear people saying: "Why this waste?" They complained that I thought only of myself when, in their view, I could be working for the welfare of others. . . . But let those who accuse me of indolence listen to the Lord who takes my part with the query: "Why are you upsetting this woman?" By this he means: "You are looking at the surface of things and therefore you judge superficially."[97]

I think it is reasonable to say that Bernard wishes to disparage neither the active nor the contemplative life. Indeed, the two are complementary. Just as the active life feeds the life of contemplation, so contemplation leads to zeal for service:

> It is characteristic of true and pure contemplation that when the mind is ardently aglow with God's love, it is sometimes so filled with zeal and the desire to gather to God those who will love him with equal abandon that it gladly foregoes contemplative leisure for the endeavor of preaching.[98]

In another place, he says of contemplation and action that "these two are comrades and live together, for Martha is sister to Mary."[99]

Bernard notes that sometimes "the mind is tossed to and fro" as it alternates between contemplation and preaching, "fearful and violently agitated lest it cling more than is justified to one or the other of these rival attractions and so deviate from God's will even momentarily."[100] Here he gets to the heart of the issue: what matters is that God's will be done at all times.

In addition to his stress on Christian service, Bernard promotes the sacramental life and the other ordinary means of grace:

> We, however, who have not yet merited to be rapt into paradise, into the third heaven, let us meanwhile be fed with the flesh of Christ, let us honor his mysteries, follow his footsteps, preserve the faith, and we will certainly be living in his shadow.[101]

However, in contrast to what we shall see in Calvin, Bernard's specific references to the sacraments are relatively infrequent. Bernard McGinn makes a comment that is relevant in this regard:

> Some later medieval mystics were to find the center of their piety in contact with Christ in the sacraments, especially in the Eucharist. The abbot of Clairvaux, on the other hand, so concentrates on the *magnum mysterium*, the sacrament of the marriage of Christ and the Church, of which the other sacraments serve as exemplifications, that he did not feel compelled to discuss the latter in detail. Through the *magnum mysterium* we gain access to Christ who united flesh to himself in a personal union without abandoning his substantial union with the Father.[102]

McGinn points to a passage in *De diversis* that illustrates this aspect of Bernard's thought:

Christ the Lord is a mountain, a mountain gathered [coagulatus] and rich. He is a mountain in sublimity, gathered in the bringing together of a multitude, rich in charity. Now see how he draws all things to himself, how he unites all things in unity, substantial, personal, spiritual, sacramental [Et nunc vide quomodo trahat ad se omnia, quomodo et omnia uniantur unitate substantiali, personali, spirituali, sacramentali]. He has the Father in himself, with whom he is one substance. He has the assumed humanity, with which he is one person. He has the faithful soul clinging to him, with whom he is one spirit. He has the one Church of all the elect, with which he is one flesh.[103]

The conclusions that can be drawn from this discussion of Bernard's ecclesiology are best summarized by Leclercq. He notes that "charity . . . is the fundamental constitutive law" in Bernard, whether he is speaking of the individual or the church. He continues:

In the order of salvation . . . it is a matter of participating in the Church, sharing what the Church has and what the Church is with all those who live by her and in her; as scripture must be read in Church, the sacraments must be received from her, prayer must be in union with her: a Christian's contemplation must be part of hers, for it is she who, in us, is united with God.[104]

In short, Bernard's theology is anything but individualistic.

I would like to add just a word about sanctification. We saw in chapter 3 that Bernard does not distinguish this from justification in the same way as Calvin. Sanctification, which in Bernard's understanding is virtually equivalent to "growth in love," is always partial in our present existence. Neither affective nor active love is perfectly fulfilled in this life.[105] Indeed, Bernard insists that the Christian life is a never-ending process of growth. This is clear in a letter he wrote to a group of abbots assembled at Soissons:

We have not here an abiding city nor do we yet possess it, but we are still seeking the one that is to come. Either you must go up or you must come down, you inevitably fall if you try to stand still [Aut ascendas necesse est, aut descendas: si attentas stare, ruas necesse est]. It is certain that the man who does not try to be better is not even good; when you stop trying to be better, then you cease to be good.[106]

The fullness of love will finally be experienced permanently after the final resurrection.[107]

Looking back to Gerson's definition of mystical union, we can see that Bernard's mystical theology fits it perfectly:

Mystical theology is experiential knowledge of God attained through the union of spiritual affection with Him. Through this union the words of the Apostle are fulfilled: "He who clings to God is one spirit with Him

(1 Cor. 6:17)." This adherence, as the blessed Dionysius witnesses, occurs unquestionably through ecstatic love.[108]

This could hardly be a more fitting summary of Bernard's understanding. Indeed, for Bernard, to know God is to love God, and to become "one spirit" with him. Let us now turn to Calvin and see how his mystical theology will relate to this definition.

5

JOHN CALVIN ON MYSTICAL UNION

THE NATURE OF MYSTICAL UNION

The term *unio mystica* is not, to my knowledge, ever employed by Bernard in his discussion of union with God. In contrast, the term *is* used by Calvin, in two places in the *Institutes*. The most important of these is found in *Institutes* 3.11.10:

> Therefore, that joining together of Head and members, that indwelling of Christ in our hearts—in short, that mystical union [mystica . . . unio]—are accorded by us the highest degree of importance, so that Christ, having been made ours, makes us sharers with him in the gifts with which he has been endowed. We do not, therefore, contemplate [speculamur] him outside ourselves from afar in order that his righteousness may be imputed to us but because we put on Christ and are engrafted into his body [sed quia ipsum induimus, et insiti sumus in eius corpus]—in short, because he deigns to make us one with him. For this reason, we glory that we have fellowship of righteousness with him [ideo iustitiae societatem nobis cum eo esse gloriamur].[1]

This single quotation embraces many of the themes that are central in Calvin's understanding of union with God or Christ. An earlier reference occurs in *Institutes* 2.12.7, where Calvin is commenting on Matt. 19:4–6 ("the two shall become one flesh," in the context of a discussion about divorce). He states, "Here he [Jesus] is not discussing the mystical union [mystica unione] with which he graced the church, but only fidelity in marriage."[2] Interestingly, the context of both passages where Calvin actually employs the term *unio mystica* is a refutation of the ideas of Osiander, to whom we shall return below.

Calvin's understanding of what he calls mystical union correlates directly with his understanding of justification and sanctification. Indeed,

Kolfhaus rightly speaks of "engrafting into Christ" as providing the "inner indissoluble cohesion" of Calvin's conception of the salvific work of God. He explains, "Justification and sanctification, faith and morality, are seen [by Calvin] in light of engrafting into Christ. Calvin thinks from this point out, and his thoughts always turn back to it."[3] My own research has confirmed that this is so. While "engrafting" is only one of several terms Calvin uses in describing union with Christ, it certainly is the most frequent.

If Bernard's notion of union with God (or Christ) revolves around love, Calvin's surely revolves around faith. It is not that Bernard does not see mystical union as rooted in faith; we have seen that he certainly does. We are saved by grace through faith; and while contemplative experiences of union are not essential, faith is absolutely essential.[4] Calvin more characteristically speaks of union with Christ (or God) in relation to faith than to love; but love is definitely a part of the picture. Calvin makes a succinct statement about faith and union in *Institutes* 3.2.25: "Christ, when he illumines us into faith by the power of his Spirit, at the same time so engrafts us into his body that we become partakers of every good."[5] It is clear that he considers engrafting to be "simultaneous" with faith. What exactly is the relationship here?

At one point in his analysis, Kolfhaus states that according to Calvin, faith *is* union with Christ. This is surely mistaken, as Kolfhaus's own examples and further explanations show.[6] Admittedly, some of the confusion may be rooted in the many different connections Calvin makes when discussing this theme. Calvin wants to speak of *unio* in relation to faith, the Holy Spirit, the gospel (scripture), the sacraments, and election. It is intimately connected with all of these, but identical with none of them.

S. P. Dee's opinion is of some help in resolving this question. He says that "where Calvin distinguishes between faith and *unio mystica*, he is only referring to a logical distinction." According to Dee, faith yields *unio mystica* as an immediate result, and conversely, faith always remains dependent on *unio mystica*.[7]

I believe that Dee is basically on the mark here. Calvin himself speaks of "that sacred wedlock through which we are made flesh of his flesh and bone of his bone, and thus one with him. But he unites himself to us by the Spirit alone." He goes on to say that "faith is the principal work of the Holy Spirit."[8] Thus, we can agree with this summary by Kolfhaus: "The Holy Spirit alone, and indeed alone through faith, engrafts us into Christ."[9]

Kolfhaus also notes that Calvin "occasionally specifies the Gospel or the Word of God as the means for the realization of unio cum Christo, and says that engrafting into Christ takes place through the Gospel." Kolfhaus insists that this is not a contradiction or even a major deviation from

Calvin's conviction about the centrality of faith: "For faith and the Word belong together; the foundation of both expressions is always the *faith produced by the Spirit through the Gospel*."[10]

Let us look at a few of Calvin's own words on this point. In his commentary on 1 Cor. 1:9 ("God is faithful, through whom ye were called into the fellowship of his Son Jesus Christ our Lord"), Calvin says, "Since you have been brought into fellowship with Christ *through the Gospel, which you have received by faith,* there is no reason for you to be afraid of the danger of death, since you have been made partakers of Him who rose, the Victor over death."[11] In the commentary on Rom. 1:17, he states, "Righteousness is offered by the Gospel, and is received by faith."[12]

I would like to stress here that it is the *Spirit* who effects this faith, which is, to use Kolfhaus's words, "aroused through the Word."[13] We have already discussed the crucial role of the Holy Spirit in Calvin's notion of faith, so I will not repeat that here.[14]

Faith, in turn, is preceded by election. Kolfhaus rightly notes that in Calvin, "faith, election, and engrafting belong together."[15] Calvin himself speaks of election as "antecedent to faith" and as "the mother of faith."[16] Therefore, only the elect in Calvin's sense can experience union with Christ.

I would like to summarize what I have presented thus far about the *basis* of unity with Christ. It is certainly by grace through faith, as Bernard would confirm. I would suggest the following sentence as clarifying the relationship of the various themes that Calvin includes under this rubric: The Holy Spirit brings the elect, through the hearing of the gospel, to faith; in so doing, the Spirit engrafts them into Christ.

To situate our discussion of the nature of mystical union in Calvin, it is necessary to sketch its general relationship to justification and sanctification. Later we will discuss in greater detail the relationship to sanctification.

Calvin actually speaks of a twofold communion with Christ, which corresponds to the twofold grace of justification and sanctification. Let us look at some specific examples. In his commentary on Gal. 2:20 ("It is no longer I that live, but Christ liveth in me"), Calvin says:

> Christ lives in us in two ways. The one consists in His governing us by his Spirit and directing all our actions. The other is what He grants us by participation in His righteousness, that, since we can do nothing of ourselves, we are accepted in Him by God. The first relates to regeneration, the second to the free acceptance of righteousness.[17]

Another important reference to this twofold communion is found in a letter of Calvin to Peter Martyr. Again Calvin speaks of two communions with Christ. The first communion is that Christ lives in us through the power of the Spirit:

> I know only this: that through the power of the Holy Spirit the life of heaven flows down to earth, for the flesh of Christ is neither life-giving in itself nor can its effect reach us without the unmeasurable work of the Spirit. Thus it is the Spirit who makes Christ live in us, who sustains and nourishes us, who accomplishes everything on behalf of the Head.[18]

The second communion, whereby Christ makes us rich in spiritual gifts, "is . . . the fruit and effect of the first [illius prioris . . . fructus est ac affectus]."[19] It is interesting to note that this second communion "grows" whereas the first is "total." This corresponds exactly to Calvin's theology of justification and sanctification. Just as justification for Calvin is always total while sanctification is always partial, so our participation in Christ's righteousness is total while the union of regeneration is partial.[20]

What, then, is the nature of mystical union? Calvin does at times speak of our having a share in the "substance" of Christ. An example of this is his comment on Eph. 5:30 (the reference to Genesis, "flesh of my flesh, bone of my bone"):

> As Eve was formed out of the substance of her husband Adam, and thus was a part of him, so, if we are to be the true members of Christ, we grow into one Body by the communication of His substance [ita nos, ut simus vera Christi membra, substantiae eius communicare, et hac communicatione nos coalescere in unum corpus]. In short, Paul describes our union to Christ, a symbol and pledge of which is given to us in the holy Supper.[21]

However, Calvin is referring here to what happens in the power of the Holy Spirit, not to a crass mixture of substances, which elsewhere he rejects in the most emphatic terms. Commenting on the next verse from Ephesians 5, he says:

> Such is the union between us and Christ, that *in a sense* he pours Himself into us. For we are not bone of His bone, and flesh of His flesh, because, like ourselves, He is man, but because, *by the power of His Spirit*, He engrafts us into His Body, so that from him we derive life.[22]

Indeed, Calvin is tireless in his stress on the Holy Spirit as the bond of a spiritual (yet absolutely real) union with Christ.

Calvin's rejection of the idea of a strictly substantial union is most clearly expressed in his criticisms of Osiander, whose doctrine of "essential righteousness" was tantamount to a kind of pantheistic mixture of substances between God and humans. This dispute takes up a great deal of Calvin's attention in *Institutes* 3.11. Against Osiander, Calvin insists:

For we hold ourselves to be united with Christ by the secret power of his Spirit [tenemus nos cum Christo uniri arcana Spiritus eius virtute].

That gentleman had conceived something bordering on Manicheism, in his desire to transfuse the essence of God into men. . . .

He says that we are one with Christ. We agree. But we deny that Christ's essence is mixed with our own [interea negamus misceri Christi essentiam cum nostra].[23]

This statement is corroborated in other writings of Calvin. In his commentary on John 17:21 ("That they all may be one"), he remarks:

From this, too, we infer that we are one with Christ; not because he transfuses His substance into us, but because by the power of His Spirit he communicates to us His life and all the blessings He has received from the Father.[24]

In Sermon 42 on Eph. 5:31–33, Calvin states:

I have told you briefly already how we are bone of our Lord Jesus Christ's bone, and how we are his flesh. It is not that we are taken out of his body, for we come of the lineage of Adam, but because we live of his own substance [sa propre substance], according to this saying that his flesh is our meat and his blood our drink, by which he means that we live in him—spiritually, however.[25]

It is clear, then, that Calvin wishes to speak of a spiritual union between Christ and believers, effected by the Spirit.[26] This union embraces both the body and the soul of the believer:

We should note that the spiritual union which we have with Christ is not a matter of the soul alone, but of the body also, so that we are flesh of his flesh etc. (Eph. 5:30). The hope of the resurrection would be faint, if our union with Him were not complete and total like that.[27]

Interestingly, Calvin does not make much use of 1 Cor. 6:17 (which figures so prominently in Bernard) in describing the nature of union. He does cite it once in the *Institutes*, but in reference to love of neighbor.[28] Even in his Commentary on 1 Corinthians, where one might expect a greater expansion on this verse, Calvin has little to say except that "the union [coniunctionem] of Christ with us is closer than that of husband and wife"; and that believers "are not only one flesh with Christ, but also one Spirit [non una tantum caro sunt cum Christo, sed unus etiam spiritus]."[29] In any case, I know of no instance where Calvin disputes Bernard's use of this passage. This is not surprising, given Calvin's own strong statements about spiritual union.

When Calvin speaks of union with Christ as "spiritual," he does not mean "figurative." This is clear in passages like the following:

Christ is not outside us but dwells within us. Not only does he cleave to us by an indivisible bond of fellowship, but with a wonderful communion, day by day, he grows more and more into one body with us, until he becomes completely one with us.[30]

Indeed, this union is so intimate that Calvin sees it as the ground of faith's certitude.[31] At the same time, while union is "real," it is not a union of identity or essence (as the rejection of "substantive" union clearly shows). As Kolfhaus puts it:

> For union with Christ, however intimately it may be conceived—and it cannot be conceived profoundly enough, for we are "bone of his bone, flesh of his flesh"—nevertheless cannot entail the substitution of our "I" by a numinous "I" or an identity with the victorious Redeemer. The person who is engrafted in Christ is, even as such, a person who participates in Christ through faith alone, i.e., who always stands [before him] empty-handed. . . . The boundary between Christ and ourselves is never obliterated or unclear.[32]

Bernard, too, speaks of an intimate union with Christ, but not a union of essences.[33] Thus, Kolfhaus is clearly wrong, at least in relation to Bernard, when he says that "*unio cum Christo* allows Calvin to observe respectfully the boundaries which have been fixed for us sinful people in this lifetime, boundaries which do not exist for the mystic in his ecstasy."[34] In this connection we may note that there is certainly no question of a "union of equals" in Calvin, any more than there is in Bernard.[35]

When Calvin brings up the question of the exact nature of the union, he always insists that it is "mysterious." There is an especially candid statement about this in his letter to Peter Martyr, "How this happens far exceeds the limits of my understanding, I must confess; thus I have more of an impression of this mystery than I strive to comprehend it."[36] In his commentary on Eph. 5:32 ("This mystery is great"—referring to the "bone of my bones, flesh of my flesh" metaphor), Calvin suggests: "Let us therefore labour more to feel Christ living in us, than to discover the nature of that communication."[37] At least seven instances occur in the *Institutes* where Calvin uses the word *arcanus* or *incomprehensibilis* to describe union with Christ.[38]

Another issue that I discussed in relation to Bernard was that union with God, whether conceived in terms of active or contemplative love, is incomplete in this life. Even the contemplative's vision is fleeting, and does not show God "as he is."[39] For Calvin (whose view of the active and contemplative lives will be discussed later on), there is one sense in which union with Christ is complete in the present life. Seen in relation to justification, our engrafting into Christ is "total"; in relation to sanctification, it is "partial" and "grows." We have already seen this in the letter to

Peter Martyr.[40] At the same time, Calvin, like Bernard, looks to the final resurrection as the ultimate locus of union with God. This resurrection includes both body and soul.[41]

Let us turn now to the images used by Calvin in describing union with Christ. By far the most numerous references in the *Institutes* are to "engrafting" (Latin *insero* or *insitio*), with "communion" (*communio* or *communico*) and "fellowship" (*societas*) being next in frequency. Calvin also speaks in terms of participation (usually translated "partaking," Latin *participes*) and "adoption" (*adoptio*) in Christ. These terms are used both in Calvin's general discussion of *unio* as a direct consequence of justification, and in his discussion of *unio* in relation to the church and sacraments. Calvin often combines images, particularly engrafting and communion or fellowship.[42]

Calvin also uses the image of the spiritual marriage. We have already seen how prominent an image this is in Bernard; indeed, we can say that it is his primary image.[43] It is much less prominent in Calvin. The *Institutes*, for example, contain four references to spiritual marriage. Reflecting on Eph. 5:30–32 (which we might say is as important a passage for Calvin as 1 Cor. 6:17 is for Bernard), Calvin states:

> When Paul has said that we are flesh of the flesh of Christ, he adds at once: "This is a mystery [mysterium]." For Paul did not mean to tell in what sense Adam uttered the words, but to set forth under the figure and likeness of marriage the holy union that makes us one with Christ [sed sub figura et similitudine coniugii sacram coniunctionem proponere, quae nos unum cum Christo facit].[44]

In another place, reflecting on the moral law in the light of the Second Commandment (Ex. 20:5–6), Calvin remarks:

> God very commonly takes on the character of a husband to us. Indeed, the union by which he binds us to himself when he receives us into the bosom of the church is like sacred wedlock [sacri . . . coniugii], which must rest upon mutual faithfulness.[45]

Still later in the *Institutes*, at the beginning of his discussion of justification by faith, Calvin speaks of the Holy Spirit as our link to faith. Christ has only come profitably for those for whom he is their Head, and who have "put Christ on." He continues:

> This union alone ensures that, as far as we are concerned, he has not unprofitably come with the name of Savior. The same purpose is served by that sacred wedlock [sacrum illud coniugium] through which we are made flesh of his flesh and bone of his bone, and thus one with him. But he unites himself to us by the Spirit alone. By the grace and power of the same Spirit we are made his members [efficimur illius membra], to keep us under himself and in turn to possess him.[46]

It is clear that for Calvin, the image of the spiritual marriage is applied not to the contemplative experience, but to the union that flows from faith. Thus, he really uses it in a different way than Bernard.[47]

What is the role of knowledge in this mystical union of the believer with Christ? We have already seen that Calvin regards the union as "mysterious," and that we should "labour more to feel Christ living in us, than to discover the nature of that communication."[48] This dovetails well with what was said earlier about Calvin's notion of knowledge, viz., that true knowledge of God is the knowledge of faith, which "consists in assurance rather than in comprehension."[49]

Bernard, as we saw, also does not fully specify the nature of knowledge in union with God. He does say that God is "never fully known until he is perfectly loved," and that "love itself is a form of knowing."[50] Bernard's understanding of the knowledge that accompanies faith is that it is experiential, a knowledge of God's goodness.[51] Calvin, in turn, speaks of piety as the context of true knowledge of God: "Faith can in no wise be separated from a devout disposition."[52] Since Calvin defines piety as "that reverence joined with *love* of God which the knowledge of his benefits induces,"[53] it is clear that he intends to include "love" in his definition of knowledge of God.

Calvin does not characteristically speak explicitly of "love" in passages dealing with union with Christ, as does Bernard. However, he echoes Bernard in those places where he does speak of love of God and neighbor. For example, there is a passage in his commentary on 2 Cor. 5:14 ("the love of Christ constraineth us") that is reminiscent of Bernard's description of the second stage of loving God:

> The word "love" can be understood either actively or passively but I prefer the former. For unless our hearts are harder than iron, the remembrance of the great love Christ has shown us by submitting to death for our sakes is bound to make us devote ourselves entirely to Him. . . . The knowledge of this love should constrain our feelings so that we cannot but love Him in return.[54]

In *Institutes* 3.16.2, Calvin speaks of love in a way similar to Bernard's third stage of loving God in *De diligendo Deo:*

> For if it is only a matter of men looking for reward when they serve God, and hiring or selling their labor to him, it is of little profit. *God wills to be freely worshipped, freely loved.* That worshiper, I say, he approves who, when all hope of receiving reward has been cut off, still ceases not to serve him.[55]

It is important to recall that for Calvin, love is subordinate to faith. In *Institutes* 3.9.13, he declares, "For as our freedom must be subordinated to love, so in turn ought love itself to abide under purity of faith."[56] I do not think that Bernard would have difficulty with this emphasis. For example, in *De diligendo Deo*, he remarks, "If we wish to have Christ for a guest often, we must keep our hearts fortified by the testimony of our faith in the mercy of him who died for us and in the power of him who rose from the dead."[57] There are also two other passages in *De diligendo Deo* where Bernard gives priority to faith. Speaking of all the gifts that come to us from God, and in particular of redemption, Bernard says, "Faith certainly bids me love him all the more whom I regard as that much greater than I, for he not only gives me myself, he also gives me himself." Later in the treatise, speaking of the soul that is in the flesh, he notes that "it moves by faith which necessarily acts through charity."[58]

I now turn to the crucial issue of the role of Christ. It is clear by now, I trust, that Calvin's tendency is to speak most often of union with Christ, to whom he even refers at times as the "Bridegroom."[59] As Bernard promoted devotion to the humanity of Christ,[60] Calvin is emphatic that our union with Christ is with his humanity. For example, in *Institutes* 3.2.1, Calvin speaks of the goal of faith, saying of Jesus that "as God he is the destination to which we move; as man, the path by which we go."[61] That Jesus' human nature is the source of our sanctification is especially clear in Calvin's comment on John 6:51 ("The bread that I will give . . ."):

> Since this secret power of bestowing life of which He is speaking might be referred to His divine essence, He now comes to the second step and tells them that this life resides in His flesh so that it may be drawn from it. . . . For as the eternal Word of God is the fountain of life, so His Flesh is a channel to pour out to us the life which resides intrinsically, as they say, in His divinity. In this sense it is called life-giving, because it communicates to us a life that it borrows from elsewhere. . . . Although righteousness flows from God alone, we shall not have the full manifestation of it anywhere else than in Christ's flesh.[62]

This passage also makes clear a point that is stressed by Ronald Wallace: that "in discussing the mystery of how we can be . . . united to the human nature of Christ . . . Calvin does not forget that in the Ascension Jesus Christ has taken His human nature beyond this earth to Heaven where it will remain until His second coming in glory."[63] Calvin himself shuns speculation about how Christ can be in heaven and at the same time be united with us:

> Therefore, if we find here any contradiction, and it puzzles us to wonder how it is possible that our Lord Jesus Christ who is in heaven should nourish us with his own substance [sa propre substance], so that his body should be our meat and his blood our drink—I say, if we fall into such fancies, we must repulse them all with what is said here, namely,

that it is a secret [C'est un secret], and we must rebuke our own folly and rashness in trying to measure what is infinite.[64]

Calvin will only say that this mysterious union takes place in the power of the Holy Spirit.[65]

On the basis of this analysis, I would say that Calvin might not be comfortable with the language that we saw in Bernard's *Sermons on the Canticles* 20, of Jesus first drawing people "to the salutary love of his own humanity," then raising them "gradually . . . to a spiritual love."[66] I do not think that Calvin would make such a distinction. Indeed, union with the humanity of Christ *is* a spiritual union for Calvin; and the flesh of Christ is the "channel" by which his divine life flows into us.

While Calvin's concept of union is emphatically Christ-centered (perhaps more so than Bernard's), Calvin is not opposed to speaking of union with God. He does it himself in several places in both the *Institutes* and the commentaries, and in a comment on 1 John 4:15, he implies that the terminology makes no difference: "We are united to God by Christ and . . . we can only be joined to Christ if God abides in us"; and "men are so engrafted into Christ by faith that Christ joins them to God."[67]

There is a place where Calvin assigns different roles for each person of the Trinity in relation to *unio*. In *Institutes* 4.15.6, he speaks of the Father, who sends the mediator; Christ, in whom we are engrafted; and the Spirit, who sanctifies us. They are respectively the cause, matter, and effect of our purgation and regeneration.[68] We have seen that Bernard also distinguishes roles within the Trinity at times, but not in this fashion (and not consistently throughout his works).[69]

Overall, I think it is appropriate to say that Calvin's notion of *unio*, like Bernard's, contains a trinitarian element. Calvin does more characteristically speak of union with Christ, but he speaks frequently enough of union with the Father, and quite frequently of union being in the power of the Spirit. Real differences do exist in the way Bernard and Calvin incorporate the Trinity, but I do not see any great oppositions here.[70]

THE SCOPE OF MYSTICAL UNION

To whom is the experience of mystical union granted? We have already seen Calvin's answer: to the elect.[71] All those who are among the chosen are de facto in union with Christ as an immediate consequence of justification by faith. In Calvin's understanding, some people are definitely excluded from election, and therefore from being engrafted into Christ. As he puts it in *Institutes* 3.22.10: "If [God] willed all to be saved, he would set his Son over them, and would engraft all into his body with the sacred bond of faith." However, "it is clear that the doctrine of salvation, which is said to be reserved solely and individually for the sons of the church, is falsely debased when presented as effectually profitable for all."[72]

This is one of the passages in the *Institutes* where Calvin cites Bernard in support of his position. The reference is to Bernard's letter to Thomas of Beverly, where Bernard says that God "does not vouchsafe to others participation in so great a mystery [God's plan], save to those whom he has foreknown and predestined to become his own." As Jill Raitt points out, Calvin does not use the passage inappropriately.[73] However, I do not think that Bernard understands or speaks of predestination in quite the same way as Calvin. Specifically, he does not expressly support a doctrine either of double predestination or of the certitude of election. In the letter to Thomas of Beverly, he goes on to say that "each one who is called by fear and justified by love *dares* to believe that he also *may* be among the blessed, knowing that 'whom he has justified, them also he has glorified.' "[74] The qualifiers here, in my view, reflect Bernard's hesitancy to talk about a certitude of election.[75] In a later section of the same letter, Bernard speaks of the conversion of one who "by his former life and conscience was doomed as a true son of perdition." He goes on:

> A great secret which from all eternity has remained hidden in the bosom of eternity has now been revealed in the light of day for the consolation of the wretched: God does not want the death of a sinner but that he should be converted and live.[76]

In other words, Bernard does not say that certain people are incapable a priori of converting and receiving the gift of salvation. Nevertheless, there *is* a "particularity" of election, which is what Calvin correctly appropriates from this letter of Bernard.[77]

Herein lies a significant difference between Bernard and Calvin on mystical union: while Bernard would tend to exclude most Christians from an experience of contemplative union (but not of the union of "active love" such as he describes in the third stage in *De diligendo Deo*), Calvin would exclude a definite part of humanity a priori from justification and therefore from the *unio* that accompanies it. In any case, for Calvin, every one of the elect share in *unio mystica* as soon as they have come to faith.

It is time to take a closer look at what Calvin thinks of both the monastic life and contemplation. While he is willing to grant that ancient monasticism had some good points, he believes that the monasticism of his own day is an odious distortion of the gospel:

> Our present-day monks find in idleness the chief part of their sanctity. For if you take idleness [otium] away from them, where will that contemplative life [contemplativa vita] be, in which they boast they excel all others and draw nigh to the angels?[78]

It is interesting how Calvin connects contemplation with idleness in this passage. We shall see shortly that he does not totally disparage contemplation.

At times Calvin becomes downright caustic in his criticism of monks. For example, reflecting on 2 Cor. 10:12 ("measuring themselves by themselves"), he remarks:

> To find an application for this passage we need look no further than the monks, for though they are all completely unlearned asses [indoctissimi asini], yet solely on account of their long robes and hoods they have the reputation of being learned men. . . . The excessively insolent pride of the monks comes chiefly from the fact that they measure themselves by themselves, and since in their cloisters there is nothing but barbarism, it is no wonder if the one-eyed man is king in the country of the blind.[79]

Again, it is to be emphasized that Calvin recognizes a time when monasteries served a positive purpose in the church.[80] I know of no place where he singles out Bernard's approach to monasticism as flawed. Calvin's biggest problem with monasticism is that it sets up a "double Christianity."[81] He states that he would like to ask monks "why they dignify their order alone with the title of perfection, and take the same title away from all God's callings."[82] Calvin is strictly opposed to the idea that monks have greater or higher demands to fulfill than other Christians.[83] Thus, it is clear that he would have problems with Bernard's preference for the monastic life, particularly the notion that monastic life is a "better" or "higher" calling, which Bernard, as we saw, certainly believed (and which is stated with particular directness in *De gradibus*).[84] Interestingly, Calvin never calls Bernard directly to task on this point. But he certainly believed that union with Christ is lived out in the world. To him, the gospel is a transformative social power. This will be discussed below under sanctification.

It would seem that Calvin has little use for any experience of contemplation. Kolfhaus certainly thinks that this is the case:

> Calvin does not desire with the mystics to catch a glimpse here and now of the mystery of God, for in communion with Christ the Christian is given everything that he needs for time and eternity. Communion with Christ through faith has cut off all impertinent questions, and therefore has also made ecstasies and visions (which seem to the mystics as especially desirable) superfluous.[85]

However, let us take a closer look at what Calvin actually says about contemplative experiences. A key passage here is 2 Cor. 12:1–5, where Paul speaks of being taken up into the "third heaven." When Calvin speaks of this passage in the *Institutes*, he also takes the opportunity to criticize Pseudo-Dionysius:

No one will deny that Dionysius, whoever he was, subtly and skillfully discussed many matters in his *Celestial Hierarchy*. But if anyone examine it more closely, he will find it for the most part nothing but talk. The theologian's task is not to divert the ears with chatter, but to strengthen consciences by teaching things true, sure, and profitable. If you read that book, you would think a man fallen from heaven recounted, not what he had learned, but what he had seen with his own eyes. Yet Paul, who had been caught up beyond the third heaven, not only said nothing about it, but also testified that it is unlawful for any man to speak of the secret things that he has seen.[86]

Calvin uses similar terms in his commentary on 2 Corinthians 12. There he speaks of Paul being "admitted into these secrets" that are described in verses 1–5. He continues:

Also the word heaven by itself means here God's blessed and glorious kingdom above all spheres and the firmament itself and all the framework of the world. But not content with using the simple word heaven, Paul adds that he had reached its utmost height and its innermost chambers. Our faith climbs up and enters heaven and those who excel in knowledge penetrate higher and further, but to reach the third heaven has been given to very few.[87]

Here Calvin uses language that is reminiscent of Bernard's in the *Sermones super Cantica*, for example, in talking about reaching heaven's "innermost chambers." In any case, he speaks without disparagement of Paul's "unspeakable" experience (note that he makes a connection with faith). With regard to Paul's not speaking about it, Calvin draws the conclusion, "From this passage we should allow ourselves to be reminded of the bounds we must set to our knowledge." He goes on to make a negative remark about "everything that that trifler Dionysius has had the audacity to invent about the hierarchies of heaven."[88]

This passage suggests that Calvin would not totally rule out a contemplative experience of union, even if he wouldn't consider it "especially desirable," to use Kolfhaus's phrase. Calvin also speaks in positive terms of other visions, particularly the ones that are described in the Acts of the Apostles.[89] Bernard, of course, *does* see contemplative union as especially desirable, but he also would insist that it is not necessary.[90]

To sum up, the "scope" of mystical union is definitely an area in which there is a great deal of contrast (but not total mutual exclusivity) between the thought of Bernard and Calvin. Bernard would extol the monastic life as preferable, while Calvin would shun such a distinction. Bernard sees contemplation as highly desirable, while Calvin does not. Yet Calvin does not totally rule out such an experience, just as Bernard would not insist on its necessity even in the life of a monk.

MYSTICISM, ECCLESIOLOGY,
AND THE CHRISTIAN LIFE

In our discussion of Bernard, we saw that he considers the church as the necessary context for both active and contemplative love. Calvin is even more explicit on this point than Bernard, referring as frequently to union with Christ in an ecclesiological context (particularly in relation to the sacraments), as he does in the context of justification.[91] Indeed, Kolfhaus would insist that "the teaching on union with Christ is the bond that ties together [Calvin's] soteriology and ecclesiology."[92]

For Calvin, the church is necessary as an aid to our faith:

> It is by the faith in the gospel that Christ becomes ours and we are made partakers of the salvation and eternal blessedness brought by him. Since, however, in our ignorance and sloth (to which I add fickleness of disposition) we need outward helps to beget and increase faith within us, and advance it to its goal, God has also added these aids that he may provide for our weakness.

Thus, God has given the church "pastors and teachers," and he also has "instituted sacraments, which we who have experienced them feel to be highly useful aids to foster and strengthen faith." In all of this, God is "accommodating himself to our capacity," providing a way for us to "draw near" to him, even though we are "still far off."[93]

Kolfhaus asserts that for Calvin, "belonging to the church was nothing short of a condition for being in Christ." He further notes that Calvin regards the church as the "exposition and realization of *insitio in Christum.*"[94] It would appear that *insitio* is the primary reality, but that membership in the church is a necessary correlate. In fact, the two cannot really be separated. As Calvin himself says, "But all the elect are so united in Christ that as they are dependent on one Head, they also grow together in one body, being joined and knit together as are the limbs of a body."[95] Thus, Christ's promises are made to individuals, but only insofar as they are members of the community.[96]

According to Kolfhaus, it is fair to say that for Calvin, the church is first and foremost a "living organism" and not primarily a visible "institution" (although it is that too). Calvin's concept of church "embraces above all the community of the elect," which is known to God alone. At the same time, the elect are members of the visible church, with which they are "commanded to revere and keep communion."[97] Calvin therefore is emphatic that Christians must love not only God but also one another.

I see Calvin's understanding of love of neighbor as corresponding fairly well to Bernard's notion of "active love," which was discussed earlier.[98] First I wish to point out that like Bernard, Calvin places a higher value on the love of God. In his commentary on Gal. 5:14 ("for the whole law is fulfilled in one word, even in this: Thou shalt love thy neighbour as thyself"), he outlines the relationship between love of God and neighbor:

> Piety towards God is, I confess, higher than love of the brethren; and therefore the observance of the first table is more valuable in the sight of God than that of the second. But as God Himself is invisible, so godliness is something hidden from the human senses. . . . God therefore wants to make trial of our love for Him by that love of our brother which He commends to us. This is why not here alone, but also in Rom 13.8 and 10, love is called the fulfilling of the law, not because it is superior to the worship of God, but because it is the proof of it. God, as I said, is invisible; but He represents Himself to us in the brethren and in their persons demands what is due to Himself. Love to men springs only from the fear and love of God.[99]

This idea is echoed in the *Institutes* 2.8.51, where Calvin says, "First, indeed, our soul should be entirely filled with the love of God [Dei dilectione]. From this will flow directly the love of neighbor [proximi dilectio]."[100]

Actually, what we love in other people is the image of God in them. As Calvin says in *Institutes* 3.7.6, "We are not to consider that men merit of themselves [to be loved] but to look upon the image of God [imaginem Dei] in all men, to which we owe all honor and love."[101] Indeed, Calvin says that we should love others in proportion to their closeness to God. In his commentary on John 13:23 (a reference to the "disciple whom Jesus loved"), Calvin asserts, "But everything depends on our love being directed towards God and on our loving every man the more in proportion as he excels in the gifts of God."[102]

In short, Calvin is clear that union with Christ must have consequences for our relationships with each other. As Calvin puts it in *Institutes* 2.8.54, "Our life shall best conform to God's will [ad Dei voluntatem] and the prescription of the law when it is in every respect most fruitful for our brethren."[103] Later in the *Institutes*, he states, "We must at all times seek after love [charitati] and look toward the edification of our neighbor."[104] Thus, Calvin promotes love of neighbor as aggressively as Bernard does, and indeed, he sees love of neighbor as flowing from a genuine love of God (comparable to what Bernard says about the third stage of loving God in *De diligendo Deo*).[105]

Turning now to the sacraments, I would suggest that Calvin is decidedly more thorough in relating them to *unio* than Bernard. While Bernard loves and defends the sacraments,[106] Calvin speaks explicitly of their relation to *unio* with great frequency. I would only like to summarize the relationship here; the Appendix gives a listing of texts.

Kolfhaus situates the discussion of sacraments by saying that Calvin "is no more able to conceive of communion with Christ without the sacraments than he is of communion with Christ without faith. . . . The sacraments are signs, witnesses, pledges that Christ has taken us into his community."[107] Kolfhaus particularly points to a passage from Calvin's Sermons on Ephesians, where he says that Baptism and the Lord's Supper "are like a ladder to us so that we may seek our Lord Jesus Christ, and so that we may be fully convinced that he lives in us and we are united to him."[108]

Calvin directly connects both Baptism and the Lord's Supper with his favorite image of "engrafting." He defines Baptism as "the sign of the initiation by which we are received into the society of the church, in order that, engrafted in Christ [Christo insiti], we may be reckoned among God's children."[109] Through Baptism, Christ "makes us sharers in his death, that we may be engrafted in it [nos mortis suae fecerit participes, ut in eam inseramur]"; at the same time, Calvin refers to it as "the washing of regeneration and of renewal [lavacrum regenerationis et renovationis]."[110] Thus does Baptism relate to the *unio* both of justification and of sanctification.

True to what he says elsewhere, Calvin insists in this context as well that all of this takes place through the power of the Holy Spirit. For example, in his comment on Titus 3:5–7, he remarks:

> Although he [Paul] mentions the sign to exhibit God's grace clearly to us, yet to prevent us from fixing our whole attention upon it, he soon reminds us of the Spirit, that we know that we are not washed by water but by His power. . . . It is God's Spirit who regenerates us and makes us new creatures, but since His grace is invisible and hidden, a visible symbol of it is given to us in baptism.[111]

In addition to engrafting, Calvin describes Baptism in terms of communion, fellowship, and "cleaving" (*cohaereo*) to Christ. He often combines several of these terms in one reference.[112]

Calvin's understanding of the Eucharist also is related to his favorite image of "engrafting." In *Institutes* 4.17.33 he describes the Eucharist as "a help whereby we may be engrafted into Christ's body, or, engrafted, may grow more and more together with him, until he perfectly joins us with him in the heavenly life."[113] Notice how this citation embraces several of Calvin's beliefs about *unio*: its connection with justification, sanctification, and our ultimate union with God in heaven.

Again, Calvin insists in discussing the Lord's supper that "a serious wrong is done to the Holy Spirit, unless we believe that it is through his incomprehensible power that we come to partake of Christ's flesh and blood."[114] In this connection Calvin also insists that our union with Christ in the Lord's Supper is both spiritual and real. Opposing those who would posit the idea that "Christ is attached to the element of bread [acsi panis elemento affixus esset Christus]," Calvin asserts that the bond of our connection with Christ is "the Spirit of Christ, with whom we are joined in unity, and who is like a channel through which all that Christ himself is and has is conveyed to us."[115] He chides those who claim that "spiritual" eating cannot be "true" eating:

> They falsely boast that all we teach of spiritual eating is contrary, as they say, to true and real eating, seeing that we pay attention only to the manner, which with them is carnal, while they enclose Christ in bread. For us the manner is spiritual because the secret power of the Spirit is the bond of our union with Christ [nobis spiritualis, qui vis arcana Spiritus nostrae cum Christo coniunctionis vinculum est].[116]

Thus, Calvin rejects any interpretation of the Lord's Supper that would smack of Osiander's "mixing of substances." Of course, he also criticizes here the Roman understanding of the transformation of bread and wine.

As in his treatment of Baptism, Calvin uses several other terms besides engrafting in relating the Eucharist to *unio*. These include communion, fellowship, partaking, and adoption. As is the case with Baptism, he frequently combines these terms in a single reference.[117]

Kolfhaus's summary of the significance of the sacraments is worth quoting:

> The sacraments do not have any meaning of their own; they serve the goal of sealing an already existing *unio mystica cum Christo*, of making it more emphatic and clear, of strengthening communion with the Head, and of nourishing the soul as living food.[118]

Let us move finally to sanctification. As I have already noted, *unio* embraces both justification and sanctification. The latter follows as a direct consequence of the former:

> When we hear mention of our union with God, let us remember that holiness must be its bond; not because we come into communion with him by virtue of our holiness! Rather, we ought first to cleave unto him so that, infused with his holiness, we may follow whither he calls [quum potius adhaerere primo illi oporteat ut eius sanctitate perfusi sequamur quo vocat].[119]

Calvin goes so far as to state that people who show virtue, apart from Christ, are headed for hell, "since there is no sanctification apart from union with Christ."[120] Conversely, Calvin speaks of the goodness of the works of those who have been engrafted into Christ.[121]

While the *unio* of justification is in a sense total, the *unio* of sanctification is always partial and growing. We saw this already in chapter 3, in our discussion of repentance as a lifelong process.[122] Calvin also speaks of repentance in direct connection with *unio*. For example, in *Institutes* 3.3.20, he states:

> Therefore, I think he has profited greatly who has learned to be very much displeased with himself, not so as to stick fast in this mire and progress no farther, but rather to hasten to God and yearn for him in order that, having been engrafted into the life and death of Christ, he may give attention to continual repentance [quo morti vitaeque Christi insertus, perpetuam poenitentiam meditetur].[123]

Here again, we see Calvin's stress on repentance as continual. This notion of progress in sanctification is a frequent one in Calvin.[124]

Calvin is not opposed to mortification, as long as it is not done in a spirit of works righteousness.[125] Indeed, "God reigns where men, both by denial of themselves and by contempt of the world and of the earthly life, pledge themselves to his righteousness in order to aspire to a heavenly life."[126] Calvin states directly that he is not opposed to outward penance, but he thinks that the "old writers [vetusti scriptores]" stressed it too much. What matters is the "inner disposition of the heart [interiore cordis affectu]."[127] In any case, Calvin sees the struggle for holiness as properly taking place not in the monastery, but in the world.[128] On the other hand, as we have seen, he agrees with Bernard that only in the final resurrection will the struggle be over.[129]

How would Calvin's understanding of *unio mystica* measure up to Gerson's definition? Calvin would certainly see union with Christ as a "spiritual" union that brings "experiential knowledge of God." He does not speak explicitly of a "union of wills," but he does speak of the desire to follow God's will and to keep his commandments as a direct result of engrafting into Christ.[130] I believe that Calvin's major disagreement with Gerson would be in his claim that "this adherence, as the blessed Dionysius witnesses, occurs unquestionably through ecstatic love." Calvin would say, I think, that it occurs unquestionably through faith, and the life of active love that flows from faith.[131] We have seen that Bernard would also affirm the priority of faith and active love.

In the next and final chapter, I summarize the findings of my textual comparison and state their implications for Calvin studies.

6

CONCLUSIONS

T. F. Torrance, in his Preface to *Calvin's Doctrine of Man*, makes the following comment that I believe is relevant to this work:

> One of the calamities of traditional exposition and interpretation of Calvin's theology has been, by means of arid logical forms, to make Calvin's own distinctions too clean and too rigid. This has resulted in an oversimplification which has obscured the flexibility as well as the range and profundity of his thought.[1]

I can think of no other topic to which this statement applies more perfectly than the discussion of a mystical strand in Calvin's thought. More recent studies of Calvin have stressed that Calvin saw himself as a spiritual writer and not primarily as a dogmatician. As William Bouwsma puts it:

> That Calvin's religion has not been generally treated as "spirituality" is largely a result of the widespread notion of Calvin as a systematic and dogmatic theologian, a conception that probably says more about later Calvinism than about Calvin. Calvin thought of himself as an exclusively biblical theologian, and he was well aware of what this implied about all human theologizing. He valued system and expressed himself systematically only for limited, practical, and pedagogical purposes. Otherwise he distrusted the all-too-human impulse to systematize, above all in religious matters.[2]

One might disagree with Bouwsma's negative assessment of Calvin as a systematician. Nevertheless, I believe he is correct in stressing the spiritual nature of Calvin's writing. We have already seen that piety is the context for all of Calvin's theology; indeed, Calvin saw his *Institutes* as a *summa pietatis*.[3]

I hope that this book has adequately shown that Calvin, who used the term "mystical union," did so in a way that is compatible with the definitions of mysticism I offered in chapter 1. Of course, it must be noted that Calvin himself never gives a precise definition of what he means by *unio mystica*.[4] Nevertheless, his treatment of union with Christ unquestionably contains parallels to the medieval mystical tradition. Although it is true that Calvin also departs from the tradition in significant ways, in my view the similarities are at least as striking as the differences.

Generally, it can be said that the denial of a "mystical" element in Calvin's theology is rooted in an inaccurate definition of mysticism, which then leads to an a priori exclusion of a mystical strand in Calvin. This is certainly the case with Kolfhaus, who understands mystical union as always fundamentally the same, involving a union of essences or "absorption" into the divine.[5] He goes on to claim that:

> the Christian does not seek spiritual enjoyment, but rather is happy to be counted among the members of his Lord, and wants nothing more than that the Lord alone receive the glory. This is not Christ-mysticism, which wishes to pass over the barrier between head and members and runs the risk of irreverence, but communion with Christ, being united with him.[6]

However, we have seen that Bernard's mysticism, at least, in no way wishes to "pass over the barrier between head and members." It is a union in love, a union of wills. Calvin will speak of union in much the same way, except that he will generally correlate union more with faith than love. (It is really a matter of emphasis here, and not mutual exclusivity, as noted earlier.) Therefore, I would say that Kolfhaus's distinction between Calvin's "communion with Christ" and a "Christ-mysticism" is in fact a false distinction.

Kolfhaus, writing in the 1930s (before the current revival in the study of spirituality), and in the light of the many fine insights in his study that have withstood the test of time, may perhaps be forgiven for his narrow definition of mysticism and the consequent exclusion of any "mystical" element in Calvin. However, studies that have appeared as recently as the late 1970s have continued to insist on a "dogmatic" Calvin, who can in no way be associated with the mystical.[7]

Whether mysticism is conceived in the "generic" sense as the experiential element of religion, or in the more specific sense of a definition like Gerson's, I think we can say that both Bernard and Calvin express a genuine mysticism. Since, for Calvin, union with Christ is an immediate consequence of faith, and is therefore fundamental to the Christian experience, I believe that it is *not* too bold (despite the claims of much of the secondary literature) to speak of a positive relationship between Calvin and mysticism.

At the same time, it must be admitted that Calvin did not have a great interest in "contemplative" mysticism, as Bernard did. Calvin's mysticism was a fact of Christian existence, the fruits of which were expressed primarily in the active love of God and neighbor. Bernard also stressed "active love," but embraced contemplation in a way that is not found in Calvin. It is perhaps significant that while Bernard wrote an extensive commentary on the Song of Songs, Calvin did not write a commentary on this work. (He did, however, quote this work of Bernard more than any other in the *Institutes*).[8] The key point I am making here is that for both Bernard and Calvin, mysticism embraces more than just contemplation. Nevertheless, it might be suggested that their differences on the role of contemplation explain why we would continue to call Bernard a mystic while withholding the title from Calvin.[9]

William Siktberg, in his 1951 thesis on "The Mystical Element in the Theology of John Calvin," makes some judgments that are worth considering. At the beginning of his inquiry, he expresses the hope that his study "will help bring to light the warm and pious nature of this reformer so ill-conceived by some as a cold, logical theologian."[10] In my opinion, Siktberg is correct in pointing to Calvin's mystical sensitivity as exemplifying his "warmer side"; however, Siktberg has a tendency throughout his thesis to identify as "mystical" anything that is "warm" or "personal" in Calvin.[11] I believe that this conception is a little *too* broad.

At the end of his work, Siktberg draws an important conclusion about mysticism in relation to the whole of Calvin's thought. In his view, the mystical element in Calvin is always bound by the authoritative:

> Calvin was most concerned to establish the validity of the authoritative level of his thought. . . . His burning interest is not so much in Christian experience as it is in logical apologetics.[12]

However, this assertion does not hold up under the weight of the evidence. Nowhere have I found such a statement in Calvin's works. On the contrary, I find Calvin's "burning interest" to be precisely "Christian experience." Almost immediately in Book 1 of the *Institutes*, Calvin makes it clear that he wants nothing to do with any purely intellectual knowledge of God; that, indeed, the promotion of *piety* is what concerns him most deeply.[13]

To sum up, I would suggest that much of what has been written until recently about Calvin and mysticism suffers from misconceptions both about Calvin's thought and about the nature of mysticism. Admittedly, part of the problem is that it is difficult to get people to agree on what mysticism means. If one is willing to accept the two definitions (generic and specific) adopted for this study, I believe that a more positive and accurate assessment of mysticism in Calvin results.

In support of these conclusions, I would now like to review the main points of similarity and difference between Bernard and Calvin with respect to the notion of *unio mystica*.

SUMMARY

We can summarize the similarities between Bernard and Calvin on *unio mystica* as follows:

1. However union with God is conceived (and there are certainly some differences here that will be described below), both Bernard and Calvin insist that *unio* is an effect of grace and not of any "works" of the believer. Although Bernard speaks of *unio* more in terms of love and Calvin more in terms of faith, their approaches to this notion are not mutually exclusive. Bernard recognizes the priority of faith, just as Calvin sees a relationship between love and the engrafting into Christ that the Holy Spirit effects through faith.

2. In speaking of union with God (or Christ), both Bernard and Calvin emphatically reject any notion of a union of essences. The union between God and the believer is rather a "spiritual" union. Bernard characteristically speaks of this in terms of the theme of *unus spiritus* in 1 Cor. 6:17; Calvin more characteristically refers to Eph. 5:31–33, "flesh of my flesh, bone of my bones." Both see this union as taking place in or through the Holy Spirit. In no sense would either Bernard or Calvin conceive of union as a "union of equals."

3. I think it would be fair to characterize both Bernard's and Calvin's notions of union as a "union of wills." Bernard makes a direct connection in his description of the highest degree of love in *De diligendo Deo*:

> It is therefore necessary for our souls to reach a similar state in which, just as God willed everything to exist for himself, so we wish that [*sic*] neither ourselves nor other beings to have been nor to be except for his will alone, not for our pleasure. The satisfaction of our wants, chance happiness, delights us less than to see his will done in us and for us.[14]

While Calvin does not speak directly of a "union of wills" in discussing *unio cum Christo*, he does believe that those who have faith will inevitably keep God's commandments, particularly the greatest commandments of the love of God and neighbor. Indeed, for Calvin, the cognitive component of faith is knowledge of God's will and God's goodness.

4. Bernard and Calvin agree that God is only loved properly when he is loved unselfishly, that is, when God is loved for God's own glory. I see Bernard's understanding of love as quite compatible with Calvin's definition of piety as "that reverence joined with love of God which the knowledge of his benefits induces."[15]

5. This authentic love of God will flow over into love of neighbor. Both Bernard and Calvin give priority to active love of the neighbor in need, even though they also both value the love of God more highly.

6. Both Bernard and Calvin speak of a "knowledge" that corresponds to union with God. Neither of them speaks with perfect clarity of the nature of this knowledge. Bernard connects it explicitly with love, just as Calvin, true to form, connects it with faith (although love is also included, as his definition of piety makes clear). In any case, Bernard and Calvin are in agreement about this much: true knowledge of God is *experiential* and not theoretical. It is a knowledge of God's goodness and not of God's essence. Both Bernard and Calvin would see the latter kind of knowledge as essentially useless—and, in any case, impossible.

7. Both Bernard and Calvin speak often of union specifically with Christ, Calvin perhaps more characteristically than Bernard (although it really depends on which of their works one is reading). At the same time, both of them speak of "union with God, through Christ, in the Holy Spirit," or some variant of this—the point being that they both see the whole Trinity as "involved" in *unio*. Therefore, I think it is fair to say that both their notions of union contain a trinitarian element.

8. Both Bernard and Calvin see the church as the indispensable context for *unio*, however it may be conceived. Calvin is more frequently explicit about this connection than Bernard is, weaving his notion of *unio* throughout the ecclesiology presented in Book 4 of the *Institutes*.

9. Both Bernard and Calvin conceive of sanctification as a lifelong process of growth in our love of God and neighbor. Union with God will be consummated only in the final resurrection.

10. Both Bernard and Calvin both use the image of the spiritual marriage. It is much more prominent in Bernard, however.

Let us now turn to the differences between Bernard and Calvin when they discuss union with God or Christ.

1. Bernard is much more interested in the contemplative life than is Calvin. Indeed, Bernard sees the contemplative life as in some sense "higher" because it is directed toward God and not humans. Calvin would not disagree that God should be loved above all things, including all human beings. Calvin even speaks in positive terms at times about contemplation. He does not deny the possibility of a contemplative experience of union. (How could he, when Paul describes one in 2 Cor. 12:1–5?) He regards such experiences, however, as "secret things," which should not be discussed with others. In this connection, he criticizes Pseudo-Dionysius for trying to speak about the unspeakable. In short, Calvin has little interest in pursuing the subject. This being the case, it is certainly curious that the work of Bernard that Calvin quotes most

frequently is the *Sermones super Cantica,* a work that is unabashedly concerned with contemplation.

2. Related to this first difference is Calvin's disdain for the monastic life. While Bernard extols the monastic life as a "higher" calling than that received by other Christians, Calvin will have nothing to do with such a distinction. For Calvin, salvation is accomplished "in the world" and not in isolation from it. Thus, he makes a distinction between ancient and contemporary monasteries; the former, in his view, were acceptable because they integrated themselves into the public life of the church.

3. Both Bernard and Calvin "exclude" certain individuals from particular experiences of *unio,* but they do so in different ways. Bernard tends to describe contemplative union as something that can happen only within the monastery, and that is rare even there. The ordinary experience of "union in love" (i.e., stage three as described in *De diligendo Deo*) would appear to be open to all Christians. Calvin would not disagree with this (since he himself regards contemplative union as rare, I suspect as being rarer than Bernard does): all true Christians are de facto in union with Christ. However, Calvin has his own principle of exclusion, in that double predestination excludes certain individuals a priori from union with Christ.

4. There is no question that Bernard speaks of *unio* more in terms of love and Calvin more in terms of faith. This is consistent with their overall approaches to theology.[16] However, I have tried to show that these approaches are not mutually exclusive. I would say that for Bernard, love in a real sense "constitutes" (is a constitutive component of) union with God (or Christ), whereas for Calvin love is an *effect* of that union. Another difference is that Bernard makes a distinction between carnal and spiritual love of Christ, a distinction that is foreign to Calvin.

5. Calvin is meticulous in describing *unio* in relation to the ordinary means of grace, particularly the sacraments. This connection, while not absent from Bernard, is less emphasized.

6. Since Bernard does not conceive of justification and sanctification as distinct in the sense in which Calvin distinguishes them, he does not speak of *unio* as total in one sense (justification) and partial in another (sanctification). Like other medieval theologians, Bernard subsumes sanctification under justification and therefore speaks of a single, "growing" union.

SIGNIFICANCE OF THIS WORK

It is perhaps rash to try to predict how this work might be significant for future discussions on Christian spirituality, and specifically for dialogue between Roman Catholics and Protestants. Nevertheless, a number of possibilities clearly suggest themselves, which I humbly offer for consideration by both academic and ecclesial communities.

Until very recently, it has been common for Protestant thinkers to be almost embarrassed by the presence of a mystical strand in the works of their classic theologians and pastors. Often they have dealt with the embarrassment either by attempting to deny that a mystical dimension is really present (as we have seen in Kolfhaus) or by claiming that it is an alien intrusion and not part of the fabric of a true evangelical theology (as we have seen in Ritschl). Similarly, Roman Catholic and Orthodox thinkers have sometimes spoken of mysticism as if their own traditions have the exclusive right to this phenomenon. They often have not even looked for its manifestations in Reformation thought, probably because they have assumed that it must not be there. The Reformers, after all, stress faith and not love. We have seen that Calvin in particular is often misread as a rigid dogmatist who did not have a heart for spiritual matters. In short, thinkers on "both sides" of the Reformation have tended to dismiss the mystical dimension of Reformation theology either as nonexistent or as an aberration.

I hope that this book—along with many of the other studies I have cited here—has shown that nothing could be further from the truth. Slowly but surely, the point has been gaining ground in recent scholarship that the Reformation was at least as much a spiritual phenomenon as it was a dogmatic one. The Reformers drew from the well of medieval spirituality in numerous ways, perhaps not all of them direct or even conscious. It is common knowledge that the late Middle Ages was a time of resurgence of spiritual movements, and the classic Reformers were certainly affected in various ways by their exposure to them. Although "influence" is a word that must be used sparingly and carefully when comparing the writings of theologians, the evidence does at least point to some influence of the medieval mystics on the Reformers.

We have certainly seen that this is true in Calvin's case. By the very fact of quoting Bernard, Calvin acknowledges a certain debt to Bernard's way of thinking. As for the clear parallels to Bernard's theology that we have found in Calvin's writings where Calvin does not make an explicit reference to Bernard, I personally would oppose describing these as "examples of Bernard's influence on Calvin." In some instances this may very well be the case; but it would be impossible to prove this, especially since Calvin may have come to the same insight as Bernard either independently or through some other avenue that may or may not be directly traceable back to Bernard.

There is, however, at least one example of a medieval mystical movement which can be said to have "influenced" Calvin's thought and work:

the Brethren of the Common Life. As we saw in chapter 1, Kenneth Strand has presented a strong argument for the influence of the Brethren's educational programs on Calvin's own program in Geneva.[17] Other attempts to connect Calvin's insights with those of the *Devotio moderna* have been less successful.[18]

If nothing else, I hope that this book, and others like it, will make future scholars hesitant to speak of mysticism in rigid or narrow categories that exclude a priori its presence in any Christian tradition. In this day and age, Roman Catholics and Protestants alike should be able to turn to the writings of Protestant mystics such as Johann Arndt and Jakob Boehme and draw inspiration from them without having to excuse themselves for doing so. Furthermore, Roman Catholic and Protestant dialogue can only benefit from the insight that we share a significant spiritual legacy, which we have had in common from the very dawn of the Reformation. The unapologetic and generally positive citation of medieval mystics in the works of Luther and Calvin can be seen as a reminder that the classic Reformers were themselves well aware of this connection, and if they were not afraid of it, neither should we be. Spirituality is not Catholic or Protestant—it is simply, as von Hügel would say, an essential element in all religious life.

In hindsight, we might observe that it is a pity that until recently so many debates about the Reformation have centered on dogmatic issues. The blame for this probably lies to some degree on all sides. It is common knowledge that a rigid dogmatism developed fairly early in the history of Protestantism, despite this being contrary to the fundamental principles that drove the Reformation. Similarly, at the Council of Trent, the Roman Catholic Church adopted its own rigid dogmatism in reaction against the teachings of the Reformers. The healthy diversity of late medieval theology gave way after Trent to a narrow approach to doctrine that was characterized above all by anti-Protestantism. Thus, for centuries, the relationship between Catholics and Protestants was reduced to hurling anathemas at each other.

This sad state of affairs finally came to an end with the Second Vatican Council, which has led to a series of friendly dialogues between Catholics and Protestants on several fundamental dogmatic issues. As theologians begin to listen to one another and struggle to come to a genuine appreciation of one another's insights, they are finding that what unites us is far more compelling than what divides us.

My own participation in ecumenical studies has led me to the conclusion that spirituality, in the sense in which I have understood it in this book,[19] is perhaps a better starting point than dogmatics for fruitful dialogue today. This is not to say that dogmatic issues are no longer important; only that they need to be seen, as Calvin himself would boldly say, in the context of a life of Christian piety.

Interestingly, it is precisely in the area of praxis (spirituality in action) that many Christians find themselves coming together today in ways that transcend denominational differences. Catholics and Protestants often work side by side in feeding the hungry and working to secure justice for all the oppressed. Perhaps these rank-and-file Christians are ahead of many scholars in their discernment of what is most important in contemporary interreligious dialogue. Thankfully, the academic world seems slowly to be getting this message, aided to an extent by such movements as feminist and liberation theology, which stress the primacy of experience in the construction of a theological worldview.

I believe that this book has shown both Bernard and Calvin to be positive resources for this kind of theological reconstruction. Far from giving us theologies of merely historical interest, they offer us numerous insights that have withstood well the test of time. The primacy of religious experience is surely one of the most central of these. We have nothing to lose, and everything to gain, from continuing to draw from the richness of these authors in our ongoing interreligious dialogue, especially their profound appreciation of the meaning of mystical union.

I would like to conclude with a brief confession: Despite my fascination with the mysticism of Bernard and Calvin, I wonder if sometimes the word "mysticism" may get in the way of understanding their thought. Neither Bernard nor Calvin was caught up in arguments about definitions of mysticism. Rather, both authors were ultimately concerned about the unity of the believer with God, rooted in faith and expressed primarily through love and service of God and others. Their agreement on this matter quietly transcends Christianity's later obsession with defining and delimiting mystical experience. We would do well to take a cue from them and from von Hügel, and remember that mysticism, however it is conceived, is only one of several essential dimensions of the Christian experience.

APPENDIX

REFERENCES TO UNION WITH CHRIST IN THE 1559 *INSTITUTES* AND OTHER SELECTED CALVIN TEXTS

The references are arranged topically by concept or image. Texts preceded by "Com." refer to Commentaries, "Serm." to Sermons.

Engrafting
(Latin *insero, insitio*)

2.8.57	O.S. 3:396
3.1.1	O.S. 4:1
3.2.24	O.S. 4:34
3.2.35	O.S. 4:46
3.3.20	O.S. 4:78
3.6.3	O.S. 4:148
3.11.10	O.S. 4:191
3.14.6	O.S. 4:225
3.15.5	O.S. 4:244
3.17.10	O.S. 4:263
3.22.7	O.S. 4:388
3.22.10	O.S. 4:392
3.24.5	O.S. 4:416
4.15.1	O.S. 5:285
4.15.5	O.S. 5:288
4.15.6	O.S. 5:289
4.15.12	O.S. 5:294
4.16.17	O.S. 5:321
4.17.1	O.S. 5:342
4.17.33	O.S. 5:394
Com. on John 15:1	C.O. 47:338
Com. on John 17:3	C.O. 47:376
Com. on 1 Cor. 1:2	C.O. 49:308
Com. on 1 Cor. 4:15	C.O. 49:372
Com. on 1 Cor. 10:16	C.O. 49:464
Com. on 1 Cor. 12:13	C.O. 49:501

Com. on Gal. 2:19	C.O. 50:198
Com. on Gal. 6:15	C.O. 50:266
Com. on Eph. 5:31	C.O. 51:226
Com. on Titus 3:5	C.O. 52:430
Com. on 1 John 3:5	C.O. 55:334
Com. on 1 John 5:11	C.O. 55:368
Com. on 1 John 5:20	C.O. 55:375

Communion
(Latin *communio, communico,* etc.)

3.1.1	O.S. 4:1
3.2.24	O.S. 4:35
3.6.2	O.S. 4:147
3.14.4	O.S. 4:223
3.14.6	O.S. 4:225
3.15.1	O.S. 4:239
3.20.24	O.S. 4:329
3.24.5	O.S. 4:416
4.15.12	O.S. 5:294
4.16.7	O.S. 5:310
4.16.17	O.S. 5:320
4.17.6	O.S. 5:348
4.17.7	O.S. 5:348
4.17.9	O.S. 5:351
4.17.11	O.S. 5:354
4.17.38	O.S. 5:402
Com. on 1 Cor. 1:9	C.O. 49:313

Com. on Eph. 5:30   C.O. 51:225
Com. on Phil. 3:10   C.O. 52:50

Fellowship
(Latin *societas*)
3.2.24   O.S. 4:35
3.11.10   O.S. 4:191
3.25.3   O.S. 4:435
4.15.6   O.S. 5:289
4.16.2   O.S. 5:306
4.16.7   O.S. 5:310
4.17.1   O.S. 5:342
4.17.9   O.S. 5:351
Com. on 1 Cor. 1:9   C.O. 49:313
Com. on 1 Cor. 10:16   C.O. 49:464
Com. on Phil. 3:10   C.O. 52:50

In the Spirit
3.1.1   O.S. 4:2
3.1.3   O.S. 4:5
3.2.35   O.S. 4:46
3.11.5   O.S. 4:185
4.17.12   O.S. 5:355–56
4.17.31   O.S. 5:389
4.17.33   O.S. 5:391–92
Com. on Eph. 5:31   C.O. 51:226
Com. on Gal. 3:20   C.O. 50:199
Com. on Titus 3:5   C.O. 52:431
Com. on 1 John 17:21   C.O. 47:387
Letter to P. Martyr,
   8 Aug. 1555   C.O. 15:723
Short Treatise on
   Lord's Supper   C.O. 5:460

Mysterious/Incomprehensible
(Latin *arcanus, incomprehensibilis,*
   mysterium; French *secret*)
2.12.7   O.S. 3:447
3.11.5   O.S. 4:185
4.17.1   O.S. 5:342
4.17.9   O.S. 5:351
4.17.31   O.S. 5:389
4.17.33   O.S. 5:391–92
4.19.35   O.S. 5:469
Com. on Eph. 2:6   C.O. 51:164
Com. on Eph. 5:32   C.O. 51:227
Serm. on Eph. 5:31–33   C.O. 51:782
Letter to P. Martyr,
   8 Aug. 1555   C.O. 15:723

Not a mixture of substances
3.11.5   O.S. 4:186
3.11.10   O.S. 4:192
4.17.30   O.S. 5:387–89
4.17.32   O.S. 5:391
Com. on John 17:21   C.O. 47:387

One flesh/spiritual marriage
(Latin *caro in carnem Christi,*
   coniugium)
2.8.18   O.S. 3:360
2.12.7   O.S. 3:447
3.1.3   O.S. 4:5
4.19.35   O.S. 5:469
Com. on 1 Cor.
   11:3   C.O. 49:474–75
Com. on Eph. 5:30   C.O. 51:225
Serm. on Dt. 24:1–6   C.O. 28:152
Serm. on Eph. 5:31–33   C.O. 51:780

Spiritual union
(Latin *coniunctio spiritualis*)
2.12.7   O.S. 3:447
3.11.10   O.S. 4:192
Com. on 1 Cor. 6:15   C.O. 49:398
Com. on 1 Cor. 6:16   C.O. 49:398
Com. on 1 Cor. 10:16   C.O. 49:464
Com. on 1 Cor. 11:3   C.O. 49:474
Serm. on Eph. 5:31–33   C.O. 51:780
Letter to Bullinger,
   25 Feb. 1547   C.O. 12:482
Short Treatise on
   Lord's Supper   C.O. 5:460

Mystical union
(Latin *unio mystica*)
2.12.7   O.S. 3:446
3.11.10   O.S. 4:191

Growing together/becoming one
(Latin *coalesco*)
3.1.1   O.S. 4:1
3.2.24   O.S. 4:35
4.17.9   O.S. 5:351
4.17.10   O.S. 5:351
4.17.11   O.S. 5:354
4.17.33   O.S. 5:394
Com. on 1 Cor. 6:15   C.O. 49:398
Com. on Eph. 5:30   C.O. 51:225

Union with God

2.8.18	O.S. 3:360
2.15.5	O.S. 3:478
2.16.3	O.S. 3:485
3.6.2	O.S. 4:147
3.25.2	O.S. 4:433
Com. on 1 Cor. 3:23	C.O. 49:361
Com. on 1 John 4:15	C.O. 47:145
Com. on 1 John 5:20	C.O. 55:375

Adoption
(Latin *adoptio*)

3.15.5	O.S. 4:244
4.17.1	O.S. 5:342
Com. on John 17:3	C.O. 47:376

Regeneration
(Latin *regeneratio*)

3.3.9	O.S. 4:63
4.15.5	O.S. 5:289
4.15.6	O.S. 5:289
4.15.12	O.S. 5:293

4.16.2	O.S. 5:306
4.16.17	O.S. 5:320
4.17.1	O.S. 5:342
Com. on Gal. 2:20	C.O. 50:199
Com. on Titus 3:5	C.O. 52:431

Partakers of Christ
(Latin *participes*)

3.2.24	O.S. 4:34
3.11.23	O.S. 4:206
3.15.5	O.S. 4:244
4.15.6	O.S. 5:289
4.16.17	O.S. 5:320
4.17.5	O.S. 5:346
4.17.8	O.S. 5:350
4.17.9	O.S. 5:350
4.17.11	O.S. 5:354
4.17.38	O.S. 5:402
Com. on John 17:3	C.O. 47:376
Com. on 1 Cor. 1:9	C.O. 49:313
Com. on Eph. 3:17	C.O. 51:187
Com. on Gal. 2:20	C.O. 50:199

NOTES

CHAPTER 1. CALVIN AND MYSTICISM: THE STATE OF THE QUESTION

1. Georgia Harkness, *Mysticism: Its Meaning and Message*, 124.
2. Calvin's letter to the Congregation at Frankfurt, 23 February 1559. C.O. 47:442. "Ordures" can be rendered as "trash" but also as "excrement" (translation mine). Calvin citations other than those from the *Institutes* are referenced to the *Calvini Opera* of the *Corpus Reformatorum* (hereafter C.O.). References in parentheses for Bernard citations are to the critical Latin edition, *Sancti Bernardi Opera* (hereafter B.O.).
3. John Calvin, *Institutes of the Christian Religion,* ed. John T. McNeill, trans. Ford Lewis Battles, 1.14.4 (O.S. 3:157). References in parentheses after citations from the *Institutes* are to the *Iohannis Calvini Opera Selecta* (hereafter O.S.).
4. *Institutes* 3.11 (O.S. 4:181ff.).
5. See especially the studies by Kenneth Strand, "John Calvin and the Brethren of the Common Life," in *Andrews University Seminary Studies* 13 (1975): 67–78 and 15 (1977):43–56 ("The Role of Strassburg"); also Jean Boisset, *Sagesse et sainteté dans la pensée de Jean Calvin,* and Charles Partee, "The Soul in Plato, Platonism, and Calvin," 278–96.
6. *Institutes* 3.11.10 (O.S. 4:191).
7. The reference, in *Institutes* 3.22.10 (O.S. 4:392), is to one of Bernard's letters (107.4,5; B.O. 7:269–71).
8. A. N. S. Lane, "Calvin's Sources of St. Bernard," 253–83.
9. Jill Raitt, "Calvin's Use of Bernard of Clairvaux," 118, 99.
10. Ibid., 118.
11. Lane, "Calvin's Sources of St. Bernard," 277. On Calvin's medieval antecedents, see also A. N. S. Lane, "Calvin's Use of the Fathers and the Medievals," 149–205, and Karl Reuter, *Das Grundverständnis der Theologie Calvins unter Einbeziehung ihrer geschichtlichen Abhängigkeiten,* esp. chap. 1, pp. 9–87.
12. Albrecht Ritschl, *The Christian Doctrine of Justification and Reconciliation,* 3:113.

13. Evelyn Underhill, *Mysticism*, xii.

14. Albrecht Ritschl, *A Critical History of the Christian Doctrine of Justification and Reconciliation*, 1:99–101.

15. Ibid., 95–97.

16. Albrecht Ritschl, *Geschichte des Pietismus*, vol. 1: *Der Pietismus in der reformierten Kirche*, 47, 45–46.

17. Ritschl, *Justification and Reconciliation*, 3:593–94. See also *Geschichte des Pietismus*, 1:49, where Ritschl speaks of the barrier between God (Christ) and ourselves being removed by love-mysticism.

18. Ritschl, *Justification and Reconciliation*, 3:112.

19. "The Pietistic or mystical directions are always so stated as though the Christian existed only for contemplation, and as though work, which interrupts his meditations, were worth nothing." Ibid., 163.

20. Wilhelm Kolfhaus, *Christusgemeinschaft bei Johannes Calvin*, 126. Translations from Kolfhaus are my own.

21. Ibid., 127.

22. Ibid., 126.

23. Ibid., 132. Here he accepts Peter Brunner's claim that "the same words in Calvin have a different meaning than they have in Bernard."

24. Ibid., 133.

25. Ibid.

26. Ibid.

27. *New Catholic Encyclopedia*, 1967 ed., s.v. "Mysticism," by T. Corbishley, 10:175.

28. Jerald C. Brauer, "Francis Rous, Puritan Mystic, 1579–1659: An Introduction to the Study of the Mystical Element in Puritanism," 4.

29. This book will attempt to deal only with Christian understandings of mysticism—a sufficiently monumental task!

30. Bernard McGinn, "Love, Knowledge, and Mystical Union in Western Christianity: Twelfth to Sixteenth Centuries," 7 (emphasis added).

31. McGinn notes: "The classic schools of mysticism in the Western Church from the twelfth through the sixteenth centuries saw the experience of union with God as the favored way of characterizing the goal of their beliefs and practices." Ibid.

32. To give but one example, Evelyn Underhill states: "Mysticism, in its pure form, is . . . the science of union with the Absolute, and nothing else, and . . . the mystic is the person who attains to this union, not the person who talks about it." *Mysticism*, 72.

33. Ernst Troeltsch, *The Social Teachings of the Christian Churches*, 2:730.

34. Friedrich von Hügel, *The Mystical Element of Religion as Studied in St. Catherine of Genoa and Her Friends*, 2d ed., 1:51–53.

35. Ibid., 1:53, 65–66.

36. Ibid., 1:66, 70.

37. Ibid., 2:283.

38. Ibid., 2:282–83. We shall see that there is a strong parallel here to a notion of *sensus divinitatis* that is found in both Bernard and Calvin.

39. Rufus M. Jones, *Studies in Mystical Religion*, xv (emphasis added).

40. Brauer, "Francis Rous," 5.

41. John Baillie, *Our Knowledge of God*, 178, 181. The "other presences" of which Baillie speaks are the presence of God, the corporeal world, and other people (181).

42. Ibid., 182–89.
43. Bernard J. F. Lonergan, *Method in Theology*, 76–77.
44. Von Hügel, *Mystical Element of Religion*, 1:69–70.
45. Ibid., 1:63.
46. William R. Siktberg, "The Mystical Element in the Theology of John Calvin," 115.
47. Von Hügel, *Mystical Element of Religion*, 2:269.
48. Ibid., 2:263–64.
49. "Theologia mystica est experimentalis cognitio habita de Deo per amoris unitivi complexum." Jean Gerson, *Selections from "A Deo exivit," "Contra curiositatem studentium" and "De mystica theologia speculativa"*, 64–65. There are other definitions given by Gerson, but they are not substantially different from this one. See Steven E. Ozment, *Homo Spiritualis: A Comparative Study of Johannes Tauler, Jean Gerson and Martin Luther (1509–16) in the Context of Their Theological Thought*, 78–79.
50. Gerson, *Selections*, 48–49. The *unus spiritus* theme is one that is also found in Bernard, e.g., in *Sermons on the Canticles* (hereafter *SC*) 71:6–8 (B.O. 2:217–220).
51. Gerson, *Selections*, 50–51. Gerson's reference to the soul "becoming like" God is certainly problematic in relation to Reformation thought. As Ozment puts it: "Gerson . . . preserves the distance between God and man in the mystical union. But it is a distance and otherness of two generic 'likes.' The radical opposition between a righteous God and a sinful man disappears in the union of likes." *Homo Spiritualis*, 83. This point will be examined in relation to Bernard and Calvin in chaps. 4 and 5.
52. Ozment, *Homo Spiritualis*, 71. See *De mystica theologia speculativa* in Ioannis Carlerii de Gerson, *De Mystica Theologia*, ed. André Combes (Lucani, Italy: In Aedibus Thesauri Mundi), cons. 17, 39.17–26, quoted in Ozment, *Homo Spiritualis*, 64–65.
53. See McGinn, "Love, Knowledge, and Mystical Union," 8, 21.
54. Gerson, *De mystica theologia speculativa* (Combes), cons. 30, 78.33–36 (translation mine). See Ozment, *Homo Spiritualis*, 52.
55. See Ozment, *Homo Spiritualis*, 76–77, esp. 76 n. 2.
56. Calvin's opinion of Pseudo-Dionysius has already been noted (above, pp. 1–2, n. 3). In this connection, Calvin refers to Paul's account of being "caught up beyond the third heaven" in 2 Cor. 12:2—but unlike Pseudo-Dionysius, who gives the impression of recounting "not what he had learned, but what he had seen with his own eyes," Paul "not only said nothing about it, but also testified that it is unlawful for any man to speak of the secret things that he has seen" (2 Cor. 12:4). *Institutes* 1.14.4 (O.S. 3:157). As for Ignatius Loyola, there is an indirect reference to the *Spiritual Exercises* (First Week, Section 82) in which Calvin rejects the need for several days of penance by converts as a prologue to acceptance into the church (*Institutes* 3.3.2, O.S. 4:57). It is doubtful whether Calvin knew much about Ignatius. They were both students at the College of Montaigu in Paris, although Ignatius arrived there in 1528, just as Calvin was leaving. See Strand, "Calvin and the Brethren," 72.
57. W. Stanford Reid, "Bernard of Clairvaux in the Thought of John Calvin," 127–45. There is also an earlier article by George Bavaud, "Dialogue entre saint Bernard, saint Thomas d'Aquin et Calvin," 328–38.
58. Reid, "Clairvaux in the Thought of Calvin," 129–35.

59. Ibid., 135–44. This latter point will be discussed further in chap. 2, as part of the treatment of the *sensus divinitatis*.

60. See above, nn. 8 and 9.

61. Raitt, "Calvin's Use of Bernard," 100–102.

62. See the Appendix of Raitt's article, ibid., 119–20. The relevant material regarding the doctrinal loci (Sec. III, pp. 102–18) will be discussed in chaps. 2–5.

63. Ibid., 118. We shall see that although Calvin generally *quotes* Bernard accurately from the time of the 1543 edition, his *interpretations* are not always true to Bernard's context.

64. Ibid., 118–19. On Lombard, see also 102.

65. See Raitt's comment, ibid., 118. It should be noted that there are other areas of conflict between Calvin and Bernard besides the ones treated by Raitt (i.e., where Bernard is specifically cited by Calvin as an opponent). For example, Calvin rejects the doctrine of purgatory, which Bernard upholds. Calvin, *Institutes*, 3.5.7 (O.S. 4:139); Bernard, *SC* 66.11 (B.O. 2:185).

66. Regarding this last point (Calvin's view of his contemporaries), the few studies that have been done generally treat "mysticism" in terms of a pantheistic "union of essences," i.e., the understanding accepted by Ritschl and Kolfhaus (which I have already criticized as an oversimplification). See, for example, Benjamin Wirt Farley's summary of modern assessments of Calvin's treatise against the Libertines, in John Calvin, *Treatises Against the Anabaptists and Against the Libertines*, trans. and ed. B. W. Farley (Grand Rapids: Baker Book House, 1982), 164–73.

67. Boisset, *Sagesse et sainteté*, 254–55.

68. Ibid., 255–84.

69. Ibid., 256. Translations from Boisset are my own. See *Institutes* 1.15.6 (O.S. 3:182).

70. For example, in *Institutes* 3.9.4 (O.S. 4:174) and 1.15.2 (O.S. 3:176).

71. Boisset, *Sagesse et sainteté*, 257. Boisset does note (p. 260) that Plato tones down the anticorporeal rhetoric in works other than the *Phaedo*.

72. *Institutes* 3.25.2 (O.S. 4:433–34); Boisset, *Sagesse et sainteté*, 258.

73. Boisset, *Sagesse et sainteté*, 261–62.

74. Ibid., 313.

75. Partee, "The Soul in Plato, Platonism, and Calvin," 295. See C.O. 6:599.

76. A helpful summary of the Neoplatonic grounds of Christian mysticism is found in Thomas M. Tomasic, "Neoplatonism and the Mysticism of William of St.-Thierry," in *An Introduction to the Medieval Mystics of Europe*, ed. Paul Szarmach, 53–75.

77. See especially Roy W. Battenhouse, "The Doctrine of Man in Calvin and in Renaissance Platonism," 448. On 468, Battenhouse refers to Calvin's "fundamental Platonism" with regard to his teaching on soul and body. It is precisely Partee's intention, in the article cited above (n. 75), to refute this thesis.

78. Lucien Joseph Richard, *The Spirituality of John Calvin*, 122.

79. Alexandre Ganoczy, *Calvin, théologien de l'Eglise et du ministère*, 22–24 (translation mine).

80. Albert Hyma, *The Christian Renaissance: A History of the "Devotio Moderna,"* 283–84.

81. Richard, *Spirituality of Calvin*, 122.

82. Ibid., 122–27.

83. Ibid., 180–83. Richard's thesis is fully expounded with textual references in chap. 5, 136–73. I frankly find his reading of Calvin to be deeply flawed, and will be challenging many of his conclusions in the chapters that follow. For example, the Holy Spirit certainly does *not* "create" the *sensus divinitatis*, which Calvin takes to be a natural endowment. Furthermore, I do not see the strong "individualism" that Richard sees in Calvin's spirituality. These points will be taken up in chaps. 2 and 5, respectively.

84. Ibid., 174. On the unity of Christian life and theology, see esp. 186–87.

85. Strand, "Calvin and the Brethren," 67. Note that this study appears in two parts, the second bearing the subtitle "The Role of Strassburg." See above, n. 5.

86. Strand, "Calvin and the Brethren," 70–71.

87. Ibid., 72–73. Strand points to "clear indications of a strong impact of the Montaigu's reform program *and its library* on Loyola," and suggests that Calvin must have been similarly touched by these ideals, since he spent several years at Montaigu just prior to Loyola's arrival.

88. Ibid., 73–74.

89. Ibid., 75–76. See C. Louise Salley, "Jacques Lefèvre d'Etaples: Heir of the Dutch Reformers of the Fifteenth Century," in *The Dawn of Modern Civilization*, ed. Kenneth Strand, 2d ed., 75–124. Of particular interest is the reference to "mystical union."

90. Strand, "Calvin and the Brethren," 76–77. On good works, see his remark on 77: "Calvin's belief that Christ does not justify anyone whom he does not also sanctify is more akin to the emphasis revealed in expressions in the writings of Lefèvre and the Devotio Moderna." See *Institutes* 3.16.1 (O.S. 4:248–49) and Salley, "Lefèvre," 107–9.

91. Strand, "Calvin and the Brethren," 77–78.

92. Strand, "The Role of Strassburg," 43–47.

93. Ibid., 48–49.

94. Ibid., 50.

95. See especially Richard, *Spirituality of Calvin*, 13–39.

96. Kenneth Strand, "Additional Note on Calvin and the Influence of the Brethren of the Common Life in France," 51–52.

97. Ibid., 52–54.

98. See above, n. 78.

99. Strand, "Additional Note," 55.

100. See Richard, *Spirituality of Calvin*, 122.

101. Siktberg, "Mystical Element in Calvin," 24–31. See Jules Bonnet, *Letters of John Calvin*, trans. D. Constable (Edinburgh: Constable, 1855), 1:356, 431. On the Libertines, see the references listed on p. 1722 of the McNeill-Battles edition of the *Institutes*, and Calvin's *Contre la secte des Libertins* in C.O. 7:145–252. This treatise is translated in Calvin, *Treatises Against the Anabaptists and Against the Libertines*, 187–326. B. W. Farley's excellent introduction notes that "a careful study of the *Libertines* piece may shed light on Calvin's rejection of any mystical identification of man with God or Christ while sharpening an understanding of his use of the term *mystica unio* and *union sacrée*" (p. 186). I hope to explore the connections in a future study.

102. Siktberg, "Mystical Element in Calvin," 28; Bonnet, *Letters* 4:21–23. For the correction of Bonnet's view, see C.O. 47:441–42 (fn. 2).

103. Willem Balke, *Calvin and the Anabaptist Radicals*, trans. William Heynen

(Grand Rapids: Wm. B. Eerdmans Publishing Co., 1981), 46–70. Balke does not mention mysticism as an issue, although I would not want to rule out further consideration of the question. Balke is also helpful in providing a definition of Anabaptism as it is understood in contemporary scholarship. On p. 11, he notes: "The name 'Anabaptist,' or 'rebaptizer,' picks out what actually was only an incidental teaching. The central concept of the movement was not the doctrine of the sacrament but the doctrine of the church. They were committed to a congregation that demonstrated that it was a community of believers by living a life of active and practical obedience to the Scriptures. This, in turn, demanded their rejection of the established state church, or, in other words, the established church of their time." A good summary of scholarship on Calvin and the Anabaptists is provided on pp. 5–9. See also George H. Williams, *The Radical Reformation*, esp. chap. 23, "Calvin and the Radical Reformation," 580–614.

104. Siktberg, "Mystical Element in Calvin," 28.

105. Reid, "Clairvaux in the Thought of Calvin," 144.

106. *Institutes* 3.1.3 (esp. n. 6 in McNeill-Battles, 540; O.S. 4:4–5) and 3.20.28 (O.S. 4:337).

107. Siktberg, "Mystical Element in Calvin," 39–95, 109–10.

108. *Institutes* 3.11.10, n. 20; Wilhelm Niesel, *The Theology of John Calvin*, 126. Marguerite Soulié, in her essay " 'Mystique' chez Calvin et création littéraire," 136, 142, advances a similar view.

109. *Institutes* 3.11.10 (O.S. 4:191); see above, n. 50.

CHAPTER 2. THE CHRISTIAN ANTHROPOLOGY OF BERNARD AND CALVIN

1. Bernard of Clairvaux, *Sermons on Conversion, De convers.* 6.11 (B.O. 4:84). Translations of Bernard's works are from this series unless otherwise noted. See also Bernard of Clairvaux, *On the Song of Songs I, SC* 11.5 (B.O. 1:57).

2. Endre von Ivánka, "La structure de l'âme selon S. Bernard," 204. Translations from this article are my own.

3. Bernard of Clairvaux, *De diversis* 84.1 (B.O. 6–1:325). Translation mine.

4. Von Ivánka, "La structure de l'âme," 204. Wilhelm Hiss, in *Die Anthropologie Bernhards von Clairvaux*, disagrees with von Ivánka's analysis, insisting that Bernard does make real distinctions in discussing the soul. He points in particular (see esp. 75ff.) to a distinction that we will be discussing below, between the greatness (*magnitudo*) and uprightness (*rectitudo*) of the soul (see pp. 27–28 below, nn. 27 and 28). While I believe Hiss is technically correct, and in this sense provides a good corrective to von Ivánka's argument, he himself states that Bernard is ultimately more interested in the functions of the soul: "The abbot wishes to teach the art of living; his science wholly served ascetical-mystical training, above all the monk's, whose goal is deification" (p. 138, translation mine). He also acknowledges, with von Ivánka, that Bernard may have simply "adopted" elements of the tradition without going into further questions about them (p. 139).

5. Von Ivánka, "La structure de l'âme," 205–6. There is, however, one distinction that Bernard consistently maintains, that between love and knowledge (see pp. 206–8). A full discussion of this point appears in chap. 4.

6. Ibid., 208.

7. *SC* 5.8 (B.O. 1:25). An example of the "passive" language used by Bernard is in *De diligendo Deo* 10.28 (B.O. 3:143), where he speaks of union with God as being God's doing: "sic affici, deificari est": to be so affected is to be deified (translation mine). See von Ivánka, 208. Note too the language of "direct" communication, the problematic aspects of which were mentioned in chap. 1 (pp. 9–10). The mediation of grace will be taken up in more detail in chap. 3.

8. Bernard of Clairvaux, *On the Song of Songs IV*, *SC* 71.8 (B.O. 2:220). Hiss agrees that Bernard is "free from any suspicion of pantheism" (*Die Anthropologie Bernhards*, 78, translation mine).

9. Translations of *De gratia et libero arbitrio* are taken from Bernard of Clairvaux, *Treatises III: On Grace and Free Choice; In Praise of the New Knighthood.*

10. See Bernard McGinn's Introduction, ibid., 5–8.

11. Ibid., 1.1–2 (B.O. 3:165–67).

12. Ibid., 1.2 (B.O. 3:167).

13. Ibid., 2.4–5 (B.O. 3:168–70).

14. Ibid., 3.7, 9.28 (B.O. 3:170–71, 185).

15. Ibid., 3.7, 4.11 (B.O. 3:171, 173). In 5.15 (B.O. 3:177), Bernard notes that "contemplatives alone can in some way enjoy freedom of pleasure, though only in part, in very small part, and on the rarest occasions." This will be significant in our discussion of *unio mystica.*

16. Ibid., 4.11 (B.O. 3:173).

17. Etienne Gilson, *La théologie mystique de Saint Bernard*, 68 (translation mine).

18. *De gratia* 6.16 (B.O. 3:177–78).

19. *De gratia* 7.21–22 (B.O. 3:182).

20. Ibid., 7.23–8.24 (B.O. 3:183–84).

21. Ibid., 12.39 (B.O. 3:194).

22. "Itaque liberum arbitrium nos facit volentes, gratia benevolos." Ibid., 6.16 (B.O. 3:178).

23. Ibid., 1.2 (B.O. 3:167). See McGinn's Introduction, 15–16.

24. Gilson, *Théologie mystique*, 68.

25. Bernard of Clairvaux, *On the Song of Songs II*, *SC* 27.6 (B.O. 1:185) (emphasis mine).

26. *SC* 81.11 (B.O. 2:291).

27. *SC* 80.3 (B.O. 2:278).

28. *SC* 80.3–5 (B.O. 2:278–81).

29. *SC* 82.2, 5 (B.O. 2:293, 295). In a similar way, we will find Calvin speaking of the *sensus divinitatis* as distorted or suppressed.

30. In *SC* 81.11 (B.O. 2:291), Bernard explains, "In the book I have written on grace and free choice you may find other observations about the image and the likeness, but I do not think they contradict the things I have been saying. You have read them, and you have heard what I just said; I leave it to your judgement which is preferable." For a more complete discussion of the *imago Dei* in Bernard, see M. Standaert, "La doctrine de l'image chez S. Bernard," 70–129.

31. *SC* 85.1 (B.O. 2:307).

32. *On the Song of Songs I*, xi–xii. A comment by William Siktberg is relevant here: "Mysticism cannot exist in a system which sees no capability of response in man. The element of feeling demands a point of immanence where man becomes conscious of God. . . . The mystic can never consider man to be so depraved as not

to have some point of contact or natural inclination toward God." Siktberg, "Mystical Element in Calvin," 39.

33. See above, nn. 11 and 12.

34. Bernard, *De diligendo Deo* 8.23–10.29 (B.O. 3:138–44).

35. *Institutes* 1.15.2 (O.S. 3:174–75).

36. *Institutes* 1.15.5 (O.S. 3:181).

37. See *Institutes* 1.15.4 (O.S. 3:180), where Calvin says, "For that speculation of Augustine, that the soul is the reflection of the Trinity because in it reside the understanding, will and memory, is by no means sound." However, it should be noted that Calvin's objection here is more to the *assumption of an analogy* between the soul and the Trinity than to the anthropology that Augustine's formula implies. This is more clearly expressed earlier in the *Institutes* (1.13.18, O.S. 3:132), where Calvin states that the analogies advanced by "men of old" about the Trinity "were quite inadequate."

38. *Institutes* 1.15.8 (O.S. 3:185). Note that in the two previous sections, 1.15.6–7 (O.S. 3:183–85), Calvin lists other faculties as well, which he omits along with memory. Holding to two faculties, understanding and will, "is suitable to our present purpose" (*Institutes* 1.15.7, O.S. 3:185).

39. See above, n. 20.

40. *Institutes* 1.15.8 (O.S. 3:186) (emphasis added). See 2.3.13 (O.S. 3:289) where Calvin, referring to Augustine's *On Rebuke and Grace*, says, "The original freedom was to be able not to sin."

41. *Institutes* 1.15.8 (O.S. 3:186). See *Institutes* 1.16–18 (O.S. 3:187–227).

42. "For although God's glory shines forth in the outer man, yet there is no doubt that the proper seat of his image is in the soul." *Institutes* 1.15.3 (O.S. 3:176). An important new study on Calvin's use of the *imago Dei* is found in Mary Potter Engel, *John Calvin's Perspectival Anthropology*, 37–63. Of particular interest is her discussion of whether the *imago* is totally lost or only deformed as a result of the fall of humankind (54–61). Briefly, she points to Calvin's use of *both* displacement/replacement and deformed/transformed language to speak of the *imago* after the Fall. Calvin uses the former in speaking from the perspective of God as judge, and the latter in speaking from the perspective of humankind.

43. A fuller discussion of this matter is found in Jill Raitt, "Calvin's Use of Bernard," 102–11. I will only attempt to highlight the salient points here. It is worth stressing that it is free *choice* (*arbitrium*) that is under discussion, not free will (*voluntas*). The term is inaccurately translated in McNeill-Battles. See "Calvin's Use of Bernard," 103, n. 37. Recall that free choice is also the issue for Bernard (above n. 10). As Bernard McGinn notes in his Introduction to *De gratia*, "It is the term 'free choice' (*liberum arbitrium*) and not 'free will' (*libera voluntas*) which is the operative one in Bernard and throughout most of the period in question. The problem was essentially that of man's ability to perform free acts. An explanation of freedom need not be intimately involved with a developed theory of the will; particularly before the period of High Scholasticism medieval authors rarely took up their pens to write treatises *De voluntate*." *Treatises III*, 8.

44. *Institutes* 2.2.4 (O.S. 3:246–47); *De gratia* 3.6 (B.O. 3:170): "ut liberum ad voluntatem, arbitrium referatur ad rationem." In this connection, Calvin criticizes the scholastics for what is also found in Bernard, although Calvin does not attribute it to him, i.e., that "free" refers to the will, "choice" to the reason. On the other hand, Calvin accepts the threefold division of freedom (i.e., from necessity,

sin, and sorrow), which he attributes to the "schools" but is generally considered by scholars to have originated with Bernard. See *Institutes* 2.2.5 (O.S. 3:247); *De gratia* 3.7, 4.11 (B.O. 3:171, 173); Raitt, "Calvin's Use of Bernard," 104. Calvin's only reservation about the threefold understanding of freedom, noted at the end of 2.2.5, is when "necessity" is confused with "compulsion." However, he later cites Bernard in support of his notion of "willing necessity" (see 2.3.5). This will be discussed further below, but a clarification is in order here. Calvin, like Bernard, wants to argue that after the Fall, we are still free to choose, but only among evil options (see above, n. 18). As Mary Potter Engel aptly summarizes: "Though sinners have lost the ability to choose freely between good and evil (*liberum arbitrium*), they have not lost the faculty *voluntas*; for they choose evil." *Calvin's Perspectival Anthropology*, 136; see also 135. Thus, we sin of necessity, but each sin is the result of a human act of willing. As Calvin says in *Institutes* 2.3.5 (O.S. 3:277), humans after the Fall are not "deprived of will, but of soundness of will."

45. *Institutes* 2.2.6 (O.S. 3:248). The reference from *De gratia* is cited as 14.46, which Raitt notes is "clearly wrong. 14.47 seems closer, but is inaccurately remembered by Calvin who never bothered to correct it" (i.e., in the later editions). "Calvin's Use of Bernard," 103. See B.O. 3:199–200.

46. Raitt, "Calvin's Use of Bernard," 105. See above, n. 11; B.O. 3:166–67.

47. Raitt, "Calvin's Use of Bernard," 118.

48. Ibid. Later, Thomas Aquinas will speak of *gratia cooperans* (both in terms of grace as "motion" and grace as "habit") as a gift of God. Thomas, like Bernard, speaks of "consent" as a "passive" human component in justification: "God does not justify us without us, since while we are being justified, we consent to God's justice by a movement of free choice. But that movement is not the cause but the effect of grace. *Thus the whole operation belongs to grace.*" Thomas Aquinas, *Summa Theologiae* 1–2: qu. 110, art. 4; vol. 30, *The Gospel of Grace*, trans. Cornelius Ernst, O.P. (New York: McGraw–Hill Book Co., 1972), 69 (emphasis mine). I am indebted to Bernard McGinn for providing the following clarification: for Thomas, justification is the result of operative grace. We consent to that justification through the performance of good works, which are the result of cooperative grace. Similarly, Bernard says in *De gratia*, "The consent and the work, . . . though not originating from us, nevertheless are not without us. . . . Grace does the whole work, and so does free choice—with this one qualification: that whereas the whole is done *in* free choice, so is the whole done *of* grace." *De gratia* 14.46–47 (B.O. 3:199–200). See also above, nn. 11 and 46. I do not see Bernard's position here as substantially different from Thomas's. As for Calvin, he speaks of the distinction between operating and cooperating grace as a "worn distinction" (*Institutes* 2.3.11, O.S. 3:287).

49. *Institutes* 2.3.7 (O.S. 3:281). See Raitt, "Calvin's Use of Bernard," 106. The issue between Bernard and Calvin here is not, however, merely "verbal." As noted above (see nn. 12, 13, and 31), Bernard speaks of "free choice" both negatively (as freedom from necessity) and positively (as consent to the gift of salvation). It is the latter designation that Calvin rejects in *Institutes* 2.2.4. See also n. 44 above.

50. *Institutes* 1.15.4 (O.S. 3:179).

51. *Institutes* 2.2.12 (O.S. 3:255). The word for "sparks" is *scintillas*, not *synteresis*. Calvin's use of the latter term would have been significant, since it was a common one in medieval mystical texts.

52. *Institutes* 2.2.13–17 (O.S. 3:256–60). In a fine essay on the spirituality of
Calvin, William J. Bouwsma makes an important point regarding Calvin's notion
of "total depravity": "It means not that there is nothing good left in human beings
but that no part of the personality has been left untouched by sin and thus that no
area of the self can be depended on for human salvation." "The Spirituality of John
Calvin," 326. Mary Potter Engel offers a more nuanced view, based on what she
calls the "perspectival" nature of Calvin's anthropology: "Whereas from the
perspective of God as judge total depravity meant that all of God's gifts are totally
lost in the Fall, from the perspective of humankind total depravity means that the
totality of the self is affected by sin." Thus, she would see Bouwsma's comment as
true only from the human perspective. *Calvin's Perspectival Anthropology,* 59.

53. *Institutes* 2.2.18 (O.S. 3:260–61).

54. *Institutes* 2.3.5 (O.S. 3:277). See Raitt, "Calvin's Use of Bernard," 106;
Bernard, *De gratia* 6.16 (B.O. 3:177–78).

55. Jill Raitt provides a very thorough analysis in "Calvin's Use of Bernard,"
107–110.

56. *Institutes* 2.3.5 (O.S. 3:278); *SC* 81.7 (B.O. 2:288).

57. *De gratia* 3.7–4.11 (B.O. 2:171–74).

58. Raitt, "Calvin's Use of Bernard," 109.

59. Ibid., 109–10.

60. "Trahe quodammodo invitam, ut facias voluntariam; trahe torpentem, ut
reddas currentem." B.O. 1:127.

61. *Institutes* 3.9.4 (O.S. 4:174). See Raitt, "Calvin's Use of Bernard," 110–11.

62. *Institutes* 2.3.6 (O.S. 3:280); *De gratia* 6.16 (B.O. 3:178). See above, nn. 18
and 22.

63. *Institutes* 2.5.14 (O.S. 3:314). McNeill and Battles note on p. 335 of the LCC
edition that the statement from *De gratia* is also found in Augustine's works.
Calvin's argument continues in the same vein in the next section, 2.5.15 (O.S.
3:315–16).

64. Commentary on John 1:5, John Calvin, *Calvin's New Testament Commentaries,* vol. 4, *The Gospel according to St. John 1–10,* trans. T. H. L. Parker (Grand Rapids:
Wm. B. Eerdmans Publishing Co., 1961, 12 (C.O. 47:6). All translations from the
New Testament commentaries are from this series unless otherwise noted.
Reference to the "seed of religion" (*semen religionis*) is also found in the first book
of the *Institutes:* see 1.4.1 (O.S. 3:40), 1.4.4 (O.S. 3:44), and 1.5.15 (O.S. 3:59).

65. See esp. Karl Barth, "No! Answer to Emil Brunner," in Emil Brunner and
Karl Barth, *Natural Theology.*

66. *Institutes* 1.3.1, 1.4.2, 1.4.1 (O.S. 3:37, 41, 40). See above, p. 28. I would like to
recall here the difficulty with Richard's thesis about the *sensus divinitatis* that was
reviewed in chap. 1, namely that the *sensus* is "created" by the Holy Spirit. The
texts quoted here make it clear that this is not the case. See chap. 1, p. 17, n. 83.
Mary Potter Engel also makes an important point in this connection: that there *are*
texts in which Calvin speaks of the *sensus* as being erased rather than defaced. She
explains this discrepancy as a function of Calvin's perspectival anthropology,
"From the perspective of God as judge, the *sensus divinitatis,* the aspiration to
heavenly life, is completely gone; for when the issue is human sin and the need for
redemption, all piety is to be counted as nothing. However, from the perspective
of humankind, one can properly speak of a remnant of piety and worship in
human beings after the Fall, at least as the *sensus divinitatis,* which can never be

erased in human beings." Thus, "Calvin speaks seriously of the whole image being both completely erased and only defaced. Though he speaks of obliteration more frequently than retention, we are not thereby justified in omitting the latter from his anthropology." *Calvin's Perspectival Anthropology*, 59–60. I am not sure if Calvin really speaks "more frequently" of obliteration; this does not seem to be the case in the *Institutes*, at least. In any case, the argument that follows stresses the aspect of "retention" of which Engel speaks.

67. Edward A. Dowey, *The Knowledge of God in Calvin's Theology*, 2d ed., 55. *Institutes* 1.3.2 (O.S. 3:39). This passage exemplifies the "empirical effects" of the *sensus* as elucidated by Dowey: "(1) the universality of religion, which because of sin means the universality of idolatry, accompanied by (2) the servile fear of God and (3) the troubled conscience" (p. 53). Conscience, although treated by Calvin as distinct from the *sensus*, is nevertheless related to it.

68. *Institutes* 1.2.1 (O.S. 3:35).

69. *Institutes* 1.6.1 (O.S. 3:60).

70. Brian A. Gerrish, "From Calvin to Schleiermacher: The Theme and the Shape of Christian Dogmatics," 1:1043.

71. See Barth, "No!" 89. However, this remark must be qualified in the light of Mary Potter Engel's study of Calvin's anthropology. Engel remarks that if one keeps Calvin's shifting perspectives in mind, "it is easy to regard the entire Barth-Brunner controversy over the 'point of contact' as a misplaced debate, for Calvin espouses both their positions." *Calvin's Perspectival Anthropology*, 61. See above, n. 66. In deference to the Barthian position in the natural theology debate, I should at least point out why the spectacles metaphor was regarded as unpersuasive. Calvin does, after all, sometimes assert that human beings after the Fall are blinder than moles (see *Institutes* 2.2.18 [O.S. 3:260]). See also *Institutes* 2.2.19 (O.S. 3:261), where Calvin speaks of our own insight being "utterly blind and stupid in divine matters [in rebus divinis caecam prorsus . . . et stupidam]." These remarks would fit with the "divine" perspective in Calvin's anthropology, as expounded by Engel. Her point remains persuasive that Barth only acknowledged one aspect of what Calvin said on this subject. See Barth, "No!" 106–7, and Calvin's Commentary on 1 Cor. 1:21 (C.O. 49:326), which Barth cites in support of his position.

72. Barth, "No!" 109; *Institutes* 1.2.1 (O.S. 3:34) (emphasis added).

73. Barth, "No!" 74–75; *Institutes* 1.5.15 (O.S. 3:59–60).

74. Dowey, *Knowledge of God*, 72–73 (emphasis added). The debate on natural theology is a long and interesting one that I will not develop here. Key works include Peter Barth's *Das Problem der natürlichen Theologie bei Calvin* and Günter Gloede's *Theologia naturalis bei Calvin*. Gloede asks in his introductory chapter, "Is a natural theology found in Calvin? We can answer with an unqualified yes" (p. 5, translation mine). He goes on to offer a detailed study of every aspect of natural theology in Calvin.

75. *SC* 31.3 (B.O. 1:221). Note that the second point Bernard makes, "that you must seek him," corresponds to what Calvin will say about the conscience, which shows us (but does not give us the power to carry out) our duty before God. Another example of the *sensus* (although not so-called) is found in *De convers.* 2.3 (B.O. 4:72), where Bernard speaks of God's "voice" coming to all people, "Nor do we have much difficulty in hearing this voice; *the difficulty is rather in stopping our ears from hearing it* [labor est potius aures obturare ne audias]. For that voice offers

itself, presents itself, and never ceases to knock at the door of each one of us" (emphasis added).

76. John Calvin, *Calvin's Commentaries*, vol. 1, *Commentaries on the Book of Genesis*, trans. John King (Grand Rapids: Baker Book House, 1984), 118 (C.O. 23:39).

77. Dowey, *Knowledge of God*, 56. In *Institutes* 1.15.2 (O.S. 3:175), Calvin states, "Surely the conscience, which, discerning between good and evil, responds to God's judgment, is an undoubted sign of the immortal spirit." To my knowledge, Calvin himself does not directly call conscience "revelation."

78. Dowey, *Knowledge of God*, 72. As mentioned above (n. 75), Bernard makes a similar distinction in *SC* 31.3, where he speaks of both the awareness that God exists and the awareness that we must seek him. The latter point comes out even more strongly in *De diligendo Deo* 2.6 (B.O. 3:124), where Bernard declares that even the infidel is "inexcusable" for not loving God, "For an innate justice, not unknown to reason, cries interiorly to him that he ought to love with his whole being the one to whom he owes all that he is."

79. *Institutes* 4.10.3 (O.S. 5:166), translation Dowey's, in *Knowledge of God*, 57; (Latin *sensum . . . divini iudicii*).

80. Dowey, *Knowledge of God*, 57.

81. *Institutes* 2.8.1 (O.S. 3:344).

82. Dowey, *Knowledge of God*, 57.

83. See above, p. 32.

84. *De gratia* 4.11 (B.O. 3:173); see above, n. 16.

85. See above, n. 24.

86. See above, n. 75.

87. *De gratia* 6.16 (B.O. 3:173); see above, nn. 18–20.

88. See above, nn. 39 and 40.

89. *De gratia* 1.1–2 (B.O. 3:165–167).

90. *Institutes* 2.3.7 (O.S. 3:281). See above, n. 49.

91. *De gratia* 14.46 (B.O. 3:199).

92. *Institutes* 3.1.1 (O.S. 4:2).

93. See above, n. 74.

94. *De gratia* 6.17 (B.O. 3:179). The theme of love is fully developed elsewhere, particularly in the *Sermons on the Canticles* and in *De diligendo Deo*. These works will receive full attention in chap. 4.

95. For example, in *De diversis* 29.1 (B.O. 6–1:210), Bernard agrees with Gregory the Great that "love itself is a form of knowing [amor ipse notitia est]." See McGinn, "Love, Knowledge, and Mystical Union," 9. See also above, n. 34. The relationship of love and knowledge will be discussed more precisely under the rubric of *unio mystica* in chap. 4.

96. *Institutes* 1.2.2 (O.S. 3:35).

97. *Institutes* 1.2.1 (O.S. 3:35). See above, n. 68.

CHAPTER 3. THE THEOLOGY OF JUSTIFICATION IN BERNARD AND CALVIN

1. It should be noted that in Bernard's mind, the terms are almost interchangeable, as when he speaks of "this consent, in which all merit consists" in *De gratia* 14.46 (B.O. 3:199).

2. *De gratia* 14.46–47 (B.O. 3:199–200). A corroborating passage is found in 13.43 (B.O. 3:197), where Bernard asserts that "salvation is from the Lord, not from free choice [non liberi arbitrii, sed Domini est salus]."

3. Bernard of Clairvaux, *Treatises II: The Steps of Humility and Pride; On Loving God, De diligendo Deo*, 1.1 (B.O. 3:120); 2.3, 4 (B.O. 3:121–22, 123).

4. *SC* 82.7 (B.O. 2:297).

5. *SC* 67.10 (B.O. 2:194–95). See also *SC* 3.4 (B.O. 1:16) and 22.8 (B.O. 1:133–35).

6. *De convers.* 1.2 (B.O. 4:71).

7. Lenten Sermons on the Psalm "He Who Dwells," in *Sermons on Conversion,* Sermon 8.5 (B.O. 4:429). In Sermon 14.1 on the same psalm, Bernard notes that human beings owe their entire existence, body and soul, to God. Speaking of bodily limbs and of reason, he declares, "Surely the Lord your God, the bestower of all these, has made all these things out of nothing. Not only did he make them, but he also knit them together and formed them, and he showed them their functions. How should he not, by every right, demand yet more gratitude?" (B.O. 4:469).

8. *De gratia* 6.16 (B.O. 3:178).

9. *De gratia* 3.7 (B.O. 3:171); 8.24 (B.O. 3:183–84).

10. *SC* 23.15 (B.O. 1:148–49). In the same section, Bernard goes on to say, "Inability to sin constitutes God's righteousness; God's forgiveness constitutes man's" (B.O. 1:149).

11. *De gratia* 8.26 (B.O. 3:184–85).

12. *De gratia* 10.32, 8.26 (B.O. 3:188–89, 185). It has already been noted in chap. 2 that Bernard is not consistent in his use of the terms "image" and "likeness." In the *Sermones super Cantica,* it is the *likeness,* not the image, that remains intact after sin. See above, chap. 2, pp. 27–28.

13. *SC* 85.6 (B.O. 2:311).

14. *SC* 86.3 (B.O. 2:319).

15. *SC* 25.7 (B.O. 1:167).

16. *SC* 22.7 (B.O. 1:133). In another sermon from this series, Bernard states, "It is living faith which obtains for us the most exalted graces." *SC* 32.8 (translation by Halflants, from his Introduction to the Sermons in *On the Song of Songs I*, xviii; B.O. 1:231).

17. *SC* 67.11 (B.O. 2:195) (emphasis added).

18. Sermon 9.6 on Psalm 90 in *Sermons on Conversion* (B.O. 4:439).

19. "Sicut ferrum et testa iungi non possunt, sic et haec duo nequeunt commisceri, si non misceat glutinum Spiritus Dei." Bernard of Clairvaux, *St. Bernard's Sermons for the Seasons and Principal Feasts of the Year*, Third Sermon for Christmas Eve, 1:340 (B.O. 4:218). *Glutinum* here would be more accurately translated as "glue."

20. *SC* 5.8 (B.O. 1:25). I do not think that this language of "direct" communication compromises the notion of the mediation of grace. Rather, it reinforces the idea that it is God who does the mediating, through the inspiration of the Holy Spirit. Thus, faith is itself a gift from God, not something we arrive at by ourselves.

21. See chap. 2, pp. 39–40.

22. *SC* 28.9 (B.O. 1:198). In his Sixth Sermon for Christmas Eve, Bernard makes a similar comment about faith, "Faith may be regarded as an image of eternity, comprehending, as it does, in its most ample bosom, all things past, present, and to come, so that nothing escapes it, nothing is lost to it, nothing lies beyond

its range." Bernard, *Seasons and Feasts*, 1:371 (B.O. 4:237). See also 1:378 (B.O. 4:242).

23. *SC* 8.5 (B.O. 1:38–39). In another passage, Bernard insists that truly to know God is to fear him: "To know him is one thing, to fear him is another; nor does knowledge make a man wise, but the fear that motivates him. Would you then call him wise who is puffed up by his own knowledge? Who but the most witless would consider those wise who, 'although they knew God, did not honor him as God or give thanks to him?' " *SC* 23.14 (B.O. 1:147–48).

24. *SC* 11.2 (B.O. 1:55). This sermon, especially sections 2 and 3, is particularly strong on the theme of contemplating God's goodness. Calvin will later quote it in the *Institutes*. See below, p. 61.

25. *SC* 24.7 (B.O. 1:160).

26. Bernard of Clairvaux, *On the Song of Songs III*, *SC* 51.2 (B.O. 2:84–85). See also *SC* 30.6 (B.O. 1:213).

27. *De gratia* 13.45, 14.51 (B.O. 3:198, 203).

28. Sermon 6.3 on Psalm 90 from *Sermons on Conversion* (B.O. 4:406). See also Sermon 1.1 from the same series, where Bernard states that anyone who "fails to make God his refuge, trusting in his own strength and the abundance of his riches, . . . does not dwell in the shelter of God" (B.O. 4:385).

29. Bernard, *Seasons and Feasts*, First Sermon for the First Sunday after the Octave of Epiphany, 2:37–38 (B.O. 4:316).

30. Sermon 15.5 on Psalm 90 from *Sermons on Conversion* (B.O. 4:479).

31. *SC* 68.6 (B.O. 2:200).

32. See above, n. 1.

33. *De gratia* 14.49–50 (B.O. 3:201–2) (emphasis added). The Latin for the italicized passage (in brackets) suggests that it would be better translated "*with* the assent of our will," rather than "by," which implies that the will does the accomplishing. Earlier in this chapter, Bernard notes that God works three things in us: thinking, willing, and accomplishing the good; "the first he does without us; the second, with us [nobiscum]; and the third, through us" (14.46, B.O. 3:199). Thus, it is really only in the middle stage that "merit" is involved. See Bernard McGinn's Introduction to *De gratia*, in *Treatises III: On Grace and Free Choice; In Praise of the New Knighthood*, 36.

34. *SC* 3.3 (B.O. 1:16).

35. *De diligendo Deo* 6.16 (B.O. 3:133).

36. *De diligendo Deo* 8.23–10.29 (B.O. 3:138–44).

37. *De diligendo Deo* 10.27–29 (B.O. 3:142–44, esp. 144); 15.39 (B.O. 3:152–53). This point is repeated in the Sermons on the Song of Songs, e.g., in *SC* 27.13 (B.O. 1:191).

38. *De diligendo Deo* 10.29–11.31 (B.O. 3:143–46).

39. *De diligendo Deo* 9.26 (B.O. 3:141). Bernard goes on to say in this section that "this love is pleasing because it is free [Amor iste merito gratus, quia gratuitus]." In other words, it is given totally for God's sake and not for our own. In a similar way, we will see Calvin stressing that concern for our own salvation is unbecoming a Christian; he or she should rather be concerned with glorifying God (the service of the neighbor being one expression of this).

40. *SC* 24.7 (B.O. 1:159).

41. *SC* 23.12 (B.O. 1:146).

42. *SC* 9.5 (B.O. 1:45).

43. Bernard, *Seasons and Feasts* 2:56–58 (First Sermon for Septuagesima on John 8:47; B.O. 4:345).

44. Calvin, *Institutes* 3.11.1 (O.S. 4:182). This twofold understanding is echoed in the commentary on Gal. 2:20. See John Calvin, *Calvin's New Testament Commentaries*, vol. 11, *The Epistles of Paul the Apostle to the Galatians, Ephesians, Philippians, and Colossians*, trans. T. H. L. Parker (Grand Rapids: Wm. B. Eerdmans Publishing Co., 1965), 43 (C.O. 50:199).

45. *Institutes* 3.11.2 (O.S. 4:183).

46. *Institutes* 3.11.3 (O.S. 4:184) (emphasis added).

47. *Institutes* 3.11.5 (O.S. 4:185). Calvin goes on, in 3.11.10, to describe this union as *unio mystica*. We shall hold our discussion of this for chapter 5.

48. See fnn. 5 and 9 on 729 and 731 respectively in the McNeill-Battles edition of the *Institutes*.

49. *Institutes* 3.11.6 (O.S. 4:188).

50. *Institutes* 3.11.13–15 (O.S. 4:197–200). Calvin is gentle in his criticism of Augustine (like Bernard, Calvin often finds in him an ally), stating that "Augustine's view, or at any rate his manner of stating it, we must not entirely accept. For even though he admirably deprives man of all credit for righteousness and transfers it to God's grace, he still subsumes grace under sanctification, by which we are reborn in newness of life through the Spirit" (3.11.15, O.S. 4:200).

51. *Institutes* 3.11.16 (O.S. 4:200); *SC* 68.6 (B.O. 2:200, as quoted in the McNeill-Battles edition of the *Institutes*, 3.15.2; O.S. 4:241).

52. *Institutes* 3.11.22 (O.S. 4:206); *SC* 23.15 (B.O. 1:149) and 22.6, 11 (B.O. 1:133, 137). The statement that Bernard's sentences "correspond to" is found in Augustine's *City of God* 19.27, as noted in McNeill-Battles on 752.

53. Jill Raitt, "Calvin's Use of Bernard," 114.

54. *Institutes* 3.11.23 (O.S. 4:206).

55. *De gratia* 8.26 (B.O. 3:184–85). See above, n. 11.

56. *Institutes* 2.16.1 (O.S. 3:482–83); *SC* 15.6 (B.O. 1:86). For some reason, Jill Raitt does not place this quotation under the category of justification by faith, but as a "single instance" referring to the sweet name of Jesus (see "Calvin's Use of Bernard," 99, 120). However, I would argue that it *does* relate to justification. Bernard's context in *SC* 15.6 is certainly the question of salvation in Christ. He begins this section: "How shall we explain the world-wide light of faith, swift and flaming in its progress, except by the preaching of Jesus' name? Is it not by the light of this name that God has called us into his wonderful light, that irradiates our darkness and empowers us to see the light?" (B.O. 1:85–86). The earlier sections of the sermon also name salvation as one of Bernard's concerns.

57. *Institutes* 3.2.7 (O.S. 4:16). A comment from the previous section, *Institutes* 3.2.6 (O.S. 4:15), is also relevant here: "We hold faith to be a knowledge of God's will toward us, perceived from his Word. But the foundation of this is a preconceived conviction of God's truth." See above, chap. 2, p. 38. For a fuller discussion of justification and faith, see Victor A. Shepherd, *The Nature and Function of Faith in the Theology of John Calvin*, 29–34.

58. *Institutes* 3.2.7 (O.S. 4:15).

59. "Fidem a pio affectu nullo modo esse distrahendam." *Institutes* 3.2.8 (O.S. 4:18).

60. *Institutes* 3.2.14 (O.S. 4:24–25).

61. See above, nn. 23 and 24.

62. *Institutes* 3.2.14 (O.S. 4:25). Again, Calvin speaks of "assurance" because, as noted above, he wishes to speak of God's will preeminently in terms of God's "benevolence." See above, n. 58. See also Siktberg, "Mystical Element in Calvin," 72–75.

63. See above, n. 23. In the quoted passage from *SC* 8.5 (B.O. 1:38–39), Bernard speaks of people who know God but refuse to honor him. Their knowledge is paltry compared to the knowledge that comes with faith (and that is rooted in the Holy Spirit): "They were content with the knowledge that gives self-importance, but ignorant of the love that makes the building grow. . . . For if their knowledge had been complete, they would not have been blind to that goodness by which he willed to be born a human being, and to die for their sins."

64. Recall his statement from *Institutes* 1.2.2 (O.S. 3:35): "What help is it . . . to know a God with whom we have nothing to do? Rather, our knowledge should serve first to teach us fear and reverence; secondly, with it as our guide and teacher, we should learn to seek every good from him, and, having received it, to credit it to his account." Calvin's stress on experience is also prominent in *Institutes* 3.20.12 (O.S. 4:311), where he says, "No one can well perceive the power of faith unless he feels it by experience in his heart." See Siktberg, "Mystical Element in Calvin," 86.

65. *Institutes* 3.2.7 (O.S. 4:16) (emphasis added). Bernard spoke in similar terms in the Christmas Eve sermon quoted above, n. 19: "Just as iron and clay cannot be welded together, so it is equally impossible to conjoin so mighty a force of faith with the weakness and inconstancy of the human heart, without the solder [glutinum] of the Holy Spirit." See also *Institutes* 3.1.1 and esp. 3.1.4, where Calvin states that "faith is the principal work of the Holy Spirit [Verum quia fides praecipuum est eius (i.e., the Spirit's) opus]" (O.S. 4:5). William Siktberg speaks of the Holy Spirit as "the means whereby a man can be united with God; thus it is the ontological aspect of the mystical element in Calvin." In turn, he speaks of repentance and faith as the "psychological" mystical element. Siktberg, "Mystical Element in Calvin," 53, 59–82. The only problem with this is that Siktberg himself later notes that Calvin sometimes speaks of faith as standing "beyond the psychological experience of repentance and remission of sins" (Siktberg, 71), particularly when he is stressing the dogmatic point that faith produces repentance. See below, n. 107.

66. John Calvin, *The First Epistle of Paul the Apostle to the Corinthians*, trans. John W. Fraser, *Calvin's New Testament Commentaries*, vol. 9 (Grand Rapids: Wm. B. Eerdmans Publishing Co., 1960), 23–24 (C.O. 49:312–13). See above, n. 20. See also Shepherd, *Nature and Function of Faith in the Theology of Calvin*, 5–28.

67. *Institutes* 2.2.4 (O.S. 3:246–47); *De gratia* 3.6 (B.O. 3:170). See chap. 2, n. 44.

68. *Institutes* 2.3.11 (O.S. 3:287). Here Calvin accepts Augustine's "moderated" understanding of this distinction: "God by co-operating perfects that which by operating he has begun. It is the same grace but with its name changed to fit the different mode of its effect." We will see below that Calvin finds Bernard's use of the term also acceptable.

69. Chap. 2, n. 88; *De gratia* 1.1–2 (B.O. 3:165–67); see also 14.46 (B.O. 3:199).

70. *Institutes* 3.11.7 (O.S. 4:188).

71. O.S. 4:35–36. See *Seasons and Feasts* 2:419–26 (B.O. 5:390–94).

72. Raitt, "Calvin's Use of Bernard," 111–12. Her analysis on these pages is the basis for my comments.

73. O.S. 4:35.

74. This recalls another direct quote from Bernard that we discussed above (n. 51), where Calvin stresses turning to the memory of God's goodness rather than dwelling on our own sins. See Siktberg, "Mystical Element in Calvin," 82. While Bernard is not quoted inappropriately to his context in this instance, he would not agree with Calvin that faith brings certitude of election. See above, n. 43.

75. O.S. 4:218–19. The quotation is from *In ded. eccl.* 5.6 (*Seasons and Feasts* 2:424, B.O. 5:393). See Raitt, "Calvin's Use of Bernard," 112.

76. *Institutes* 3.2.41 (O.S. 4:52) (emphasis added); see B.O. 5:13–16.

77. Raitt, "Calvin's Use of Bernard," 113. I must note here that Calvin himself does not say that the foundation of faith is election, but rather "the freely given promise in Christ." See *Institutes* 3.2.7 (O.S. 4:16) and n. 57 above.

78. *Institutes* 3.15.1 (O.S. 4:240).

79. *Institutes* 3.15.2 (O.S. 4:240).

80. *Institutes* 3.15.2 (O.S. 4:241); *SC* 68.6 (B.O. 2:200). Earlier, in 3.14.21 (O.S. 4:238–39), he allows works to be seen as "inferior causes" (*causas inferiores*) in the sense that "those whom the Lord has destined by his mercy for the inheritance of eternal life he leads into possession of it, according to his ordinary dispensation, by means of good works. What goes before in the order of dispensation he calls the cause of what comes after. In this way he sometimes derives eternal life from works, not intending it to be ascribed to them." See Raitt, "Calvin's Use of Bernard," 115.

81. Again, see Raitt, "Calvin's Use of Bernard," 115–16. In this connection, Raitt recalls Calvin's doctrine of "double acceptance," which is developed in *Institutes* 3.17.5 (O.S. 4:257). We are first accepted through the "grace of adoption," but are "approved of God also in respect of works." Calvin explains this in a passage that originally appeared in the 1539 edition but is carefully emended in 1559: "But we must always remember that God 'accepts' believers by reason of works only because he is their source and graciously, by way of adding to his liberality, deigns also to show 'acceptance' toward the good works he has himself bestowed" (also in 3.17.5). Raitt goes on to quote a passage from 3.17.10 (O.S. 4:263), "Accordingly, we can deservedly [merito] say that by faith alone not only we ourselves but our works as well are justified." The Latin here reads, "Ita *merito* dicere possumus, sola fide non tantum nos sed opera etiam nostra iustificari" (emphasis added). I do not understand why Raitt calls attention to the word *merito* here, because it seems to me that in this context Calvin is not making a theological statement about merit per se. *Merito* can indeed have this meaning ("deservedly, as one deserves"), but the context suggests the other meaning: "with good cause, as a natural consequence" (these definitions are from the *Oxford Latin Dictionary* [Oxford, 1982], 1103). I would amend the translation to read, "Therefore we can justifiably say . . ."

82. *Institutes* 3.15.3 (O.S. 4:241). The Latin for "reward" here is *remunerationem*. When Calvin later speaks of "reward" in 3.18.1–4, the Latin term is *merces*. The latter term is more specific, bearing the meaning of "a payment for services rendered" (*Oxford Latin Dictionary*, 1101); the connotation here is of a "contractual" arrangement. The former term, from *remunero*, "to pay out (what is owed); pay back" (*Oxford Latin Dictionary*, 1615), often has the more general connotation of "recompense." Calvin appears to use the terms interchangeably.

83. *Institutes* 3.15.3 (O.S. 4:241).

84. See the above section "The Question of Merit," esp. n. 27.

85. *Institutes* 3.15.7 (O.S. 4:246). Translation is from McNeill-Battles except that I have changed the term "free will" to "free choice." The Latin here is *liberum arbitrium;* as already noted (chap. 2, n. 43), it is improperly translated in the McNeill-Battles edition.

86. *De gratia* 1.2 (B.O. 3:167) and 14.46 (B.O. 3:199). See chap. 2, n. 12, and above, n. 1. It bears repeating here that Bernard does not see consent as "its own doing." He explicitly states that even our yes to grace is an effect of grace. See *De gratia* 14.46 (B.O. 3:199); chap. 2, p. 39, n. 91.

87. See chap. 2, n. 44. To summarize: Calvin accuses Bernard of "obscurity" and "subtlety" in defining free choice as consent. This criticism first appeared in the 1539 edition of the *Institutes* (one of the two explicit disagreements with Bernard that appear in this edition), and was allowed to stand in the later editions. *Institutes* 2.2.4 (O.S. 3:246); *De gratia* 3.7 (B.O. 3:171), 14.46 (B.O. 3:199). It is also important to note that Calvin does not regard all the scholastics as equally odious—he speaks at times of the "sounder schoolmen [saniores scholasticos]," e.g., in *Institutes* 3.14.11 (O.S. 4:230).

88. *Institutes* 3.22.1 (O.S. 4:379–81).

89. *Institutes* 3.22.3 (O.S. 4:382).

90. *Institutes* 2.17.3 (O.S. 3:511). See also 2.17.6 (O.S. 3:514–15).

91. See *Institutes* 3.5.3 (O.S. 4:135) and 3.20.21 (O.S. 4:326).

92. See above, p. 47 (nn. 29 and 31).

93. The passages are from *SC* 61.3, 61.5, 13.4, 68.6 (B.O. 2:150, 2:151, 1:71, 2:200 [two citations]). The single passage from Sermon 15 on Psalm 90 is in 15.5 (B.O. 4:479), where Bernard says, "Man's whole merit consists in placing all his hope in him who has saved the whole man [Hoc enim totum hominis meritum, si totam spem suam ponat in eo, qui totum hominem salvum facit]." The references to *SC* 61.3 and *Qui Habitat* 15.5 were added in 1543; the rest were added in 1559.

94. Raitt, "Calvin's Use of Bernard," 114.

95. *Institutes* 3.12.3 (O.S. 4:211); Raitt, "Calvin's Use of Bernard," 115. It is worth recalling here that Calvin himself does use the term "reward," especially in *Institutes* 3.18.1–4 (O.S. 4:270–74); but again, he speaks of reward as "inheritance," that is, as the effect of our adoption by grace, not of our own works. See above, n. 82.

96. *Institutes* 3.12.8 (O.S. 4:215); *SC* 13.5 (B.O. 1:72).

97. *SC* 13.2 (B.O. 1:69).

98. Raitt, "Calvin's Use of Bernard," 116.

99. *SC* 3.3 (B.O. 1:16). See above, n. 34.

100. *Institutes* 3.16.1 (O.S. 4:249).

101. *Institutes* 3.14.11 (O.S. 4:230).

102. See above, p. 50, nn. 45 and 46.

103. *Institutes* 3.1.4 (O.S. 4:6). A more detailed example is found in 3.14.9 (O.S. 4:228): "We confess that while through the intercession of Christ's righteousness God reconciles us to himself, and by free remission of sins accounts us righteous, his beneficence is at the same time joined with such a mercy that through his Holy Spirit he dwells in us and by his power the lusts of our flesh are each day more and more mortified; we are indeed sanctified, that is, consecrated to the Lord in true purity of life, with our hearts formed to obedience to the law." Note that the Holy Spirit is the source of sanctification. Calvin often refers to the Spirit as the "Spirit of sanctification," e.g., in *Institutes* 2.2.16 (O.S. 3:259) and 2.7.10 (O.S. 3:336).

104. In *Institutes* 3.2.8 (O.S. 4:18), Calvin notes that no one can truly know Christ "without at the same time apprehending the sanctification of the Spirit."

105. *Institutes* 3.3.5 (O.S. 4:60).

106. *Institutes* 3.3.2 (O.S. 4:56). In this connection Calvin criticizes both the Anabaptists and the Jesuits, for what he takes to be their limiting "to a paltry few days a repentance that for the Christian man ought to extend throughout his life" (ibid., O.S. 4:57) This reference to repentance as lifelong is especially pertinent in relation to Bernard. See above, "Justification and Sanctification," pp. 48ff.

107. Calvin, *John 1–10*, 19 (C.O. 47:12–13). See chap. 2, n. 64. William Siktberg makes an interesting comment on the relationship of faith and repentance, "Calvin often confuses the relation of faith and repentance. When he deals with the relation from a dogmatic point of view, he says that faith produces repentance [*Institutes* 3.3.1 (O.S. 4:55)]. In this connection, faith stands beyond the psychological experience of repentance and remission of sins. But Calvin also uses faith in a psychological way, equating it with the acceptance of forgiveness which can be experienced [*Institutes* 3.20.11 (O.S. 4:310)]." Siktberg, "Mystical Element in Calvin," 70–71. I do not think that Calvin is "confused," but the point is well taken that he uses the word *fides* in more than one sense.

108. *Institutes* 3.14.4 (O.S. 4:223). See also 3.3.9 (O.S. 4:63), 3.3.20 (O.S. 4:78), and 3.6.2 (O.S. 4:147).

109. John Calvin, Preface to Commentary on Psalms, in *Calvin: Commentaries*, 52 (C.O. 31:21 [Latin]–22 [French]). I connect conversion with justification on the basis of passages like *Institutes* 2.3.6, where Calvin says, "In man's conversion what belongs to his primal nature remains entire. I also say that it is created anew; not meaning that the will now begins to exist, but that it is changed from an evil to a good will. I affirm that this is *wholly God's doing*" (O.S. 3:280). See chap. 2, n. 62.

110. *Institutes* 3.3.9 (O.S. 4:63–65). See also 3.3.10 (O.S. 4:65), 3.3.20 (O.S. 4:78), 3.6.5 (O.S. 4:150), and 3.19.2 (O.S. 4:283). See Siktberg, "Mystical Element in Calvin," 69. This theme also appears in the Short Treatise on the Lord's Supper, where Calvin remarks, "Now true repentance is firm and constant; therefore it makes us battle against the evil which is within us, not for a day or a week, but without end or intermission." John Calvin, *Calvin: Theological Treatises*, 152 (C.O. 5:445).

111. *De diligendo Deo* 10.27–11.31 (B.O. 3:142–46). See above, nn. 37 and 38.

112. *Institutes* 3.7.5 (O.S. 4:156). "Quod si ita demum sanctificantur nobis Dei dona postquam ipsi authori manu nostra ea dedicavimus: impurum esse abusum constat qui non eiusmodi dedicationem redoleat." The connotation of *dedico* here appears to be "attribute," since in this section Calvin explicitly rejects the notion that our works can "enrich" God: "Yet you wish to strive in vain to enrich the Lord by sharing your possessions; since, then, your generosity cannot extend to him, you must, as the prophet says, practice it toward the saints on earth" (Ibid.).

113. *De diligendo Deo* 9.26 (B.O. 3:141). See above, n. 39. On the four degrees of love, see 8.23–10.29 (B.O. 3:138–144).

114. *Reply to Sadolet*, in *Calvin: Theological Treatises*, 228 (C.O. 5:391–92).

115. *Institutes* 3.3.15 (O.S. 4:72), quoting SC 11.2 (B.O. 1:55). Calvin makes a similar point about turning to the memory of God's goodness in 3.11.16 (O.S. 4:200) and 3.15.2 (O.S. 4:241). In the second of these instances, he quotes Bernard's SC 68.6 (see above, n. 51). However, the context in both of these passages is

different: turning to God is contrasted not with repentance but with trust in our own works.

116. Raitt, "Calvin's Use of Bernard," 114.

117. I decided to include election in this section rather than in "Justification and the Primacy of Grace," since Calvin himself speaks of election in relation to both justification and sanctification. For example, he says that "election has as its goal holiness of life"; indeed, all our good endeavors *arise* from election. *Institutes* 3.23.12 (O.S. 4:406).

118. *Institutes* 3.21.5 (O.S. 4:374). See also 3.21.1 (O.S. 4:369).

119. *Institutes* 3.21.7 (O.S. 4:377). Later, in 4.1.8 (O.S. 5:13), Calvin speaks on the question of whether we can tell if someone *else* is among the elect. Although this is ultimately part of God's secret plan, Calvin suggests that God, knowing that it would be "of some value" for us to know who are among the elect, has substituted for the "assurance of faith . . . a certain charitable judgment whereby we recognize as members of the church those who, by confession of faith, by example of life, and by partaking of the sacraments, profess the same God and Christ with us." Thus, we have the "assurance of faith" about our own election (which is why we should not be preoccupied with it), and a "charitable judgment" with respect to the election of others.

120. See above, p. 49, n. 43.

121. Bernard, *SC* 24.7 (B.O. 1:159). See above, n. 40.

122. *Institutes* 3.21.1 (emphasis added) (O.S. 4:370); *SC* 78.4 (B.O. 2:269).

123. Raitt, "Calvin's Use of Bernard," 117. See *SC* 78.1–5 (B.O. 2:266–69).

124. *Institutes* 3.22.10 (O.S. 4:391–92); Bernard, Epistle 107.4–5 (B.O. 7:270–71). Raitt, "Calvin's Use of Bernard," 117.

125. *Institutes* 3.24.4 (O.S. 4:415); Bernard, *SC* 23.15, 16 (B.O. 1:148, 149). See above, n. 52.

126. Raitt is actually mistaken in seeing *SC* 23.15–16 as referring to the "ultimate" mystical experience. Bernard is not speaking here of the union of lovers (which to Bernard *is* the ultimate mystical experience), but of another kind of experience of God, that of the "friends" or "companions" of the divine King (this is especially clear in 23.16). I am indebted to Bernard McGinn for this clarification.

127. Raitt, "Calvin's Use of Bernard," 117–18. It is worth recalling here that Bernard denies absolute certitude of election in any case. See above, n. 43.

128. Thus, Stanford Reid's observation about Calvin's "mystical" conception of knowledge of God would appear to be on the mark. See chap. 1, p. 13, n. 59; Reid, "Bernard of Clairvaux in the Thought of Calvin," 143–44. However, Reid sees the similarity in that knowledge of God is by grace through faith. I would see the key similarity precisely in the knowledge being *experiential*.

CHAPTER 4. BERNARD OF CLAIRVAUX
ON MYSTICAL UNION

1. In the case of the second disagreement, Calvin is mistaken in thinking that Bernard holds to a natural ability to seek the good. This was clearly explained by Jill Raitt, in "Calvin's Use of Bernard," 105. See above, chap. 2, nn. 44, 46–47, and 49.

2. We have already covered most of Calvin's direct citations of Bernard in the *Institutes*. There are also three instances where Calvin refers to Bernard in his scripture commentaries, but none of these is really pertinent to our discussion here. The one citation that has any relevance at all is in his commentary on 1 Cor. 3:15, where he includes Bernard among a group of medieval theologians "whose purpose it was to build on Christ, but who, however, often turned away from the right method of building." *Commentary on First Corinthians*, trans. Fraser, 77–78 (C.O. 49:357). See chap. 3, n. 66. This commentary is dated 1546, after the third edition of the *Institutes* was published (1543). Perhaps Calvin was recalling the disagreements with Bernard that appeared in the 1539 *Institutes* (and were not removed in the later editions) in making this comment. Nevertheless, it seems to me odd that Calvin would speak negatively about Bernard in 1546, considering that in all editions of the *Institutes* after 1539, not one unfavorable word is added about Bernard.

3. Gerson, *Selections*, 64–65. See chap. 1, n. 49.

4. M. Corneille Halflants, Introduction to Bernard, *On the Song of Songs I*, xxiv.

5. Bernard, *SC* 45.8 (B.O. 2:54). Bernard actually makes a distinction between active love, which relates us to our neighbor, and contemplative love, in which the soul relates directly to God. See especially *SC* 50 (B.O. 2:78–83). This will be discussed further below. However, since I shall use the word "contemplation" fairly frequently, I would like briefly to define it here. Like "mysticism," contemplation can be a slippery term. I think Evelyn Underhill captures its essence in speaking of it as "those developed states of introversion in which the mystic attains somewhat: the results and rewards of the discipline of Recollection and Quiet." Contemplation involves the "turning of our attention from that crisp and definite world of multiplicity" to "an experience of the All, and this experience seems . . . to be *given* rather than attained." Underhill, *Mysticism*, 328, 330, 333. Thus, contemplation has to do with a total centering of one's attention on God. As we shall see, in Bernard this is not something that happens instead of, or that takes the place of, active love; indeed, the two kinds of love are complementary. Furthermore, both types of love are gifts of grace.

6. See, for example, *SC* 69.7 (B.O. 2:206), where Bernard says, "The love of God gives birth to the love of the soul for God, and his surpassing affection fills the soul with affection, and his concern evokes compassion."

7. *SC* 14.6 (B.O. 1:79). This idea is also recalled by Bernard in *De diligendo Deo* 7.22 (B.O. 3:137): "O Lord, you are so good to the soul who seeks you, what must you be to the one who finds you? More wonderful still, no one can seek you unless he has already found you."

8. In *SC* 13.3 (B.O. 1:70), Bernard says, "You are indeed a faithful servant if you do not try to grasp for yourself the manifold glory of God, which while not coming from you, nevertheless passes through you." See also *SC* 49.3, 62.4 (B.O. 2:75, 157–58).

9. *SC* 46.5 (B.O. 2:58).

10. *SC* 67.10 (B.O. 2:195). See chap. 3, n. 5. On Ritschl, see chap. 1, n. 15.

11. *De diligendo Deo* 8.23–10.29 (B.O. 3:138–44). Bernard uses the word "amor" for love until 12.34, at which point he uses "caritas" until the end of the treatise. There are other schemas used by Bernard for describing the ascent to union: most notably in *De diversis* 101 (B.O. 6–1:368) and in *De gradibus humilitatis et superbiae* 3–27 (B.O. 3:18–37). These schemata are not perfectly harmonious with each other,

but we have already seen that Bernard is willing to tolerate a variety of interpretations in diverse works of his own. See the discussion on "image" and "likeness" in chap. 2, esp. nn. 5 and 30; also McGinn, "Love, Knowledge, and Mystical Union," 9, esp. n. 7.

12. *De diligendo Deo* 8.25 (B.O. 3:139), 9.26 (B.O. 3:141). Although Bernard characterizes this love as "carnal," he sees it as a necessary step in the process. In a similar way, we find him speaking positively in the *Sermones super Cantica* of a carnal love of Christ, i.e., a love of his humanity. This will be discussed further below.

13. *De diligendo Deo* 9.26 (B.O. 3:140).

14. *De diligendo Deo* 9.26 (B.O. 3:141). See chap. 3, n. 39.

15. *De diligendo Deo* 15.39 (B.O. 3:152–53); 10.27–29 (B.O. 3:142–44, esp. 144). See chap. 3, n. 37. The "fleeting" or "momentary" character of mystical experience will be commented on further below.

16. *De diligendo Deo* 10.29–11.31 (B.O. 3:143–46). See chap. 3, n. 38.

17. *De diligendo Deo* 10.28 (B.O. 3:143).

18. An excellent analysis of this text appears in Gilson, *Théologie mystique*, 144–45. Gilson notes Bernard's careful use of language:

> The drop of water? "Deficere a se tota *videtur*"; It seems to, but we know well that it has not, ceased to exist, even if it is infinitely diluted. The inflamed iron? "Igni *simillimum* fit"; it becomes as similar to fire as possible, but it does not become fire, indeed, it must not become fire, in order that it may become like it. The air illuminated by the sun? It so absorbs its light, "ut non tam illuminatus, quam ipsum lumen esse *videatur*." Here again, it is only an appearance, the transfiguration of an indestructible substance into the glorious form that it would henceforth display. Thus, St. Bernard never spoke of an annihilation of the creature, but of a transformation.

(Translation from Gilson is my own.) His argument is further nuanced on 146–50.

19. *SC* 62.5 (B.O. 2:158). Significant here is Bernard's use of the term *pia* (pius). One of Calvin's favorite terms, *pietas*, has the same Latin root. The theme of conformity to God's will is also found in other writings of Bernard, such as his Sermons for the Liturgical Year. In his Second Sermon for Christmas Eve, he comments that "whilst we live here below, it is possible for us to be with the Lord, viz., by being conformed to His will, although He may not be with us so as to consent to our desires." Bernard, *Seasons and Feasts*, 1:321 (B.O. 4:206). We have already seen the stress on will in *De gratia* (see chap. 2, nn. 33, 94).

20. *SC* 31.6 (B.O. 1:223).

21. *SC* 71.8 (B.O. 2:220).

22. *SC* 61.1 (B.O. 2:148).

23. *SC* 26.5 (B.O. 1:173). Other examples of *unus spiritus* can be found in *SC* 2.2 (B.O. 1:9), 3.5 (B.O. 1:17), 8.9 (B.O. 1:41), 59.2 (B.O. 2:136), and 83.3 (B.O. 2:299).

24. *De diligendo Deo* 10.28 (B.O. 3:143), translation mine. In *SC*, see, for example, 67.10. See also von Ivánka, "La structure de l'âme," 208.

25. Ritschl, *Justification and Reconciliation*, 3:593–94. See above, chap. 1, n. 17.

26. *SC* 43.1 (B.O. 2:41). I believe that this last sentence would be better translated, "For a moment the *designation* of reverence has been changed into the

language of friendship; and he who was far away is quickly brought close" (emphasis mine). Bernard's mention of God's humility in this passage is also part of the key to his defense, as will be explained shortly. Another example of the language of equality is found in *SC* 45.1 (B.O. 2:50): "The master is gone, the king has disappeared, dignity is put off, reverence is laid aside, only the Beloved is present. . . . And just as Moses once spoke to God as a friend to a friend and God answered him, so now the Word and the soul converse with mutual enjoyment, like two friends [ac si inter duos vicinos]." But again, note the Latin "as if."

27. *SC* 64.9 (B.O. 2:171) (emphasis added).

28. *SC* 52.2 (B.O. 2:91).

29. *SC* 67.8 (B.O. 2:193) (emphasis added). Another example is found in *SC* 68.1 (B.O. 2:196), where he says, "Let us rejoice that this glory is ours; we are they to whom God inclines. But how unequal a partnership! [Quanta tamen disparitas!]" Bernard is emphatic that only Christ is equal with God; see, for example, *SC* 69.4 (B.O. 2:204).

30. *SC* 83.6 (B.O. 2:302).

31. Ozment, *Homo Spiritualis*, 83; Gerson, *Selections*, 50–51. See chap. 1, n. 51.

32. *SC* 81.2 (B.O. 2:285).

33. See above, nn. 5–10. The question of "likeness" and "unlikeness" is especially stressed in *SC* 81 and 82.

34. See chap. 2, p. 28, nn. 28–30; and pp. 35–39.

35. *SC* 31.2 (B.O. 1:220). Note again Bernard's belief that it is only in the final resurrection that one will achieve a permanent affective union with God.

36. *SC* 50.6 (B.O. 2:82).

37. *SC* 50.2 (B.O. 2:79). In this particular quote, Bernard is referring specifically to love as *affectus*, but in the same section he declares that the same holds true for active love.

38. *SC* 23.15 (B.O. 1:148). Another example is found in *SC* 32.2 (B.O. 1:227): "For when after vigils and prayers and a great shower of tears he who was sought presents himself, suddenly he is gone again, just when we think we hold him fast." The most famous example is found in *SC* 74:5–6 (B.O. 2:242–43), where Bernard speaks at greater length of his own experience.

39. *SC* 32.2 (B.O. 1:227).

40. *SC* 3.1 (B.O. 1:14).

41. *SC* 32.8 (B.O. 1:231), translated by Halflants, in his Introduction to *On the Song of Songs I*, xviii. For this paragraph I am especially indebted to Halflants's insights, xvii–xxv.

42. *SC* 28.9 (B.O. 1:198) (emphasis added); see also *SC* 53.2 (B.O. 2:96). The kind of knowledge that accompanies contemplation will be discussed further below.

43. *SC* 84.7 (B.O. 2:306). The Latin here reads, "Credant quod non experiuntur, ut fructum quandoque experientiae, fidei merito consequantur." I would translate this slightly differently, "Let those who do not have such an experience believe, so that by the merit of their faith they will reap the fruit of experience."

44. See above, n. 17. As Bernard McGinn points out, these metaphors were already part of the currency of philosophical and theological discussions "for more than a millennium before Bernard wrote." "Love, Knowledge, and Mystical Union," 8; see n. 4 on p. 9 of this article for a listing of studies on these comparisons.

45. *SC* 2.3 (B.O. 1:10). Bernard goes on to quote Eph. 2:14 in this connection: "he has made the two into one." Later in the sermon (*SC* 2.7, B.O. 1:12), he relates this

to the incarnation of Christ, defining the kiss as "the mystery of the incarnate Word." The context here is Christ's relationship to the church. See James Wimsatt, "St. Bernard, the Canticle of Canticles, and Mystical Poetry," in *An Introduction to the Medieval Mystics of Europe*, ed. Paul Szarmach, 79.

46. *SC* 23.3–4 (garden, B.O. 1:140–41), 46.5 (marriage bed, B.O. 2:58). See above, n. 9.

47. See chap. 3, nn. 22–24.

48. *SC* 67.3 (B.O. 2:190): ". . . affectus locutus est, non intellectus, et ideo non ad intellectum." Notice here the use of the term *affectus*. Michael Casey has done an excellent study of this term as it appears in the *Sermones super Cantica*. He notes that "Bernard often simply identifies the affect with the will." Michael Casey, *Athirst for God: Spiritual Desire in Bernard of Clairvaux's Sermons on the Song of Songs*, 101. For example, in his *Sermo in ascensione Domini* 3.2, Bernard says, "affectus, id est voluntas" (B.O. 5:135). Casey points out that *affectus* "can cover the whole field of varied manifestations of the affective nature and is equally capable of expressing the highest act of will. . . . Bernard used *affectus* equally for the fundamental dynamic principle within the human being and for the range of emotions and activities in which this underlying reality finds expression." *Athirst for God*, 97–98. See also Hiss, *Die Anthropologie Bernhards von Clairvaux*, 98–105; and von Ivánka, "La structure de l'âme," 204. Thus, for our purposes, *affectus* can be seen as included under the faculty of the will.

49. *SC* 49.4 (B.O. 2:75).

50. *SC* 8.9 (B.O. 1:41): "Felix tamen osculum, per quod non solum agnoscitur Deus, sed diligitur Pater, qui nequaquam plene cognoscitur, nisi cum perfecte diligitur."

51. Gregory's statement is found in *Homilia in Evangelia* 27. Bernard's citation is in his *De diversis* 29.1 (B.O. 6–1:210). See McGinn, "Love, Knowledge, and Mystical Union," 9, esp. n. 8.

52. In *SC* 68.1 (B.O. 2:196), Bernard says, "The Bridegroom is our God [Deus], and we, I say in all humility, are the Bride." Actually, the Bride can refer either to the church in general or to the individual soul. More will be said on this below.

53. Most of the sermons could serve as an example here. Bernard often ends with a reference to "the Bridegroom of the Church, our Lord Jesus Christ, who is God, blessed for ever. Amen." *SC* 37.7 (B.O. 2:14).

54. *De gratia* 8.26 (B.O. 3:184–85). See chap. 3, n. 11.

55. *De gratia* 10.32, 8.26 (B.O. 3:188–89, 185). See chap. 3, n. 12.

56. *De diligendo Deo* 3.7 (B.O. 3:124). Here Bernard quotes the church as saying, "Vulnerata caritate ego sum."

57. *SC* 13.1 (B.O. 1:68). Bernard goes on in this same section to say, "If you can credit yourself with wisdom or with virtue, realize that the credit is due rather to Christ, who is the Power and the Wisdom of God." In *SC* 48.6 (B.O. 2:70), Bernard makes a similar point, describing Christ as the source of all refreshment and nourishment.

58. *SC* 21.3 (B.O. 1:124). This theme runs through both *SC* 21 and 22. Notable passages are found in 21.1 (B.O. 1:121–22) and 22.5 (B.O. 1:132). At times, Bernard also speaks of the Holy Spirit in connection with being "drawn to God." For example, in *SC* 21.4 (B.O. 1:124), he says: " 'The course of man is not in his control.' It rather depends on the guidance of the Spirit who sets the pace as he pleases,

sometimes torpidly, sometimes blithely, teaching him to forget the past and to strain ahead for what is still to come."

59. *SC* 83.3 (B.O. 2:299–300).

60. In *SC* 53.3 (B.O. 2:97–98), Bernard reflects on the significance of the "mountains and hills" of Canticle 2:8. He suggests a physical image of a large man literally leaping over towering hills in search of his "absent girl-friend." He then comments, "Surely it will not do to fabricate physical images of this kind, especially when treating of this spiritual Song; and it is certainly not legitimate for us who recall reading in the Gospel that 'God is a spirit and those who worship him must worship in spirit.' " See also *SC* 63.1 (B.O. 2:161), where he rejects a literal interpretation of "catching the little foxes" in Canticle 2:15: "We must totally reject in our interpretation the common and familiar meaning of the text as absurd and insipid and clearly unworthy of inclusion in holy and authentic Scripture."

61. *SC* 20.6 (B.O. 1:118).

62. Wimsatt, "St. Bernard, the Canticle of Canticles, and Mystical Poetry," 81.

63. See above, n. 58.

64. *SC* 69.2 (B.O. 2:203)

65. *SC* 8.2–3 (B.O. 1:37) (emphasis added). Earlier, we saw that Bernard refers the kiss to the incarnation of Christ. Here, when speaking of the individual soul, the reference is to the Holy Spirit. See Wimsatt, "St. Bernard, the Canticle of Canticles, and Mystical Poetry," 79. The relationship between the church and the individual believer will be treated further below.

66. *SC* 8.4 (B.O. 1:38).

67. *SC* 8.5 (B.O. 1:38).

68. *De gradibus* 3.6 (B.O. 3:20).

69. *De gradibus* 6.19–7.20 (B.O. 3:30–31). Notice the difference here from *SC* 69.2 (n. 59 above), where Bernard correlates love with the Father rather than the Spirit.

70. *De gradibus* 7.20 (B.O. 3:31).

71. See chap. 1, n. 54.

72. *SC* 68.4 (B.O. 2:198). See also *SC* 57.3 (B.O. 2:120–21), where Bernard comments on Canticle 2:10 ("Arise, make haste, my love, my dove, my beautiful one") by saying, "These words are not so applied to the Church as to exclude any one of us, who together are the Church, from a share in its blessings. For in this respect we are all, universally and without distinction, called to possess the blessings as our heritage." Again, notice that Bernard speaks of a "share" in God's blessings. Not everyone shares in the same way, even among those who are contemplatives. For example, in *SC* 23.9 (B.O. 1:145), Bernard remarks, "All do not experience the delight of the Bridegroom's private visit in the same room, the Father has different arrangements for each."

73. *SC* 62.6 (B.O. 2:159). Note that Bernard goes on to say that such an experience is not necessary; one always has recourse to Jesus, "If . . . this is not possible to someone, let him place before him Jesus and him crucified." This is consistent with what was noted above about faith (see nn. 39–41).

74. *SC* 32.3 (B.O. 1:227). Bernard goes on in this section of the sermon (B.O. 1:227–28) to discuss the case of a person who "smarts at the remembrance of past deeds" and speaks to God "in bitterness of soul," or who is still "perilously tempted." Such a person, Bernard says, "needs a physician, not a bridegroom; hence kisses and embraces are not for him, but only oil and ointments, remedies

for his wounds." In other words, with such a person, Christ would share the grace of healing and forgiveness rather than of contemplation.

75. *SC* 46.2 (B.O. 2:56): "Et in Ecclesia quidem 'lectum' in quo quiescitur, claustra existimo esse et monasteria, in quibus quiete a curis vivitur saeculi et sollicitudinibus vitae."

76. *De conversione* 21.37 (B.O. 4:113). See Introduction to *Sermons on Conversion*, 13, 20.

77. *De gradibus*, B.O. 3:13–14: "Duo iste primi humilitatis gradus extra claustrum monasterii ascendendi sunt. . . . Duo iste ultimi superbiae gradus intra claustrum descendi non possunt." (The English translation in *Treatises II* places this "table of contents" between the *Retractio* and the Preface.) It is interesting to note that Bernard does not believe that the lowest two steps of pride are even possible outside of the monastery.

78. *SC* 64.2 (B.O. 2:167). Bernard is even suspicious of monks being "drawn from their monasteries by the attraction of the solitary life," as he explains in 64.4 (B.O. 2:168).

79. Introduction to *Sermons on Conversion*, 20.

80. See above, nn. 41–43, 73.

81. *SC* 60.2 (B.O. 2:142).

82. See chap. 1, p. 4, esp. n. 16.

83. Ritschl, *Justification and Reconciliation*, 3:112. See chap. 1, n. 18.

84. Kolfhaus, *Christusgemeinschaft bei Johannes Calvin*, 133. See chap. 1, n. 25.

85. *SC* 61.2 (B.O. 2:149). See also *SC* 69.1 (B.O. 2:201–2), and Bernard's Second Sermon for the First Sunday after Epiphany, for which the gospel text was John 2:3–7. Bernard states that the changing of water into wine signifies that "we are all invited to the spiritual nuptials in which Christ our Lord is the Bridegroom." In answer to the question, Who is the Bride? Bernard says, "We ourselves, my brethren, are the bride, incredible though it may seem to you; we are all, collectively, one same Bride of the one Christ, and, moreover, our several souls are, so to speak, several Brides." *Seasons and Feasts* 2:44 (B.O. 4:320).

86. *SC* 12.11 (B.O. 1:67). See also *SC* 68.3 (B.O. 2:198), where Bernard asks, "What is the Bride but the congregation of the righteous? What is she but the generation of those who seek the face of the bridegroom?"

87. Wimsatt, "St. Bernard, the Canticle of Canticles, and Mystical Poetry," 79. See above, n. 65.

88. Jean Leclercq, "St. Bernard on the Church," 274.

89. See, for example, *SC* 68.2 (B.O. 2:197), where Bernard speaks of God revealing "the depth of his love for the Church of the Saints" (i.e., the elect); and *De diligendo Deo* 15.40 (B.O. 3:153), where he refers to the members of the church being "caught in charity's net [sagena caritatis]." On the love of the Bride (understood as church) for Christ, see especially *SC* 21 (B.O. 1:121–29). See Leclercq, "Bernard on the Church," 274–75, esp. nn. 2–6.

90. Leclercq, "Bernard on the Church," 275.

91. "Singuli nos, qui simul Ecclesia sumus." *SC* 57.3 (B.O. 2:121). Translation by Leclercq in "Bernard on the Church," 275.

92. Leclercq, "Bernard on the Church," 275.

93. *SC* 50.2 (B.O. 2:79): "Est caritas in actu, est in affectu."

94. *SC* 50.5 (B.O. 2:80–81). In *SC* 52.7 (B.O. 2:95), Bernard comments on his own being "intruded upon" by the monks, "Let me not seek my own advantage; it is

what is useful not to me but to many that I shall judge useful to myself." See also *SC* 58.1 (B.O. 2:127).

95. *SC* 50.6 (B.O. 2:81). On this theme of the priority of service, see the excellent Introduction to *On the Song of Songs III* by Emero Stiegman, esp. p. ix.

96. *SC* 50.6 (B.O. 2:82); *SC* 47.4 (B.O. 2:64).

97. *SC* 12.8 (B.O. 1:65–66).

98. *SC* 57.9 (B.O. 2:124). In *SC* 85.13 (B.O. 2:315), Bernard speaks of two kinds of "birth" engendered by the spiritual marriage: preaching and meditation. Gilson notes that the *ordo caritatis* is the fundamental way in which Bernard relates active and contemplative love. For Bernard, an act of charity "reestablishes the order willed by God; it proves, by means of this exterior act, that the will, in its secret depths, has aligned itself with the divine will; it is therefore the concrete expression of a communion of our will with God's, which is in fact spiritual charity." *Théologie mystique*, 99 (translation mine).

99. *SC* 51.2 (B.O. 2:85).

100. *SC* 57.9 (B.O. 2:125).

101. *SC* 48.7 (B.O. 2:72). Bernard's love of the sacraments comes through especially pointedly in *SC* 66.4 (B.O. 2:180–81), where he defends them against the views of the Cathari.

102. This quotation is taken from an as yet unpublished manuscript by Bernard McGinn, *pro manuscripta*, 28.

103. *De diversis* 33.8 (B.O. 6–1:227). Translation by Bernard McGinn.

104. Leclercq, "Bernard on the Church," 276.

105. See above, n. 37; and chap. 3, pp. 47–48.

106. Bernard, Letter 91.3 (B.O. 7:240), in *The Letters of St. Bernard of Clairvaux*, 141. In this edition the letter appears as number 94.

107. See above, n. 37.

108. Gerson, *Selections*, 64–65. See above, n. 3.

CHAPTER 5. JOHN CALVIN ON MYSTICAL UNION

1. *Institutes* 3.11.10 (O.S. 4:191). I located the two references to *unio mystica* in the *Institutes* with the help of computerized data originally prepared by Ford Lewis Battles. They were revised, somewhat corrected, and given new identification codes by Richard F. Wevers of the Classics Department at Calvin College, Grand Rapids, MI 49506. I am grateful to the H. H. Meeter Center for Calvin Studies at Calvin College for access to these materials.

2. *Institutes* 2.12.7 (O.S. 3:446).

3. Kolfhaus, *Christusgemeinschaft bei Johannes Calvin*, 80.

4. See chap. 4, nn. 41–43.

5. *Institutes* 3.2.25 (O.S. 4:46). "Christum, ubi nos in fidem illuminat Spiritus sui virtute, simul inserere in corpus suum, ut fiamus bonorum omnium participes."

6. Kolfhaus, *Christusgemeinschaft*, 37: "Glaube ist nach ihm die unio cum Christo." However, even the passage Kolfhaus uses to document this statement (from Calvin's Sermons on Galatians) says that we are united to Christ *through* faith: "que *par* foy nous soyons unis à nostre S. J. Chr. comme membres de son corps." C.O. 50:293 (emphasis added). In fairness to Kolfhaus, it should be noted

that his concern here is to stress that for Calvin, there is no "higher level" of union that supersedes faith.

7. S. P. Dee quoted in Kolfhaus, *Christusgemeinschaft*, 16 (translation mine). A passage from Calvin himself confirms this. In his commentary on Eph. 3:17, Calvin remarks, "Most consider fellowship with Christ and believing in Christ to be the same thing; but the fellowship which we have with Christ is the effect of faith [fidei effectus]." Calvin, *Galatians, Ephesians, Philippians, Colossians*, 168 (C.O. 51:187). See chap. 3, n. 44. Brian Gerrish has suggested to me that this statement in the Ephesians Commentary is best understood as anti-Zwinglian. On the differences between Calvin's and Zwingli's understanding of faith, see especially his "Gospel and Eucharist: John Calvin on the Lord's Supper," in *The Old Protestantism and the New: Essays on the Reformation Heritage*, 109, 322, n. 13.

8. *Institutes* 3.1.3, 3.1.4 (O.S. 4:5).

9. Kolfhaus, *Christusgemeinschaft*, 52. See also p. 50.

10. Ibid., 39–40 (emphasis added). See also Gerrish, "Gospel and Eucharist," in *Old Protestantism and the New*, 109–110.

11. Calvin, *First Corinthians*, 24 (C.O. 49:313) (emphasis added). See chap. 3, n. 66. See Kolfhaus, *Christusgemeinschaft*, 40. See also Calvin's comment on 1 Cor. 4:15, p. 97 (C.O. 49:372).

12. John Calvin, *The Epistles of Paul the Apostle to the Romans and to the Thessalonians*, trans. Ross Mackenzie, *Calvin's New Testament Commentaries*, vol. 8 (Grand Rapids: Wm. B. Eerdmans Publishing Co., 1960), 28 (C.O. 49:21). See Kolfhaus, *Christusgemeinschaft*, 40.

13. Kolfhaus, *Christusgemeinschaft*, 44: "durch das Wort geweckte." See also Ronald S. Wallace, *Calvin's Doctrine of the Christian Life*, 19–23.

14. See chap. 3, pp. 52–54, esp. n. 65. Kolfhaus, while affirming this point, nevertheless emphasizes that "Calvin, above all, never grew tired of making a strong connection between the community's faith and the Word. But why? Because it is in the Word of God alone that Christ meets us and his Name becomes known to us." Thus, no "ranking" of "faith in Christ" and "faith in the Scripture" is present in Calvin, for, as Kolfhaus puts it, "I know Christ through the Scripture, and I can only read the Scripture in light of Christ." At the same time, he points out that for Calvin, Christ is clearly the object of faith, as in *Institutes* 3.2.1, where Calvin says of faith that "all its stability rests in Christ" (O.S. 4:9). Kolfhaus, *Christusgemeinschaft*, 42–43, esp. the footnotes.

15. Kolfhaus, *Christusgemeinschaft*, 36. See also 31–32.

16. John Calvin, *The Acts of the Apostles 1–13*, trans. John W. Fraser and W. J. G. McDonald, *Calvin's New Testament Commentaries*, vol. 6 (Grand Rapids: Wm. B. Eerdmans Publishing Co., 1965), 394 (on Acts 13:48, C.O. 48:314): "Quum electio fide superior statuitur"; *Institutes* 3.22.10: "electio . . . fidei mater est" (O.S. 4:392). See also *Institutes* 3.22.7 (O.S. 4:416), where Calvin says that God has engrafted into Christ those "whom he has willed from eternity to be his own."

17. Calvin, *Galatians, Ephesians, Philippians, Colossians*, 43 (C.O. 50:199): "Porro vivit Christus in nobis dupliciter. Una vita est, quum nos spiritu suo gubernat atque actiones nostras omnes dirigit. Altera quod participatione suae iustitiae nos donat: ut quando in nobis non possumus, in ipso accepti simus Deo. Prior ad regenerationem pertinet: secunda ad gratuitam iustitiae acceptionem." Another example is found in the commentary on Phil. 3:10, where Calvin refers to a

"twofold fellowship and communication in the death of Christ," 276 (C.O. 52:50). See Kolfhaus, *Christusgemeinschaft*, 34.

18. John Calvin, Letter 2266 to Peter Martyr Vermigli, 8 August 1555, C.O. 15:723: "nisi quod divina spiritus virtute vitam e coelis in terram transfundi agnosco: quia nec per se vivifica esset caro Christi, nec vis eius ad nos usque nisi immensa spiritus operatione perveniret. Ergo spiritus est qui facit, ut in nobis habitet Christus, nos sustineat atque vegetet, omniaque capitis officia impleat." Translations from this letter are my own. See Kolfhaus, *Christusgemeinschaft*, 24.

19. Calvin, Letter 2266 to Peter Martyr, C.O. 15:723.

20. See chap. 3 on justification and sanctification in Calvin. Kolfhaus notes that while Calvin distinguishes between "small" and "great" faith, he does not turn faith into a "quantitative measure," as if one kind of true faith unites us totally with Christ, and another (also true, but smaller) unites us only imperfectly. Thus, Kolfhaus insists: "We either partake of the whole Christ, or not at all." Kolfhaus, *Christusgemeinschaft*, 50; see also 57.

21. Calvin, *Galatians, Ephesians, Philippians, Colossians*, 208–9 (C.O. 51:225). Other examples are cited in Kolfhaus, *Christusgemeinschaft*, 93–94; see also 31.

22. Calvin, *Galatians, Ephesians, Philippians, Colossians*, 209 (C.O. 51:226) (emphasis added). The Latin reads, "Eadem ergo unionis ratio inter nos et Christum, quod se quodammodo in nos transfundit. *Neque enim ossa sumus ex ossibus eius, et caro ex carne, quia ipse nobiscum est homo: sed quia spiritus sui virtute nos in corpus suum inserit, ut vitam ex eo haurimus*" (emphasis in C.O. text).

23. *Institutes* 3.11.5 (O.S. 4:185–86). On the controversy with Osiander, see Niesel, *Theology of John Calvin*, 133f., and Wilhelm Niesel, "Calvin wider Osianders Rechtfertigungslehre," 410–30. See also Kolfhaus, *Christusgemeinschaft*, 27–28, 61–62.

24. John Calvin, *The Gospel according to St. John 11–21 and the First Epistle of John*, trans. T. H. L. Parker, *Calvin's New Testament Commentaries*, vol. 5 (Grand Rapids: Wm. B. Eerdmans Publishing Co., 1959), 148 (C.O. 47:387): "Unde etiam colligimus, nos unum cum Christo esse, non quia suum in nos substantiam transfundat, sed quia spiritus sui virtute nobiscum vitam suam et quidquid accepit a patre bonorum communicet."

25. John Calvin, *Sermons on The Epistle to the Ephesians*, 614 (C.O. 51:780).

26. Other passages dealing with this theme can be found in *Institutes* 2.12.7 (O.S. 3:446–47), 3.1.1 (O.S. 4:2), 3.11.10 (O.S. 4:191–92). See also Kolfhaus, *Christusgemeinschaft*, 31.

27. Calvin, *First Corinthians*, 130 (C.O. 49:398). See Kolfhaus, *Christusgemeinschaft*, 85.

28. *Institutes* 3.16.2 (O.S. 4:250–51).

29. Calvin, *First Corinthians*, 131 (C.O. 49:399).

30. *Institutes* 3.2.24 (O.S. 4:35): "Christus non extra nos est, sed in nobis habitat: nec solum individuo societatis nexu nobis adhaeret, sed mirabili quadam communione in unum corpus nobiscum coalescit in dies magis ac magis, donec unum penitus nobiscum fiat."

31. *Institutes* 3.2.24 (O.S. 4:34). Here Calvin opposes the idea that unbelief and hope can reign alternately: "As if we ought to think of Christ, standing afar off and not rather dwelling in us! For we await salvation from him not because he appears to us far off, but because he makes us, ingrafted into his body [nos corpori suo insitos], participants [participes], not only in all his benefits but also in himself."

32. Kolfhaus, *Christusgemeinschaft*, 71.

33. See chap. 4, n. 18.

34. Kolfhaus, *Christusgemeinschaft*, 131.

35. This is especially clear whenever Calvin speaks of our contributing nothing to our own justification. For example, in *Institutes* 3.11.23 (O.S. 4:206), he declares, "You see that our righteousness is not in us but in Christ, that we possess it only because we are partakers [participes] in Christ; indeed, with him we possess all its riches." And in his Commentary on John 15:1 ("I am the true vine . . ."), he remarks, "The heart of this comparison is that by nature we are barren and dry save in so far as we have been engrafted into Christ, and draw a new and extraneous power from Him [nisi quatenus Christo insiti novam vim et adventitiam ab eo haurimus]." Calvin, *John 11–21 and First Epistle of John*, 93 (C.O. 47:338). On Bernard, see chap. 4, pp. 69–70.

36. Letter to Peter Martyr, 8 Aug. 1555, C.O. 15:723. "Quomodo id fiat, intelligentiae meae modulo longe altius esse fateor. Itaque hoc mysterium magis suspicio, quam comprehendere laborem."

37. Calvin, *Galatians, Ephesians, Philippians, Colossians*, 210 (C.O. 51:227): "Proinde magis laborandum ut Christum sentiamus potius in nobis viventem, quam ut communicationis ratio nobis pateat."

38. *Institutes* 2.12.7 (O.S. 3:447); 3.11.5 (O.S. 4:185); 4.17.1 (O.S. 5:342); 4.17.9 (O.S. 5:351); 4.17.31 (O.S. 5:389); 4.17.33 (O.S. 5:391–92); 4.19.35 (O.S. 469).

39. See chap. 4, pp. 71–72.

40. See above, p. 87, nn. 19 and 20.

41. *Institutes* 3.25 (O.S. 4:432–56), esp. secs. 1–9 (O.S. 4:432–52). See Boisset, *Sagesse et sainteté dans la pensée de Jean Calvin*, 258. In Bernard, see esp. *De diligendo Deo* 11:30 (B.O. 3:144–45).

42. I will speak here in a summary fashion, since the references are so numerous. The Appendix gives a complete listing of references to *unio* in Calvin in the *Institutes*, and a representative listing from other Calvin writings, arranged according to the images or terms Calvin uses in the original texts.

43. See chap. 4, pp. 72.

44. *Institutes* 2.12.7 (O.S. 3:446–47).

45. *Institutes* 2.8.18 (O.S. 3:360).

46. *Institutes* 3.1.3 (O.S. 4:5).

47. It is important to recall, however, that Bernard sees the union of active love in the faithful believer as *in practice* the ordinary experience of union. We have seen that he does not claim that contemplative love is necessary—faith is what is most important. See chap. 4, p. 72, nn. 41–42.

48. See above, p. 89, nn. 36–38.

49. *Institutes* 3.2.14 (O.S. 4:25). See chap. 3, 53, nn. 62–64. Again, it is helpful to recall Calvin's statement in *Institutes* 1.2.2 (O.S. 3:35): "What help is it . . . to know a God with whom we have nothing to do? Rather, our knowledge should serve first to teach us fear and reverence; secondly, with it as our guide and teacher, we should learn to seek every good from him, and, having received it, to credit it to his account."

50. See chap. 4, p. 73, nn. 49–51.

51. See chap. 3, p. 53, nn. 61–64.

52. *Institutes* 3.2.8 (O.S. 4:18). Kolfhaus points out that for Calvin, *cognitio* is always *cognitio fidei*, and has "the same function" as faith, as in the Commentary

on 1 John 5:20, where Calvin speaks of an efficacious knowledge "by which we are engrafted into Christ and are made one with God." Calvin, *John 11–21 and First Epistle of John*, 314 (C.O. 55:375); Kolfhaus, *Christusgemeinschaft*, 48. Calvin will even at times say that knowledge is the same as faith, as in his Commentary on John 17:3 ("and this is life eternal, that they should know thee"): "But where He has shone, we possess Him by faith and also enter into the possession of life; and this is why the knowledge of Him is truly and justly called saving. . . . Indeed, it is the same as faith, by which we are incorporated into the body of Christ and made partakers of the divine adoption and heirs of heaven. [Imo eadem est cum fide, qua insiti in Christi corpus divinae adoptionis consortes et coelorum haeredes efficimur.]" Calvin, *John 11–21 and First Epistle of John*, 136 (C.O. 47:376).

53. *Institutes* 1.2.1 (O.S. 3:35): "Pietatem voco coniunctam cum *amore* Dei reverentiam quam beneficiorum eius notitia conciliat" (emphasis added).

54. John Calvin, *The Second Epistle of Paul the Apostle to the Corinthians and the Epistles to Timothy, Titus, and Philemon*, trans. T. A. Smail, *Calvin's New Testament Commentaries*, vol. 10 (Grand Rapids: Wm. B. Eerdmans Publishing Co., 1964), 74 (C.O. 50:67); *De diligendo Deo* 9.26 (B.O. 3:140). See chap. 4, p. 66, n. 13.

55. *Institutes* 3.16.2 (O.S. 4:249) (emphasis added). In *De diligendo Deo* 9.26 (B.O. 3:141), Bernard speaks of "loving God for God's sake." "This love is pleasing," Bernard says, "because it is free." It is pleasing because its sole motivation is to give glory to God. Such a person will also be able to love his or her neighbor unselfishly. See chap. 4, pp. 66–67, n. 14. In a similar way, Calvin speaks of the love of God overflowing into the love of one's neighbor. In *Institutes* 2.8.51 (O.S. 3:390), he asserts: "First, indeed, our soul should be entirely filled with the love of God [Dei dilectione]. From this will flow directly the love of neighbor [proximi dilectio]." The love of neighbor will be discussed in more detail below.

56. *Institutes* 3.9.13 (O.S. 4:292): ". . . ita sub fidei puritate subsidere vicissim charitas ipsa debet."

57. *De diligendo Deo* 3.9 (B.O. 3:126).

58. *De diligendo Deo* 5.15 (B.O. 3:131), 11.32 (B.O. 3:146).

59. For example, in his comment on Matt. 11:2 in John Calvin, *A Harmony of the Gospels Matthew, Mark and Luke, Volume 2*, trans. T. H. L. Parker, *Calvin's New Testament Commentaries*, vol. 2 (Grand Rapids: Wm. B. Eerdmans Publishing Co., 1972), 3 (C.O. 45:299).

60. See chap. 4, p. 74, nn. 59–61.

61. *Institutes* 3.2.1 (O.S. 4:9): "Deum enim esse quo tendimus, hominem qua imus."

62. Calvin, *John 1–10*, 167 (C.O. 47:152–53). See chap. 2, n. 64. Calvin also takes up this issue against Osiander in *Institutes* 3.11.8–9 (O.S. 4:189–91). See Wallace, *Calvin's Doctrine of the Christian Life*, 14–17.

63. Wallace, *Calvin's Doctrine of the Christian Life*, 19.

64. Calvin, *Sermons on Ephesians*, comment on Eph. 5:32, p. 616 (C.O. 51:782). See Wallace, *Calvin's Doctrine of the Christian Life*, 19; and above, n. 37.

65. Calvin, *Galatians, Ephesians, Philippians, Colossians*, on Gal. 2:20, p. 43 (C.O. 50:199). See Wallace, *Calvin's Doctrine of the Christian Life*, 20.

66. See chap. 4, n. 61.

67. Calvin, *John 11–21 and First Epistle of John*, 293–94 (C.O. 47:145). See *Institutes* 2.8.18 (O.S. 3:360), 2.15.5 (O.S. 3:478), 2.16.3 (O.S. 3:485), 3.6.2 (O.S. 4:147),

and 3.25.2 (O.S. 4:433). Several examples can be cited from the commentaries; see the Appendix. See also Kolfhaus, *Christusgemeinschaft*, 38.

68. *Institutes* 4.15.6 (O.S. 5:289).

69. See chap. 4, pp. 75–76.

70. See chap. 4, p. 76.

71. See above, p. 86, nn. 15–16.

72. *Institutes* 3.22.10 (O.S. 4:392, 391).

73. See chap. 3, p. 62, n. 124. The translation of Bernard's text here is as it appears in the McNeill-Battles edition of the *Institutes*.

74. Bernard, Letter 107.5 (109.5 in this translation), *Letters of St. Bernard of Clairvaux*, 161 (emphasis added) (B.O. 7:271). The Latin reads, "Dum quisque vocatus per timorem, iustificatus per amorem, praesumit se quoque de numero esse beatorum, sciens nimirum qui *quos iustificavit, illos et magnificavit.*"

75. See chap. 3, p. 49, n. 43.

76. Bernard, *Letters* 107.7 (109.7 in this translation), 162 (B.O. 7:272).

77. The issue of predestination is a thorny one that I do not think it is necessary to develop at length in this context. In fairness to Calvin, however, a few comments are in order, for which I am indebted to some clarifications offered by Brian Gerrish. In Bernard's case, I think it can be said that those who are excluded from election exclude themselves (his notion of consent preserves the free choice of the individual person to say either yes or no to God's grace). There is a sense in which Calvin would agree that the reprobate "exclude themselves," inasmuch as before God, we are *all* inexcusable. Calvin's view is technically "preterition" (Gerrish's term): all human beings are deservedly damned, but God in his mercy pulls some out of the mass of damnation. Calvin insists that God is not unjust in doing this (since no one, after all, has a claim on salvation). For specific references, see *Institutes* 3.23.3 (O.S. 4:396–97) and 3.23.11 (O.S. 4:405). It should be noted that Calvin also refers to the passage in Ezek. 33:11 which states that God does not will the death of the wicked, but that the wicked repent (to which Bernard refers in the letter to Thomas of Beverly). Calvin's explanation runs as follows: "Now if we are seeking the prophet's true meaning, it is that he would bring the hope of pardon to the penitent only. . . . God's mercy will always . . . go to meet repentance, but all the prophets and all the apostles, as well as Ezekiel himself, clearly teach to whom repentance is given." *Institutes* 3.24.15 (O.S. 4:427–28). On Calvin's view of predestination, see also Gerrish, " 'To the Unknown God': Luther and Calvin on the Hiddenness of God," in his *Old Protestantism and the New*, 141–45, particularly the discussion on 145 on Calvin's defense of predestination not only on the basis of scripture, but of experience.

78. *Institutes* 4.13.10 (O.S. 5:247).

79. Calvin, *2 Corinthians, Timothy, Titus, Philemon*, 135–36 (C.O. 50:120).

80. For example, in *Institutes* 4.13.8 (O.S. 5:245), Calvin speaks of a time when "pious men customarily prepared themselves by monastic discipline to govern the church, that thus they might be fitter and better trained to undertake so great an office."

81. *Institutes* 4.13.14: "duplicem Christianismum."

82. *Institutes* 4.13.11 (O.S. 5:248).

83. For example, in *Institutes* 2.8.56–57 (O.S. 3:394–96), he opposes the idea that love of one's enemies is an "evangelical counsel" that is only enjoined on monks. See also *Institutes* 4.13.12–14 (O.S. 5:249–52), esp. sec. 14 (O.S. 5:251–52), where

Calvin insists that present-day monks break with the church: "Do they not separate themselves from the lawful society of believers, in adopting a peculiar ministry and a private administration of the sacraments? If this is not to break the communion of the church [Ecclesiae communionem], what is?" He adds here that the ancient monks did not do this, "Even though they dwelt apart from the others, yet they had not a separate church; they partook of the sacraments with others; they attended solemn assemblies; there they were part of the people."

84. See chap. 4, pp. 77–78.

85. Kolfhaus, *Christusgemeinschaft*, 131.

86. *Institutes* 1.14.4 (O.S. 3:157). The Latin for the last sentence quoted reads: "Atqui Paulus, qui extra tertium caelum raptus fuerat, non modo nihil tale prodidit, sed testatus quoque est nefas esse homini loqui quae viderat arcana." Interestingly, the word *arcana* is also used by Calvin in describing the mysterious nature of union with Christ (see Appendix).

87. Calvin, *2 Corinthians, Timothy, Titus, Philemon*, 156 (C.O. 50:137).

88. Ibid., 157 (C.O. 50:138). Calvin does not explicitly state that he understands what happened to Paul as a "contemplative experience of union." He only speaks of a "revelation," and of Paul being "admitted into these secrets." However, he is talking about the type of experience that traditionally was connected with contemplation, and the fact that he quotes Pseudo-Dionysius here (who provided a vocabulary for articulating contemplative experience) is, I think, significant.

89. For example, in Calvin's comment on Acts 7:31–32 (dealing with Moses' vision of the burning bush), he notes that many visions are false, but that genuine ones do occur, e.g., to Moses, who was granted a "livelier awareness" of God's presence. Calvin, *Acts of the Apostles 1–13*, 191–92 (C.O. 48:145–46). Of course, this kind of "vision" is not quite the same as the vision or ecstasy of contemplative union.

90. See chap. 4, p. 72, nn. 41–43.

91. See the Appendix. There are numerous references to *unio* in Book 4 of the *Institutes*, and most are in relation to the sacraments (Baptism and the Lord's Supper). Some of these will be discussed in the body of the text below.

92. Kolfhaus, *Christusgemeinschaft*, 105.

93. *Institutes* 4.1.1 (O.S. 5:1).

94. Kolfhaus, *Christusgemeinschaft*, 98.

95. *Institutes* 4.1.2 (O.S. 5:4). In this same section Calvin says, "It is not sufficient, indeed, for us to comprehend in mind and thought the multitude of the elect, unless we consider the unity of the church as that into which we are convinced we have been truly engrafted [nisi talem Ecclesiae unitatem cogitemus in quam nos esse insitos vere simus persuasi]. For no hope of future inheritance remains to us unless we have been united with all other members under Christ, our Head." Thus, in a real sense, we are engrafted both into Christ and into his church. Calvin makes two further statements that are worth noting. In *Institutes* 4.1.3 (O.S. 5:16), he remarks, "So powerful is participation in the church that it keeps us in the society of God." And in 4.1.4 (O.S. 5:7) he says of the church that "away from her bosom one cannot hope for any forgiveness of sins or any salvation."

96. See Kolfhaus, *Christusgemeinschaft*, 99. Kolfhaus goes on to discuss how Calvin sees all gifts as being for the service of the community. He quotes him on p. 102 of *Christusgemeinschaft* as saying, "Over all our private interests must be

raised our sense of the general building up of the church." He lists the reference as O.S. 5:4, but this is incorrect (there is no such sentence in *Institutes* 4.1.2). In this connection, I would also like to recall Richard's flawed thesis that Calvin's spirituality is "individualistic" (chap. 1, p. 17). Contrary to Richard, the Holy Spirit does not act toward the individual "independent of the community"; see Richard, *Spirituality of Calvin,* 180–83. Clearly, that Spirit engrafts us into Christ *and* the church. See especially the references below in relation to the sacraments.

97. Kolfhaus, *Christusgemeinschaft,* 87; *Institutes* 4.1.7 (O.S. 4:12).

98. See chap. 4, pp. 79–81.

99. Calvin, *Galatians, Ephesians, Philippians, Colossians,* 100–101 (C.O. 50:251). See also Calvin's comment on 1 Cor. 12:12: "Therefore, we who are members of Christ, even if we are equipped with different gifts, ought nevertheless to be concerned about that union with each other, which we have in Christ." *First Corinthians,* 264 (C.O. 49:501). See above, chap. 4, pp. 79–80, n. 94.

100. *Institutes* 2.8.51 (O.S. 3:390). In this section Calvin is continuing his discussion of the Ten Commandments. He quotes Deut. 6:5, "That we should love the Lord God with all our heart"; the Latin reads, "Ut diligamus Dominum Deum . . ." This is the same Latin word, *diligo,* used by Bernard in *De diligendo Deo.*

101. *Institutes* 3.7.6 (O.S. 4:156–57).

102. Calvin, *John 11–21 and First Epistle of John,* 66 (C.O. 47:314). Another example of this point is found in Calvin's Commentary on Eph. 1:15 (part of Calvin's thanksgiving to the Ephesians): "If our love ought to look to God, the nearer any man approaches Him, the higher the place he should hold." Calvin, *Galatians, Ephesians, Philippians, Colossians,* 133 (C.O. 51:155).

103. *Institutes* 2.8.54 (O.S. 3:392). See also his Sermon 23 on Eph. 4:6–8 (C.O. 51:542), where he states, "And since we are members of his body, we must serve one another" (translation mine). See also C.O. 31:212, C.O. 32:629, and Kolfhaus, *Christusgemeinschaft,* 103, 122.

104. *Institutes* 3.19.12 (O.S. 4:292). This emphasis is also found in Calvin's discussion of the sacraments, as in the *Short Treatise on the Lord's Supper,* where Calvin says, "The third benefit [of the Lord's Supper] consists in our having a vehement incitement to holy living, and above all to observe charity and brotherly love among us." Calvin, *Short Treatise on the Lord's Supper,* in *Calvin: Theological Treatises,* trans. J. K. S. Reid, 149 (C.O. 5:441). The sacraments and *unio* will be discussed further below.

105. See chap. 4, p. 67, n. 14, and above, p. 91, n. 55.

106. See chap. 4, pp. 81–82, nn. 101–103.

107. Kolfhaus, *Christusgemeinschaft,* 108–9. See Calvin, *Harmony of the Gospels* on Matt. 26:27, p. 138 (C.O. 45:710), where Calvin says, "As Christ's purpose was to bind our whole faith to Himself, so that we should seek for nothing beyond Him, He gave two symbols to assure us that our life was established in him." In this case, the two symbols refer to bread and wine. Calvin is arguing here the return of the cup to the laity during the Lord's Supper.

108. Sermon 40 on Eph. 5:25–27 (C.O. 51:750) (translation mine). See Kolfhaus, *Christusgemeinschaft,* 109.

109. *Institutes* 4.15.1 (O.S. 5:285).

110. *Institutes* 4.15.5 (O.S. 5:288–89).

111. Calvin, *2 Corinthians, Timothy, Titus, Philemon,* 383 (C.O. 52:431). Thus

Kolfhaus can say that "it is not Baptism as an action that has this power; rather, it is only the instrument in the hand of the Holy Spirit." Calvin himself refers to Baptism as "instrument" in his 23rd Sermon on Gal. 3:26–29 (C.O. 50:562). Kolfhaus, *Christusgemeinschaft*, 113–14.

112. See the Appendix for specific examples.

113. *Institutes* 4.17.33 (O.S. 5:394): ". . . adminiculum esse quo inseramur in corpus Christi, vel insiti magis ac magis coalescamus, donec solide nos secum uniat in caelesti vita."

114. *Institutes* 4.17.33 (O.S. 5:391).

115. *Institutes* 4.17.12 (O.S. 5:355–56). See also 4.17.32 (O.S. 5:391), where he says, "I frankly confess that I reject their teaching of the mixture, or transfusion, of Christ's flesh with our soul. For it is enough for us that, from the substance of his flesh Christ breathes life into our souls—indeed, pours forth his very life into us—even though Christ's flesh itself does not enter into us." Notice how this argument parallels his argument against Osiander in *Institutes* 3.11. See also Calvin's Commentary on 1 Cor. 11:24 (C.O. 49:487), and above, n. 62.

116. *Institutes* 4.17.33 (O.S. 5:392). This insight also appears, not surprisingly, in the *Short Treatise on the Lord's Supper*, where Calvin says, "The Spirit of God is the bond of participation, for which reason it is called spiritual." With this in mind, he can also say with confidence that "Jesus Christ gives us in the Supper the real substance of his body and his blood [la propre substance de son corps et son sang]." Calvin, *Theological Treatises*, 166, 148 (C.O. 5:460, 440). On this point, see also two letters to Bullinger, C.O. 12:482 and C.O. 19:603; quoted in Kolfhaus, *Christusgemeinschaft*, 119 (and related material on 117–18).

117. See again the Appendix for specific examples.

118. Kolfhaus, *Christusgemeinschaft*, 121.

119. *Institutes* 3.6.2 (O.S. 4:147).

120. *Institutes* 3.14.4 (O.S. 4:223): "sine Christi communicatione nulla est sanctificatio."

121. See *Institutes* 3.17.10 (O.S. 4:263).

122. See chap. 3, p. 60, nn. 110 and 111. See also Calvin's commentary on 1 Cor. 13:9–12 (C.O. 49:513–14).

123. *Institutes* 3.3.20 (O.S. 4:78).

124. To give just one other example in relation to union with Christ, in his commentary on John 15:2 (on the vine and the branches), Calvin notes, "For it is not enough to have been made partakers of adoption once, unless God continues the progress of His grace in us." Calvin, *John 11–21 and First Epistle of John*, 94 (C.O. 47:339). See also Kolfhaus, *Christusgemeinschaft*, 54–85.

125. See *Institutes* 4.10.15 (O.S. 5:177–78), 4.12.19 (O.S. 5:228–29), and 4.18.1 (O.S. 5:417–18) for examples of Calvin's opposition to ceremony and fasting being "meritorious."

126. *Institutes* 3.20.42 (O.S. 4:352).

127. *Institutes* 3.3.16–17 (O.S. 4:73–74).

128. See Kolfhaus, *Christusgemeinschaft*, 132, where he notes that Calvin, like the mystics, spoke of the "nothingness" of the world—nevertheless, he knew he was called to a task in the world, for the world is a theater of God's glory.

129. See above, p. 90, n. 41.

130. See *Institutes* 3.6.2 (O.S. 4:147); and *Institutes* 2.8.54 (O.S. 3:392). See also

Calvin's commentary on John 14:21, where he says that to love God is to keep his commandments. Calvin, *John 11–21 and First Epistle of John*, 85 (C.O. 47:331).

131. Gerson, *Selections*, 64–65.

CHAPTER 6. CONCLUSIONS

1. Thomas F. Torrance, *Calvin's Doctrine of Man*, 7.

2. Bouwsma, "The Spirituality of John Calvin," 318.

3. Brian A. Gerrish is one writer who takes issue with Bouwsma's view that Calvin is not a systematic thinker. If being "systematic" means that Calvin "looked assiduously for the interconnections between doctrines, the way they 'hang together,' " then, according to Gerrish, Calvin is indeed rightly called a systematic theologian. See his *Grace and Gratitude: The Eucharistic Theology of John Calvin*, 14–16. On the significance of the *Institutes* as a *summa pietatis*, see ibid., 14–20.

4. Strictly speaking, Calvin does not use the *word* "mystical" in either my "generic" or "specific" sense. It is quite possible that in using the term, he meant nothing more than "secret" or "mysterious." See, for example, *Institutes* 2.12.17 (O.S. 3:446–47), which I cite above in chap. 5, n. 44. However, as I think the Appendix makes clear, many of the other words he uses in expounding the meaning of "union with Christ" (e.g., engrafting, communion, spiritual marriage, etc.) are reminiscent of the concept of mystical union as it is expressed in Bernard and Gerson. Even if we take the word "mysticism" in a more generic sense, as the experiential element in religion (as in von Hügel), a connection with Calvin can be made, particularly in relation to Calvin's claim of the *experiential* nature of faith.

5. Wilhelm Kolfhaus, *Christusgemeinschaft*, 126. See chap. 1, n. 20.

6. Kolfhaus, *Christusgemeinschaft*, 127–28.

7. See, for example, the article by Marguerite Soulié, " 'Mystique' chez Calvin et création littéraire," 136–42.

8. There is no question that Calvin agrees with Bernard's basic understanding of the Song of Songs, i.e., that it is an allegory on the love of Christ and his church. This became an issue with Sebastian Castellio, who denied the divine inspiration of the Song and held it to be an "obscene" work. It was partly on this basis that Calvin rejected Castellio as a candidate for ordination. See John T. McNeill, *The History and Character of Calvinism* (New York: Oxford University Press, 1954), 168, and Williams, *Radical Reformation*, 628.

9. I am indebted to Bernard McGinn for this suggestion.

10. William Siktberg, "Mystical Element in Calvin," 7. On pp. 6–7, Siktberg notes (legitimately, I think) that treatments of Calvin's theology have often stressed themes like "sovereignty" and "predestination" over faith and prayer. This relates to the criticism of Bouwsma that we saw above (n. 2).

11. See, for example, Siktberg, "Mystical Element in Calvin," 110.

12. Ibid., 109–10.

13. *Institutes* 1.2.

14. *De diligendo Deo* 10.28 (B.O. 3:143).

15. *Institutes* 1.2.1 (O.S. 3:35).

16. One might ask why, broadly speaking, Bernard assigns to "love" what Calvin assigns to "faith." This is a very difficult question to answer. In Calvin's

case, we can certainly point to the regulative nature of the Pauline vocabulary of faith in much of his writing. (I am indebted to Brian Gerrish for this suggestion.) It is tempting to think that Calvin follows Paul on faith, while Bernard follows John on love. However, both in his Pauline *and* in his Johannine New Testament commentaries, Calvin clearly has much to say on the theology of love. Bernard is similarly hard to pin down here. We have already seen that he stresses love but does not ignore faith. In speaking of love, Bernard draws freely from both Pauline and Johannine texts (as a glance at the scripture references for *De diligendo Deo*, for example, makes clear). This matter deserves further study.

17. See chap. 1, nn. 92–95.

18. See, for example, Hyma's claim in *Christian Renaissance: A History of the "Devotio Moderna,"* 283–84, that Calvin drew upon the insights of the *Devotio moderna* in writing the *Institutes*. Hyma may indeed be right; but I have found no evidence to support this thesis. Chapter 1, n. 80.

19. That is to say, understood as rooted in and energized by grace (as we have seen in Bernard and Calvin) and not as a form of works righteousness, as Ritschl charged.

SELECTED BIBLIOGRAPHY

PRIMARY SOURCES

Bernard of Clairvaux. *Sancti Bernardi Opera.* Edited by Jean Leclercq, C. H. Talbot, and Henri Rochais. 8 vols. Rome: Editiones Cistercienses, 1957–77.
Calvin, John. *Iohannis Calvini opera quae supersunt omnia.* Edited by Wilhelm Baum, Edward Cunitz, and Edward Reutz. 59 vols. *Corpus Reformatorum,* vols. 29–98. Brunswick: C. A. Schwetschke, 1863–1900.
———. *Johannes Calvin Opera Selecta.* Vols. 3–5. Edited by P. Barth and W. Niesel. Munich: Kaiser Verlag, 1926–36. 2d ed.: vol. 3 (1957); vol. 4 (1959).
Gerson, Jean. *Selections from "A Deo exivit," "Contra curiositatem studentium" and "De mystica theologia speculativa."* Edited and translated by Steven E. Ozment. Leiden: E. J. Brill, 1969.

TRANSLATIONS

Bernard of Clairvaux. *Five Books on Consideration: Advice to a Pope.* Translated by John D. Anderson and Elizabeth T. Kennan. Cistercian Fathers Series, No. 37. Kalamazoo, Mich.: Cistercian Publications, 1976.
———. *The Letters of St. Bernard of Clairvaux.* Translated by Bruno Scott James. Chicago: Henry Regnery Co., 1953.
———. *On the Song of Songs I.* Translated by Kilian Walsh, O.S.C.O. Cistercian Fathers Series, No. 4. Kalamazoo, Mich.: Cistercian Publications, 1981.
———. *On the Song of Songs II.* Translated by Kilian Walsh, O.S.C.O. Cistercian Fathers Series, No. 7. Kalamazoo, Mich.: Cistercian Publications, 1983.
———. *On the Song of Songs III.* Translated by Kilian Walsh, O.S.C.O., and Irene M. Edmonds. Cistercian Fathers Series, No. 31. Kalamazoo, Mich.: Cistercian Publications, 1979.
———. *On the Song of Songs IV.* Translated by Irene Edmonds. Cistercian Fathers Series, No. 40. Kalamazoo, Mich.: Cistercian Publications, 1980.
———. *Sermons on Conversion.* Translated by Marie-Bernard Saïd, O.S.B. Cis-

tercian Fathers Series, No. 25. Kalamazoo, Mich.: Cistercian Publications, 1981.

————. *St. Bernard's Sermons for the Seasons and Principal Feasts of the Year.* Translated by a Priest of Mount Melleray. 3 vols. Westminster, Md: Newman Press, 1921.

————. *Treatises II: The Steps of Humility and Pride; On Loving God.* Translated by M. Ambrose Conway, O.S.C.O., and Robert Walton, O.S.B. Cistercian Fathers Series, No. 13. Kalamazoo, Mich.: Cistercian Publications, 1980.

————. *Treatises III: On Grace and Free Choice; In Praise of the New Knighthood.* Translated by Daniel O'Donovan and Conrad Greenia. Cistercian Fathers Series, No. 19. Kalamazoo, Mich.: Cistercian Publications, 1977.

Calvin, John. *Calvin: Commentaries.* Edited and translated by Joseph Haroutunian in collaboration with Louise P. Smith. Library of Christian Classics, vol. 23. Philadelphia: Westminster Press, 1958.

————. *Calvin: Theological Treatises.* Edited and translated by J. K. S. Reid. Library of Christian Classics, vol. 22. Philadelphia: Westminster Press, 1954.

————. *Calvin's Commentaries.* 22 vols. Grand Rapids: Baker Book House, 1979. (Originally printed for the Calvin Translation Society, Edinburgh, Scotland.)

————. *Calvin's New Testament Commentaries.* 12 vols. Edited by David W. Torrance and Thomas F. Torrance. Grand Rapids: Wm. B. Eerdmans Publishing Co., 1959–72.

————. *Institutes of the Christian Religion.* Edited by John T. McNeill. Translated by Ford Lewis Battles. Library of Christian Classics, vols. 20 and 21. Philadelphia: Westminster Press, 1960.

————. *Letters of John Calvin.* Translated by D. Constable. Edinburgh: Constable, 1855.

————. *Sermons on The Epistle to the Ephesians.* Translated by Arthur Golding, 1577. Translation revised by Leslie Rawlinson and S. M. Houghton. Edinburgh, Scotland, Carlisle, Pa.: Banner of Truth Trust, 1973.

SECONDARY SOURCES

Baillie, John. *Our Knowledge of God.* New York: Charles Scribner's Sons, 1939.

Balke, Willem. *Calvin and the Anabaptist Radicals.* Translated by William Heynen. Grand Rapids: Wm. B. Eerdmans Publishing Co., 1981.

Barth, Peter. *Das Problem der natürlichen Theologie bei Calvin.* Munich: Chr. Kaiser Verlag, 1935.

Battenhouse, Roy W. "The Doctrine of Man in Calvin and in Renaissance Platonism." *Journal of the History of Ideas* 9 (1948):447–71.

Bavaud, George. "Dialogue entre saint Bernard, saint Thomas d'Aquin et Calvin: Les rapports de la grâce et du libre arbitre." *Verbum Caro* 14 (1960):328–38.

Boisset, Jean. *Sagesse et sainteté dans la pensée de Jean Calvin: Essai sur l'Humanisme du Réformateur français.* Paris: Presses Universitaires de France, 1959.

Bouwsma, William J. "The Spirituality of John Calvin." In *Christian Spirituality II: High Middle Ages and Reformation,* 318–33. Edited by Jill Raitt. Vol. 17 of *World Spirituality: An Encyclopedic History of the Religious Quest.* New York: Crossroad, 1987.

Brauer, Jerald C. "Francis Rous, Puritan Mystic, 1579–1659: An Introduction to the

Study of the Mystical Element in Puritanism." Ph.D. dissertation, University of Chicago, 1948.

Brunner, Emil, and Karl Barth. *Natural Theology*. Translated by Peter Fraenkel. London: Centenary Press, 1946.

Casey, Michael. *Athirst for God: Spiritual Desire in Bernard of Clairvaux's Sermons on the Song of Songs*. Cistercian Studies Series, No. 77. Kalamazoo, Mich.: Cistercian Publications, 1988.

Dowey, Edward A., Jr. *The Knowledge of God in Calvin's Theology*. 2d ed. New York: Columbia University Press, 1965.

Engel, Mary Potter. *John Calvin's Perspectival Anthropology*. Atlanta: Scholars Press, 1988.

Ganoczy, Alexandre. *Calvin, théologien de l'Eglise et du ministère*. Paris: Editions du Cerf, 1964.

Gerrish, Brian A. "From Calvin to Schleiermacher: The Theme and the Shape of Christian Dogmatics." In *Schleiermacher-Archiv*, 1:1033–51. *Internationaler Schleiermacher-Kongress, Berlin 1984*. Edited by Kurt-Victor Selge. 2 vols. Berlin: Walter de Gruyter, 1985.

———. *Grace and Gratitude: The Eucharistic Theology of John Calvin*. Minneapolis: Fortress Press, 1993.

———. *The Old Protestantism and the New: Essays on the Reformation Heritage*. Chicago: University of Chicago Press, 1982.

———, ed. *Reformers in Profile*. Philadelphia: Fortress Press, 1967.

Gilson, Etienne. *La théologie mystique de Saint Bernard*. 3d ed. Paris: Librairie Philosophique J. Vrin, 1969.

Gloede, Günter. *Theologia naturalis bei Calvin*. Stuttgart: Verlag von W. Kohlhammer, 1935.

Gründler, Otto. "John Calvin: Ingrafting into Christ." In *The Spirituality of Western Christendom*. Edited by E. Rozanne Elder. Kalamazoo, Mich.: Cistercian Publications, 1976.

Harkness, Georgia. *Mysticism: Its Meaning and Message*. Nashville: Abingdon Press, 1973.

Hiss, Wilhelm. *Die Anthropologie Bernhards von Clairvaux*. Berlin: Walter de Gruyter, 1964.

Hyma, Albert. *The Christian Renaissance: A History of the "Devotio Moderna."* New York and London: Century Co., 1924.

Jones, Rufus M. *Studies in Mystical Religion*. London: Macmillan Co., 1923.

Kolfhaus, Wilhelm. *Christusgemeinschaft bei Johannes Calvin*. Beiträge zur Geschichte und Lehre der Reformierten Kirche, vol. 3. Neukirchen: Buchhandlung d. Erziehungsvereins, 1938.

Lane, A. N. S. "Calvin's Sources of Saint Bernard." *Archive for Reformation History* 67 (1976):253–83.

———. "Calvin's Use of the Fathers and the Medievals." *Calvin Theological Journal* 16 (November 1981):149–205.

Leclercq, Jean. "St. Bernard on the Church." *Downside Review* 85 (July 1967): 274–94.

Lonergan, Bernard J. F. *Method in Theology*. New York: Herder & Herder, 1972.

Marcel, Pierre C. "The Relation between Justification and Sanctification in Calvin's Thought." *Evangelical Quarterly* 27 (July–September 1955):132–45.

Marshall, I. Howard. "Sanctification in the Teaching of John Wesley and John Calvin." *Evangelical Quarterly* 34 (April–June 1962):75–82.

McGinn, Bernard. Introduction to "On Grace and Free Choice." In *Bernard of Clairvaux, Treatises III: On Grace and Free Choice; In Praise of the New Knighthood.* Translated by Daniel O'Donovan and M. Conrad Greenia. Cistercian Fathers Series, No. 19. Kalamazoo, Mich.: Cistercian Publications, 1977.

————. "Love, Knowledge, and Mystical Union in Western Christianity: Twelfth to Sixteenth Centuries." *Church History* 56 (March 1987):7–24.

Niesel, Wilhelm. "Calvin wider Osianders Rechtfertigungslehre." *Zeitschrift für Kirchengeschichte* 46 (1927):410–30.

————. *The Theology of John Calvin.* Translated by Harold Knight. Grand Rapids: Baker Book House, 1980.

Ozment, Steven E. *Homo Spiritualis: A Comparative Study of Johannes Tauler, Jean Gerson and Martin Luther (1509–16) in the Context of Their Theological Thought.* Studies in Medieval and Reformation Thought, vol. 6. Leiden: E. J. Brill, 1969.

Parker, T. H. L. *Calvin's Doctrine of the Knowledge of God.* 2d ed. Grand Rapids: Wm. B. Eerdmans Publishing Co., 1959.

Partee, Charles. "The Soul in Plato, Platonism, and Calvin." *Scottish Journal of Theology* 22 (September 1969):278–96.

Raitt, Jill. "Calvin's Use of Bernard of Clairvaux." *Archive for Reformation History* 72 (1981):98–121.

Reid, W. Stanford. "Bernard of Clairvaux in the Thought of John Calvin." *Westminster Theological Journal* 41 (Fall 1978):127–45.

Reuter, Karl. *Das Grundverständnis der Theologie Calvins unter Einbeziehung ihrer geschichtlichen Abhängigkeiten.* Neukirchen: Verlag des Erziehungsvereins, 1963.

Richard, Lucien Joseph. *The Spirituality of John Calvin.* Atlanta: John Knox Press, 1974.

Ritschl, Albrecht. *The Christian Doctrine of Justification and Reconciliation.* Vol. 3. Edited by H. R. Mackintosh and A. B. Macaulay. New York: Charles Scribner's Sons, 1900.

————. *A Critical History of the Christian Doctrine of Justification and Reconciliation.* Vol. 1. Translated by John S. Black. Edinburgh: Edmonston and Douglas, 1872.

————. *Geschichte des Pietismus.* Vol. 1: *Der Pietismus in der reformierten Kirche.* Bonn: Adolph Marcus, 1880.

Shepherd, Victor A. *The Nature and Function of Faith in the Theology of John Calvin.* National Association of Baptist Professors of Religion Dissertation Series, No. 2. Macon, Ga.: Mercer University Press, 1983.

Siktberg, W. R. "The Mystical Element in the Theology of John Calvin." STM thesis, Union Theological Seminary, New York City, 1951.

Soulié, Marguerite. " 'Mystique' chez Calvin et création littéraire." In *L'Inspiration biblique dans la poésie religieuse d'Agrippa d'Aubigné.* Paris: Klincksieck, 1977.

Standaert, M. "La doctrine de l'image chez S. Bernard." *Ephemerides Theologiae Lovanienses* 23 (1947):70–129.

Strand, Kenneth. "John Calvin and the Brethren of the Common Life." *Andrews University Seminary Studies* 13 (1975):67–78.

————. "John Calvin and the Brethren of the Common Life: The Role of Strassburg." *Andrews University Seminary Studies* 15 (1977):43–50.

————. "Additional Note on Calvin and the Influence of the Brethren of the

Common Life in France." *Andrews University Seminary Studies* 15 (Spring 1977):51–56.

————, ed. *The Dawn of Modern Civilization: Studies in Renaissance, Reformation and Other Topics, Presented to Honor Albert Hyma.* 2d ed. Ann Arbor, Mich.: Ann Arbor Publishers, 1964.

Stuermann, Walter E. *A Critical Study of Calvin's Concept of Faith.* Tulsa, 1952.

Szarmach, Paul, ed. *An Introduction to the Medieval Mystics of Europe.* Albany, N.Y.: State University of New York Press, 1984.

Torrance, Thomas F. *Calvin's Doctrine of Man.* London: Lutterworth Press, 1949.

Troeltsch, Ernst. *The Social Teaching of the Christian Churches.* Translated by Olive Wyon. 2 vols. New York: Macmillan Co., 1931.

Underhill, Evelyn. *Mysticism.* New York: E. P. Dutton & Co., 1961.

von Hügel, Friedrich. *The Mystical Element of Religion as Studied in St. Catherine of Genoa and Her Friends.* 2d ed. 2 vols. London: J. M. Dent & Sons, 1923.

von Ivánka, Endre. "La structure de l'âme selon Saint Bernard." In *Saint Bernard Théologien,* pp. 202–8. Actes du Congrès de Dijon, 15–19 septembre 1953. Deuxième édition. Rome: Editiones Cistercienses, 1954.

Wallace, Ronald S. *Calvin's Doctrine of the Christian Life.* Edinburgh/London: Oliver & Boyd, 1959.

————. *Calvin's Doctrine of the Word and Sacrament.* Edinburgh/London: Oliver & Boyd, 1953.

Weis, James. "Calvin versus Osiander on Justification." *The Springfielder* 29 (Autumn 1965):31–47.

Williams, George H. *The Radical Reformation.* Philadelphia: Westminster Press, 1962.

Woods, Richard, ed. *Understanding Mysticism.* Garden City, N.Y.: Doubleday & Co., 1980.

INDEX OF NAMES

INDEX OF SUBJECTS